The Undergraduate's Companion to Arab Writers and Their Web Sites

Recent titles in the Undergraduate Companion Series
James K. Bracken, Series Editor

The Undergraduate's Companion to American Writers and Their Web Sites
James K. Bracken and Larry G. Hinman

The Undergraduate's Companion to Women Writers and Their Web Sites
Katharine A. Dean, Miriam Conteh-Morgan, and James K. Bracken

The Undergraduate's Companion to English Renaissance Writers and Their Web Sites
Steven Kenneth Galbraith

The Undergraduate's Companion to Women Poets of the World and Their Web Sites
Katharine A. Dean

The Undergraduate's Companion to Arab Writers and Their Web Sites

Dona S. Straley

Undergraduate Companion Series
James K. Bracken, Series Editor

LIBRARIES
UNLIMITED
A Member of the Greenwood Publishing Group

Westport, Connecticut • London

Library of Congress Cataloging-in-Publication Data

Straley, Dona S.
    The undergraduate's companion to Arab writers and their web sites / by Dona S.
Straley.
      p. cm. — (Undergraduate companion series)
    Includes bibliographical references (p.) and index.
    ISBN 1–59158–118–4 (alk. paper)
    1. Arabic literature—Computer network resources. 2. Authors,
Arab—Computer network resources. I. Title. II. Series.
Z3014.L56S77   2004
[PJ7517]
892.7'02854678—dc22   2004046582

British Library Cataloguing in Publication Data is available.

Library of Congress Catalog Card Number: 2004046582
ISBN:1–59158–118–4

First published in 2004

Libraries Unlimited, 88 Post Road West, Westport, CT 06881
A Member of Greenwood Publishing Group, Inc.
www.lu.com

Printed in the United States of America

The paper used in this book complies with the
Permanent Paper Standard issued by the National
Information Standards Organization (Z39.48–1984).

10 9 8 7 6 5 4 3 2 1

Contents

Acknowledgments

At The Ohio State University Libraries, Joseph Branin, Director, and the Advisory Committee on Research granted me a special research leave in the summer of 2003. Jim Bracken, Assistant Director of Main Library Research and Reference Services, encouraged me to undertake this project. Patrick Visel, of the Middle East Studies Library, was always willing to track down another book. Heidi Hoerman, University of South Carolina, commented on drafts of the introduction.

For F.C.M. and A.Z., departed friends.

—D.S.S.

Introduction

In October 1988, a literary tradition stretching back fifteen centuries came into the spotlight. The Swedish Academy awarded the Nobel Prize for Literature to the Egyptian novelist and short-story writer Najib Mahfuz, the first and still the only Arabic-language writer so honored. As a result, interest in other writers from the Arab world, especially those whose works interpret the political and social milieus of their cultures, grew in the media, the publishing industry, college and university programs, and the general reading public. Poets like Adunis and Mahmud Darwish and female authors like Nawal al-Sa'dawi became more widely available in translation and more studied within the classroom. Magazines devoted to Arabic writing began to be published in Los Angeles (*Aljadid*, 1995; on the Web at http://www.aljadid.com/, with archives of selected articles back to 1998) and in London (*Banipal*, 1998; on the Web at http://www.banipal.co.uk/, with contents of all issues). As more information became available through the Web, magazines published in English in the Arab world became available to worldwide audiences. Such titles as *Al-Ahram Weekly On-Line* (http://weekly.ahram.org.eg/, with archives back to 1998) and *Cairo Times* (http://www.cairotimes.com/, with archives of selected articles back to 1999) provide readers with insight into the political and cultural life that Arab writers depict.

Today, the interested reader can learn more about Arabic literature by consulting one of a number of excellent introductions to the topic, such as Roger Allen's *An Introduction to Arabic Literature,* the same author's *The Arabic Literary Heritage,* or *Arabic Literature: An Overview* by Pierre Cachia. Journals such as *Journal of Arabic Literature* or *Middle Eastern Literatures* publish both scholarly articles and translations. The more dedicated might wish to dip into the five volumes of *The Cambridge History of Arabic Literature.*

Undergraduates seeking information on Arab writers will have different needs from those looking for British or American authors. First, very few of you will have any familiarity with the Arab literary tradition or with Arab culture in general. Few will have read even a short piece by any Arab author or will know that there are no set spellings for Arab author's names in English. Once you start researching an author, you may become easily frustrated at the lack of quick and plentiful information like that available for Shakespeare or Toni Morrison. Finally, you may not have access in your own libraries to some of the specialized resources such as *Index Islamicus*, which are the mainstays of the field of Arabic literature.

Arab Writers

The writers and stories found in this volume cover fifteen centuries of Arabic literary and intellectual writings, from the poets of the sixth and seventh centuries to the experimental fiction authors of the twenty-first. The one common element among the over 200 writers included is that they all wrote primarily in Arabic. Thus, Tahar Benjelloun and Assia Djebar, who write in French, are excluded; Kahlil Gibran, who wrote in both Arabic and English, is included, because he was as prolific in Arabic as in English.

Literary authors and anonymous works such as the *Arabian Nights* account for the bulk of the listings, but writers of historical, geographical, philosophical, and religious texts are also included, primarily for the period before 1800. "Literature" in the Western meaning of the word is restricted to poetry in the premodern Arab world, with the exception of the epic story cycles such as *Sirat Bani Hilal* or *Arabian Nights*. Philosophy, history, and religion—disciplines that were intertwined and often indistinguishable—provided the intellectual output that filled the niches of high culture among the Arabs. Many of these authors were true polymaths; they wrote not only histories, commentaries on the Qur'an, and works on astrology but also poetry.

The original list of authors considered was formed on the basis of those found in *Encyclopedia of Arabic Literature*, and was then augmented, especially for current writers, chosen primarily by what is available on the Web. All writers in the final cut have at least one work or extract or one biographical sketch on the Web, and at least one substantial entry in one of the other three categories (autobiography and interviews, translations, biography and criticism). In other words, there had to be enough information on the Web and in print to give an undergraduate a basic understanding of the author's life and works and a starting point for further research.

There are some very well-known names missing from this volume. There is little or no information available on the Web for some. For others, what is available is not on a stable site or lacks analytical or other critical apparatus, which would make it useful to an undergraduate or a general reader. The latter is particularly true of texts relating to the religion of Islam.

Organization of Entries

Each entry includes the author's name and dates of birth and death, if available, in one alphabetical order. Web sites are listed first. The next three categories of material all refer to printed sources: autobiographies and interviews, translations, and biography and criticism.

Authors' Names

Arabic names may be spelled in a variety of ways in our Latin alphabet. The Arabic alphabet contains letters that do not exist in English, such as *'ayn* and *ghayn*.

Arabic names contain elements that we often find confusing. For example, many names begin with the element *al-* (sometimes spelled in English *el-*), the word for "the," which to our eyes is a somewhat odd addition to a name. Even more confusingly, this element is sometimes eliminated or alphabetically ignored in indexes in English books, magazines, and newspapers. Nor is there agreement among scholars on how Arabic words and names should be spelled in English; they consider all of these factors, as well as the fact that not all words and names are pronounced the same way by all Arab speakers. (Think of the differences in pronunciation between American and British English: Americans pronounce the name *Maurice* with the accent on the second syllable, whereas the British pronounce it with the accent on the first syllable, like *Morris*.)

Because the primary audience of this book will be using library resources, this book uses the standardized form used by the Library of Congress (LC). This is the form used by libraries throughout the United States and is based on a systematic table which converts the letters of the Arabic alphabet into letters and signs of the English alphabet. (For those readers who are interested in learning more about the LC system of romanization of Arabic and other alphabets into English, see http://www.loc.gov/catdir/ cpso/roman.html). Readers will be able to switch seamlessly between the entries in this book and their own library's catalog using the LC form of name. Three modifications are made to these names:

1. The definite article prefix al- to the surname is included, where LC has deleted it, but it is not used to alphabetize. Thus, al-Idlibi would be alphabetized among those names beginning with "i" and not those beginning with "a."
2. Birth and death dates are included even if the LC form of the name did not include them.
3. Diacritical marks used by LC, such as the long mark on top of a vowel or the dot underneath a consonant, are not included, as these are not necessary for you to use when searching.

One diacritical mark is retained: the apostrophe, which is used to show two different Arabic letters with no English equivalents. Some Internet search engines treat words containing apostrophes differently from the same words without the apostrophe. For example, Google searches the name "Mikha'il" as one word when it does not contain the apostrophe on the Web site (Mikhail), but as two words when it does (Mikha and il). To obtain the best results, readers should search such names both ways. Remember that in most print sources, diacritics do not make any difference in the order of the entries.

Web sites about an author do not use a standard form for the author's name; each Web site may use a different spelling. You need to be a little creative—but not too creative—when searching for individual authors on the Web. Some variant spellings are included in this book to help identify authors when different spellings are common. An excellent illustration of the many ways to spell one name is the name Muhammad, which may also appear as Mohammad, Mohammed, Mohamed, and even Mahomet.

When searching, consider using some of these equivalencies if you don't get results with your first spelling:

u and o (for example, Uthman and Othman)

i or a and e (for example, Hatatah and Hetahah)

q and k (for example, Shawqi and Shawki)

j and g (for example, Jamil and Gamil)

i and ui (for example, Nagib and Naguib)

w and ou (for example, Wattar and Ouattar)

names that end in -ah may also end in just an -a (for example, Ibn Taymiyah and Ibn Taymiya)

names that have the same letter twice may also spell it with that letter used only once (for example, Mohammed and Mohamed)

There are several excellent articles, which nicely summarize the difficulties in spelling Arab names. One, by the British journalist Brian Whitaker, can be found at http://www.guardian.co.uk/elsewhere/journalist/story/0,7792,730805,00.html. Another, part of the Arab Gateway Web site cited throughout this book, can be read at http://www.al-bab.com/arab/language/roman1.htm.

Dates of Birth and Death

For many centuries, the Islamic world used a calendar based on the moon, not the sun, as the Christian world does. Called the Hijri calendar, year 1 began when the Prophet Muhammad and his followers emigrated (or made a hijrah) from the city of Mecca to the city of Medina in Saudi Arabia in A.D. 622. Therefore, years from the Hijri calendar are not the exact equivalent of Christian dates, since each Hijri year is shorter and begins on a date other than January 1. (For an explanation of the Islamic calendar, see http://webexhibits.org/calendars/calendar-islamic.html; Freeman-Grenville, G.S.P. *The Islamic and Christian Calendars.*) For some of the authors listed in this book, you will find dates such as "1426 or 1427–1512 or 1513," which means that although we know the Hijri years of the author's birth and death, we do not know the exact month and day, and therefore cannot narrow the dates down to the exact year in the Christian calendar. In addition, the dates of birth and death for some authors are not known. Dates using question marks (1256?–1321?), a specific century (10th century), and abbreviations such as *ca.* (meaning "circa" or "approximately") are used to show that the exact dates are not known.

Although most Arab countries today have adopted the Western calendar (at least for the purposes of foreign affairs), there are still problems with dates of birth and death for authors in the 19th and 20th centuries. Here question marks, abbreviations, and other conventions are also used to mark uncertainty of the date. Note that if only a birth date followed by a dash (1935–) is given, the author is still living.

Authors' birth and death dates are those used by the Library of Congress, if available. If these are not available, dates from the *Encyclopedia of Arabic Literature* are used. Dates from the Web and other printed sources are used if neither of the first two provides that information. You may find different dates for an author's birth or death in other sources.

Web Sites

Much of the information about Arab writers can only be found piecemeal on the Web. There are but a handful of sites devoted to a single author, and very few that are completely about Arabic literature or culture. Unlike the sites listed in previous volumes of this series, there are virtually no sites established and maintained by institutions or scholarly organizations. In addition, it is common to find the same information on a half-dozen Web sites, without any acknowledgement of its originator. I have tried to ensure that each Web site presents unique content, or at least added value.

Students can expect to find, at a minimum, either an English translation of a work by the author or biographical information about the author. I have listed the English titles of translated works in the annotations. Many Web sites include photographs or artists' portraits of the author. Please note that any such depiction of a person living before 1800 is not likely to be an actual portrait, and is often based on a romanticized Western notion of what that person might have looked like.

All Web sites have English content. Some are bilingual, in English and Arabic; this is noted in the annotations. Advanced undergraduates studying Arabic may find these sites of particular interest, as there is often more content available in Arabic than in English.

Many of the Web sites listed in this volume have been established and are maintained by individuals, sometimes scholars, but often enthusiasts of a group of novelists, early Arab poets, or Muslim philosophers. Some sites espouse a particular political, religious, cultural, or ethnic view with which you may not agree, however, this does not mean that you cannot use the information provided. In some cases, such sites may provide you with clues to how a particular writer or group of writers is viewed within their own culture. Some of these Web sites have many pop-up ads, which can become very annoying and intrusive. Such sites were not included if another site had essentially the same information, but there are still a number of them listed and a site may have changed its advertising policy since this book went to press.

I have generally excluded publishers' Web sites, although you can often find biographical information as well as samples of the text on sites that publish translations, biographies, and critical studies. Be very careful about using the quotes found on such sites, even if signed by scholars. These are marketing blurbs, meant to enhance the salability of the book, and should not be used as research material.

Translations

Each work is generally listed only once, whether in print or on the Web. However, many of the poems of the more popular authors, like Mahmud Darwish, have been anthologized frequently, and so may appear more than once. Translations of complete works, which have been published in multiple editions, are generally listed only once, usually in the most recent edition. An earlier edition may be listed in preference if it is more widely held by libraries or is more readily available for purchase. Translations issued under different titles or by different translators are listed separately. Reading translations of the same work by different translators is an enlightening way to discover nuances of language and interpretation.

The editions listed are to those titles expected to be commonly held by most larger public and university libraries or that are available for sale. Thus, I have not listed the excellent and many translations published by the General Egyptian Book Organization in Cairo, or those published by other governmental or commercial publishers in the Middle East. I have listed works published by such entities as the American University in Cairo Press, since these are distributed in this country and can be easily purchased. If you have time to wait to receive a book through Interlibrary Loan, then check OCLC's (Online Computer Library Center's) WorldCat or a consortial catalog (one that lists the holdings of a group of libraries) to find other translations.

Biography and Criticism

I have searched commonly available databases, including OCLC's WorldCat, the MLA Bibliography, and Literary Index, to find citations that will be easily accessible to most students, and that will be at a suitable level for undergraduates. I have turned to more specialized resources, primarily *Index Islamicus*, to find appropriate material for less prominent authors.

Research Tips

- Consult your teacher about your topic. Be sure you understand how long your paper or presentation must be. This will help you judge how much material you will need to find.

- Consult a librarian to help you form a research strategy. If you're looking for information on a person, what are the best sources to read? What are the subjects that can lead you to Web sites, books, and articles about the author or similar authors? Librarians are trained to find information efficiently and can help you learn how to do the same.

- Keep a list of where you look—what Web sites, reference books, and online databases you used. Write down how you searched them—the spelling of the author's name, the subject headings, or keywords you used. Doing this as you go along can save you a lot of trouble later.

- Check your library's catalog for books by and about the person or subject you're researching.

- Look for online databases available in your library or through your library's Web page. Be sure to choose those that are appropriate to your subject. If you're not sure which ones contain information on your subject, ask the librarian. Most online databases will give you citations to journal and magazine articles; some also give you the actual text of the articles. If you're in a hurry, be sure to try the latter ones first. It will save you the time of having to look for the volume of the journal in your library's stacks.

- Learn the limitations and features of the Web search engine(s) you frequently use. Many libraries have developed online courses to help you learn how to search the Web efficiently. Check the home page of the search engine and look for the link marked "Help" or "Advanced Search" to learn about what terms to use, how to search more than one term at a time, how to exclude a term from your search, and many other useful tips.

- Evaluate any Web site you want to use for your research. Who is the person or group responsible for the site? When was the site first established? When was it last updated? Where did the information on the site originate? When was the information gathered, published, or collected? For example, there is a Web site that contains the contents of the Encyclopedia Britannica—the 1911 edition. Much of the information on this site is out of date. Furthermore, the text was prepared for the Web using optical character recognition scanning and is rife with mistakes.

- Still haven't found what you're looking for? Go back and tell the librarian what you've done, what databases and reference sources you've searched, and how you searched them. Did you overlook something? Are there more sources that you can consult?

- Is there a specialist librarian who knows the field in depth? If there is not one at your library, is there one at another library that can be contacted for help? The Middle East Librarians Association has a Web site that lists libraries with Middle East collections (http://depts.washington.edu/wsx9/melainlc.html). These are likely to have specialist librarians in Middle East studies. Try looking for similar sites for other subjects.

- Now that you have your data, remember that you must cite your sources properly. Follow the citation format preferred by your instructor. Library reference desks often have handouts of examples of the more commonly used citation formats. These citation formats are fully explained in style guides such as *The MLA Handbook for Writers of Research Papers* (6th ed.), edited by Joseph Gibaldi (New York: MLA, 2003). Citation formats in the MLA Handbook were used in the preparation of this book, with some modifications.

Alphabetical List of Authors

Abazah, 'Aziz, 1898–1969

Abazah, Tharwat, 1927–2002

'Abd al-Hakim, Shawqi, 1936?–

'Abd Allah, Muhammad 'Abd al-Halim, 1913–1970

'Abd al-Qaddus, Ihsan, 1919–1990

'Abd al-Rahman, 'A'ishah. See Bint al-Shati', 1913–1998

'Abd al-Sabur, Salah, 1931–1981

Abdel Hakim, Shawki. See 'Abd al-Hakim, Shawqi, 1936?–

Abdel Kouddous, Ihsan. See 'Abd al-Qaddus, Ihsan, 1919–1990

Abdelrahman, Aisha. See Bint al-Shati', 1913–1998

'Abduh, Muhammad. See Muhammad 'Abduh, 1849–1905

'Abid ibn al-Abras, fl. 6th century

Abu al-'Ala' al-Ma'arri, 973–1057

Abu al-Fida' Isma'il ibn 'Ali, 1273–1331

Abu al-Qasim Khalaf ibn 'Abbas al-Zahrawi, d. 1013?

Abu Hadid, Muhammad Farid, 1893–1968

Abu Hamid al-Ghazali. See al-Ghazzali, 1058–1111

Abu Hanifah al-Dinawari. See al-Dinawari, Abu Hanifah Ahmad ibn Dawud, d. ca. 895

Abu Khalid, Fawziyah

Abu Naddarah. See Sannu', Ya'qub ibn Rafa'il, 1839–1912

Abu Nuwas, ca. 756–ca. 810

Abu Rayhan al-Biruni. See al-Biruni, Muhammad ibn Ahmad, 973?–1048

Abu Salma. See al-Karmi, Abu Salma 'Abd al–Karim, 1907–1980

Abu Shadi, Ahmad Zaki, 1892–1955

Abu Shayib, Zuhayr, 1958–

Abu Tammam Habib ibn Aws al-Ta'i, fl. 808–842

Abu Ya'qub al-Sijistani, Ishaq ibn Ahmad, 10th century

Abu Yusuf al-Kindi. See al-Kindi, d. ca. 873

Adunis, 1930–

al-Afghani, Jamal al-Din, 1838–1897

al-Akhyaliyah, Layla. See Layla al-Akhyaliyah, d. ca. 700

Aladdin. See Arabian Nights, The

Albategnius. See al-Battani, Muhammad ibn Jabir, d. 929

Albatenius. See al-Battani, Muhammad ibn Jabir, d. 929

Albucasis. See Abu al-Qasim Khalaf ibn 'Abbas al-Zahrawi, d. 1013?

Alf Laylah wa-Laylah. See Arabian Nights, The

Alfraganus. See al-Farghani, fl. 861

Algosaibi, Ghazi. See al-Qusaybi, Ghazi 'Abd al-Rahman, 1940–

Alhazen, 965–1039

'Ali Mubarak, Basha, 1823 or 1824–1893

Amin, Ahmad, 1886–1954

Amin, Qasim. *See* Qasim Amin, 1863–1908

'Antarah ibn Shaddad, 6th century

'Aql, 'Abd al-Latif, 1942–

al-'Aqqad, 'Abbas Mahmud, 1889–1964

Arabian Nights, The

'Aridah, Nasib, 1887–1946

Arna'ut, 'A'ishah

Asbar, 'Ali Ahmad Sa'id. *See* Adunis, 1930–

Aslan, Ibrahim, 1939–

Avempace, d. 1138 or 1139

Averroes, 1126–1198

Avicenna, 980–1037

'Awad, Luwis, 1915–1990

'Awwad, Tawfiq Yusuf, 1911–1989

'Azzam, Samirah, 1925–1967

al-'Azzawi, Fadil, 1940–

Badr, Liyanah, 1950–

Baghdadi, Shawqi, 1928–

Baha' al-Din Ibn Shaddad. *See* Ibn Shaddad, Baha' al-Din Yusuf ibn Rafi', 1145–1234 or 1235

Bahithat al-Badiyah. *See* Nasif, Malak Hifni, 1886–1918

Ba Kathir, 'Ali Ahmad, 1910–1969

Bakr, Salwa, 1949–

al-Baladhuri, Ahmad ibn Yahya, d. 892

al-Banna', Hasan, 1906–1949

Banu Hilal, Romance of. *See* Sirat Bani Hilal

al-Baradduni, 'Abd Allah, 1926–1999

Barakat, Halim Isber, 1936–

Barakat, Huda, 1952–

al-Barghuthi, Murid, 1944–

al-Barudi, Mahmud Sami, 1839–1904

al-Battani, Muhammad ibn Jabir, d. 929

al-Bayati, 'Abd al-Wahhab, 1926–1999

Baydun, 'Abbas, 1945–

Bayram al-Tunisi, Mahmud, 1893–1961

al-Bayyati, 'Abd al-Wahhab. *See* al-Bayati, 'Abd al-Wahhab, 1926–1999

Bek, Khalil Mardam. *See* Mardam, Khalil, 1895?–1959

Benhadouga, Abdelhamid, 1925–

Beydhoun, Abbas. *See* Baydun, 'Abbas, 1945–

Bin Haduqah, 'Abd al-Hamid. *See* Benhadouga, Abdelhamid, 1925–

Bint al-Shati', 1913–1998

al-Biruni, Muhammad ibn Ahmad, 973?–1048

al-Bisati, Muhammad, 1937–

Book of Sindbad. *See Arabian Nights, The*

Boulus, Sargon. *See* Bulus, Sarkun, 1943–

Bulus, Sarkun, 1943–

al-Busiri, Sharaf al-Din Muhammad ibn Sa'id, 1213?–1296?

Buzurg ibn Shahriyar, 10th century

Chabbi, Abul Kacem. *See* al-Shabbi, Abu al-Qasim, 1909–1934

Chahin, Salah, 1930–1986

Charaoui, Hoda. *See* Sha'rawi, Huda, 1879–1947

Choukeir, Mahmoud. *See* Shuqayr, Mahmud, 1941–

Dahbur, Ahmad, 1946–

al-Da'if, Rashid, 1945–

Darwish, Mahmud, 1941–

Dhu al-Rummah, Ghaylan ibn 'Uqbah, 696–735

al-Dinawari, Abu Hanifah Ahmad ibn Dawud, d. ca. 895

Djabarti, 'Abd al-Rahman. *See* al-Jabarti, 'Abd al-Rahman, 1754–1822

Dunqul, Amal, d. 1983

El Daif, Rachid. *See* al-Da'if, Rashid, 1945–

El Saadawi, Nawal. *See* al-Sa'dawi, Nawal, 1931–

al-Faqih, Ahmad Ibrahim, 1942–

al-Farabi, ca. 872–950

al-Farazdaq, ca. 641–728

al-Farghani, fl. 861

al-Fasi, al-Hasan ibn Muhammad al-Wazzan. *See* Leo, *Africanus*, ca. 1492–ca.1550

al-Fituri, Muhammad, 1936?–

Gabarti, 'Abd al-Rahman. *See* al-Jabarti, 'Abd al-Rahman, 1754–1822

Ghanim, Fathi, 1924–1999

al-Ghazali, Zaynab, 1917–

al-Ghazzali, 1058–1111

al-Ghitani, Jamal, 1945–

Gibran, Kahlil, 1883–1931

al-Gosaibi, Ghazi. *See* al-Qusaybi, Ghazi 'Abd al-Rahman, 1940–

Habibi, Imil, 1921–1996

Haddad, Qasim, 1948–

Hafiz Ibrahim, Muhammad, 1872?–1932

Haidari, Buland. *See* al-Haydari, Buland, 1926–1996

al-Hakim, Tawfiq, 1898–1987

Hakki, Yehia. *See* Haqqi, Yahya, 1905–1993

al-Hallaj, al-Husayn ibn Mansur, 858 or 859–922

Hammam ibn Ghalib ibn Sa'sa'ah. *See* al-Farazdaq, ca. 641–728

Haqqi, Yahya, 1905–1993

al-Hariri, 1054–1122

al-Hasan ibn Muhammad al-Wazzan al-Fasi. *See* Leo, *Africanus*, ca. 1492–ca.1550

Hassan ibn Thabit, d. 674

Hatatah, Sharif, 1923–

Hawi, Khalil S., 1925–1982

Haydar, Haydar, 1936–

al-Haydari, Buland, 1926–1996

Haykal, Muhammad Husayn, 1888–1956

Hetata, Sharif. *See* Hatatah, Sharif, 1923–

Hunayn ibn Ishaq al-'Ibadi, 809?–873

Husayn, Taha, 1889–1937

Ibn 'Abd al-Hakam, d. 870 or 871

Ibn al-'Arabi, 1165–1240

Ibn al-Athir, 'Izz al-Din, 1160–1233

Ibn al-Haytham, al-Hasan. *See* Alhazen, 965–1039

Ibn al-Nadim, Muhammad ibn Ishaq, fl. 987

Ibn al-Nafis, 'Ali ibn Abi al-Hazm, 1210 or 1211–1288

Ibn al-Qalanisi, Abu Ya'la Hamzah ibn Asad, d. 1160

Ibn al-Rumi, 836–896

Ibn 'Arabi. *See* Ibn al-'Arabi, 1165–1240

Ibn 'Ata' Allah, Ahmad ibn Muhammad, d. 1309

Ibn Bajjah. *See* Avempace, d. 1138 or 1139

Ibn Batuta, 1304–1377

Ibn Daniyal, Muhammad, 1249 or 1250–1310 or 1311

Ibn Fadlan, Ahmad, fl. 922

Ibn Haduvah, 'Abd al-Hamid. *See* Benhadouga, Abdelhamid, 1925–

Ibn Hawqal, Muhammad, 10th century

Ibn Hazm, 'Ali ibn Ahmad, 994–1064

Ibn Ishaq, Muhammad, d. ca. 768

Ibn Jubayr, Muhammad ibn Ahmad,
1145–1217

Ibn Khaldun, 1332–1406

Ibn Masarrah, Muhammad ibn 'Abd
Allah, 882 or 883–931

Ibn Miskawayh, Ahmad ibn Muhammad,
d. 1030

Ibn Qayyim al-Jawziyah, Muhammad
ibn Abi Bakr, 1292–1350

Ibn Rushd. *See* Averroes, 1126–1198

Ibn Sa'id, 'Ali ibn Musa, 1213–1286

Ibn Shaddad, Baha' al-Din Yusuf ibn
Rafi', 1145–1234 or 1235

Ibn Sina. *See* Avicenna, 980–1037

Ibn Sinan, Ibrahim, 908–946

Ibn Taymiyah, Ahmad ibn 'Abd
al-Halim, 1263–1328

Ibn Tufayl, Muhammad ibn 'Abd
al-Malik, d. 1185

Ibrahim, Jamil 'Atiyah, 1937–

Ibrahim, Sun' Allah, 1937–

Ibrahim Hafiz. *See* Hafiz Ibrahim,
Muhammad, 1872?–1932

Ibrahim ibn Sinan ibn Thabit ibn Qurrah.
See Ibn Sinan, Ibrahim, 908-946

al-Idlibi, Ulfat, 1912–

Idris, Yusuf, 1927–1991

al-Idrisi, ca. 1100–1166

'Imad al-Din al-Isfahani. *See* al-Katib
al-Isfahani, 'Imad al-Din
Muhammad ibn
Muhammad, 1125–1201

Imru' al-Qays, 497–545

Istakhri, Ibrahim ibn Muhammad,
d. 957 or 958

al-Jabarti, 'Abd al-Rahman, 1754–1822

Jabir ibn Hayyan, ca. 721–815?

Jabra, Jabra Ibrahim, 1920–1994

Jahin, Salah. *See* Chahin, Salah,
1930–1986

al-Jahiz, d. 868 or 869

Jamal al-Din al-Afghani. *See* al-Afghani,
Jamal al-Din, 1838–1897

al-Jawahiri, Muhammad Mahdi,
1900–1997

Jayyusi, Salma Khadra, 1926–

Jibran, Jibran Khalil. *See* Gibran, Kahlil,
1883–1931

Jubran, Jubran Khalil. *See* Gibran,
Kahlil, 1883–1931

al-Juburi, Amal, 1967–

Kanafani, Ghassan, 1936–1972

al-Karmi, Abu Salma 'Abd al-Karim,
1907–1980

Kashghari, Badi'ah Dawud

al-Katib al-Isfahani, 'Imad al-Din
Muhammad ibn Muhammad,
1125–1201

al-Khal, Yusuf, 1917–1988

Khalifah, Sahar, 1941–

al-Khalili, 'Ali, 1943–

al-Khansa', d. ca. 645

al-Kharrat, Idwar, 1926–

Khazindar, Walid, 1950–

Khoury, Elias. *See* al-Khuri, Ilyas,
1948–

al-Khuli, Lutfi, 1928–1999

al-Khuri, Ilyas, 1948–

al-Khuwarizmi, Muhammad ibn Musa,
fl. 813–846

al-Kindi, d. ca. 873

Kutub, Sayyid. *See* Qutb, Sayyid,
1903–1966

Layla al-Akhyaliyah, d. ca. 700

Leo, *Africanus*, ca. 1492–ca. 1550

Leone, Giovanni. *See* Leo, *Africanus*, ca.
1492–ca. 1550

al-Ma'arri, Abu al-'Ala'. *See* Abu
   al-'Ala' al-Ma'arri, 973–1057
al-Maghut, Muhammad, 1934–
Mahfuz, Najib, 1912–
Mahmud, Zaki Najib, 1905–1993
al-Majdhub, Muhammad al-Mahdi,
   1919–1982
al-Mala'ikah, Nazik, 1923–
Mamduh, 'Aliyah, 1944–
al-Manfaluti, Mustafa, 1876?–1924
al-Maqdisi, Muhammad ibn Ahmad. *See*
   al-Muqaddasi, Muhammad ibn
   Ahmad, b. ca. 946
al-Maqrizi, Ahmad ibn 'Ali, 1364–1442
Mardam, Khalil, 1895?–1959
al-Mas'udi, d. 956?
Matar, Muhammad Afifi, 1935–
al-Mawardi, 'Ali ibn Muhammad,
   974?–1058
al-Mazini, Ibrahim 'Abd al-Qadir,
   1889–1949
Mikha'il, Dunya, 1965–
Minah, Hanna, 1924–
Mirsal, Iman, 1966–
Mohammed, Zakaria. *See* Muhammad,
   Zakariya, 1951–
Mosteghanemi, Ahlem, 1953–
Mubarak, 'Ali. *See* 'Ali Mubarak, *Basha*,
   1823 or 1824–1893
Muhammad 'Abduh, 1849–1905
Muhammad Farid, 1868–1919
Muhammad ibn Jarir al-Tabari. *See*
   al-Tabari, 838?–923
Muhammad ibn Zakariya al-Razi. *See*
   al-Razi, Abu Bakr Muhammad ibn
   Zakariya, 865?–925?
Muhammad Rashid Rida, 1865–1935
Muhammad, Zakariya, 1951–
Mulla Sadra. *See* Sadr al-Din Shirazi,
   Muhammad ibn Ibrahim, d. 1641
Munif, 'Abd al-Rahman, 1933–

al-Muqaddasi, Muhammad ibn Ahmad,
   b. ca. 946
Musa, Nabawiyah, 1886–1951
Musa, Salamah, 1887–1958
Mustaghanimi, Ahlam. *See*
   Mosteghanemi, Ahlem, 1953–
al-Mutanabbi, Abu al-Tayyib Ahmad ibn
   al-Husayn, 915 or 916–965

Nabarawi, Sayza, 1897–1985
al-Nafzawi, 'Umar ibn Muhammad, fl.
   1410–1434
Naimy, Mikhail. *See* Nu'aymah,
   Mikha'il, 1889–1989
Naji, Ibrahim, 1898–1953
Naqqash, Samir
Nasif, Malak Hifni, 1886–1918
Nasir, Amjad, 1955–
Nasir, Kamal, 1925–1973
Nasir al-Din al-Tusi. *See* al-Tusi, Nasir
   al-Din Muhammad ibn
   Muhammad, 1201–1274
Nasr Allah, Ibrahim, 1954–
Nasr Allah, Imili, 1931–
al-Nawwab, Muzaffar, 1934–
Nu'aymah, Mikha'il, 1889–1989

Othman, Leila. *See* al-'Uthman, Layla
Ousama ibn Mounqidh. *See* Usamah ibn
   Munqidh, 1095–1188

Qabbani, Nizar, 1923–1998
Qasim Amin, 1863–1908
al-Qasim, Samih, 1939–
al-Qasimi, Maysun Saqr
al-Qusaybi, Ghazi 'Abd al-Rahman,
   1940–
Qutb, Sayyid, 1903–1966

Rabi'ah al-'Adawiyah, d. 801?
al-Rafi'i, Mustafa Sadiq, d. 1937

Rashid Rida. *See* Muhammad Rashid Rida, 1865–1935

al-Rayhani, Amin. *See* Rihani, Ameen Fares, 1876–1940

al-Razi, Abu Bakr Muhammad ibn Zakariya, 865?–925?

al-Razi, Fakhr al-Din Muhammad ibn 'Umar, 1149 or 1150–1210

Rhazes. *See* al-Razi, Abu Bakr Muhammad ibn Zakariya, 865?–925?

Rida, Muhammad Rashid. *See* Muhammad Rashid Rida, 1865–1935

Rif'at, Alifah

Rifqah, Fu'ad, 1930–

Rihani, Ameen Fares, 1876–1940

al-Rimawi, Mahmud, 1948–

Sa'adah, Antun, 1904–1949

Al-Sabah S.M., 1942–

al-Sabah, Su'ad al-Mubarak 1942–

Sabri, Isma'il, 1854–1923

al-Sa'dawi, Nawal, 1931–

Sadr al-Din Shirazi, Muhammad ibn Ibrahim, d. 1641

Sa'id, 'Ali Ahmad. *See* Adunis, 1930–

al-Sa'id, Aminah, 1914–1995

Salih, al-Tayyib, 1929–

Salim, 'Ali, 1936–

al-Samman, Ghadah, 1942–

Sannu', Ya'qub ibn Rafa'il, 1839–1912

Sanua, James. *See* Sannu', Ya'qub ibn Rafa'il, 1839–1912

Saqr, Maysun. *See* al-Qasimi, Maysun Saqr

al-Sa'udi, Muna, 1945–

Sayf ibn Dhi Yazan, Romance of. *See Sirat Sayf ibn Dhi Yazan*

al-Sayigh, Mayy, 1940–

Sayigh, Tawfiq, 1924–1971

al-Sayyab, Badr Shakir, 1926–1964

Sebaie, Youssef. *See* al-Siba'i, Yusuf, 1917–1978

Seven Viziers, Story of. *See Arabian Nights, The*

al-Shabbi, Abu al-Qasim, 1909–1934

Shafiq, Durriyah, 1908–1975

Sha'rawi, Huda, 1879–1947

al-Sharqawi, 'Abd al-Rahman, 1920–1987

al-Sharuni, Yusuf, 1924–

Shawqi, Ahmad, 1868–1932

al-Shaykh, Hanan, 1945–

al-Shidyaq, Ahmad Faris, 1804?–1887

Shihab al-Din al-Suhrawardi. *See* al-Suhrawardi, Yahya ibn Habash, 1152 or 1153–1191

Shumayyil, Shibli, d. 1917

Shuqayr, Mahmud, 1941–

al-Siba'i, Yusuf, 1917–1978

al-Sijistani, Abu Ya'qub. *See* Abu Ya'qub al-Sijistani, Ishaq ibn Ahmad, 10th century

al-Sijzi, Abu Ya'qub. *See* Abu Ya'qub al-Sijistani, Ishaq ibn Ahmad, 10th century

Sindbad, Book of. *See Arabian Nights, The*

Sindbad the Sailor. *See Arabian Nights, The*

Sirat Bani Hilal

Sirat Sayf ibn Dhi Yazan

Story of the Seven Viziers. *See Arabian Nights, The*

al-Suhrawardi, Yahya ibn Habash, 1152 or 1153–1191

Sultan, Nur al-Huda. *See* Sha'rawi, Huda, 1879–1947

Surur, Najib, 1932–1978

al-Suyuti, 1445–1505

al-Tabari, 838?–923

al-Tabari, 'Ali ibn Sahl Rabban, 9th
  century

Taha, 'Ali Mahmud, 1903 or 1904–1949

al-Tahawi, Miral, 1968–

Tahir, Baha', 1935–

al-Tahtawi, Rifa'ah Rafi', 1801–1873

al-Takarli, Fu'ad, 1927–

al-Tanukhi, al-Muhassin ibn 'Ali,
  940?–994

Tarafah ibn al-'Abd, 6th century

Taymur, 'A'ishah. *See* al-Taymuriyah,
  'A'ishah, 1840 or 1841–1902 or
  1903

Taymur, Mahmud, 1894–1973

al-Taymuriyah, 'A'ishah, 1840 or
  1841–1902 or 1903

Thabit ibn Qurrah al-Harrani, d. 901

Thousand and One Nights. *See Arabian
  Nights, The*

al-Tikirli, Fu'ad. *See* al-Takarli, Fu'ad,
  1927–

Tuqan, Fadwa, 1917–

Tuqan, Ibrahim 'Abd al-Fattah,
  1905–1941

al-Tusi, Nasir al-Din Muhammad ibn
  Muhammad, 1201–1274

'Umar ibn Abi Rabi'ah, 643 or 644–711
  or 712

Usamah ibn Munqidh, 1095–1188

al-'Uthman, Layla

Waddah al-Yaman, 'Abd al-Rahman ibn
  Isma'il, d. ca. 708

Walladah bint al-Mustakfi, d. 1091 or
  1092

Wannus, Sa'd Allah, 1941–1997

Wattar, al-Tahir, 1936–

al-Wazzan al-Fasi, al-Hasan ibn
  Muhammad. *See* Leo, *Africanus*,
  ca. 1492–ca.1550

Yakhlif, Yahya, 1944–

Ya'qub ibn Ishaq al-Kindi. *See* al-Kindi,
  d. ca. 873

Yaqut ibn 'Abd Allah al-Hamawi,
  1179?–1229

Yusuf, Sa'di, 1934–

Zafzaf, Muhammad, 1945–2001

Zaqtan, Ghassan, 1954–

Zayyad, Tawfiq, 1932–1994

al-Zayyat, Latifah, 1923–1996

Zefzaf, Mohammad. *See* Zafzaf,
  Muhammad, 1945–2001

Zhahin, Salah. *See* Chahin, Salah,
  1930–1986

Ziyad, Tawfik. *See* Zayyad, Tawfiq,
  1932–1994

Ziyadah, Mayy, 1886–1941

Zu al-Rummah. *See* Dhu al-Rummah,
  Ghaylan ibn 'Uqbah, 696–735

Zuhayr ibn Abi Sulma, d. 609

Zurayq, Qustantin, 1909–2000

Authors by Nationality

Authors are listed under the nationality with which they are most often associated, not necessarily that into which they were born. Some authors are listed more than once; for example, Kahlil Gibran is listed under both American and Lebanese. Authors whose work was written before 622 are listed under Pre-Islamic, those between 622 and 1800 under Islamic.

Algerian

Benhadouga, Abdelhamid, 1925–
Mosteghanemi, Ahlem, 1953–

Wattar, al-Tahir, 1936–

American

'Aridah, Nasib, 1887–1946
Barakat, Halim Isber, 1936–
Gibran, Kahlil, 1883–1931

Nu'aymah, Mikha'il, 1889–1989
Rihani, Ameen Fares, 1876–1940

Australian

al-Hajj, Jad

Bahraini

Haddad, Qasim, 1948–

Egyptian

Abazah, 'Aziz, 1898–1969
Abazah, Tharwat, 1927–2002
'Abd al-Hakim, Shawqi, 1936?–
'Abd Allah, Muhammad 'Abd al-Halim, 1913–1970
'Abd al-Qaddus, Ihsan, 1919–1990
'Abd al-Sabur, Salah, 1931–1981
Abu Hadid, Muhammad Farid, 1893–1968
Abu Shadi, Ahmad Zaki, 1892–1955
'Ali Mubarak, *Basha*, 1823 or 1824–1893
Amin, Ahmad, 1886–1954

al-'Aqqad, 'Abbas Mahmud, 1889–1964
Aslan, Ibrahim, 1939–
'Awad, Luwis, 1915–1990
Ba Kathir, 'Ali Ahmad, 1910–1969
Bakr, Salwa, 1949–
al-Banna', Hasan, 1906–1949
al-Barudi, Mahmud Sami, 1839–1904
Bayram al-Tunisi, Mahmud, 1893–1961
Bint al-Shati', 1913–1998
al-Bisati, Muhammad, 1937–
Chahin, Salah, 1930–1986
Dunqul, Amal, d. 1983
al-Fituri, Muhammad, 1936?–

Ghanim, Fathi, 1924–1999

al-Ghazali, Zaynab, 1917–

al-Ghitani, Jamal, 1945–

Hafiz Ibrahim, Muhammad, 1872?–1932

al-Hakim, Tawfiq, 1898–1987

Haqqi, Yahya, 1905–1993

Hatatah, Sharif, 1923–

Haykal, Muhammad Husayn,
    1888–1956

Husayn, Taha, 1889–1937

Ibrahim, Jamil 'Atiyah, 1937–

Ibrahim, Sun' Allah, 1937–

Idris, Yusuf, 1927–1991

al-Jabarti, 'Abd al-Rahman,
    1754–1822

al-Kharrat, Idwar, 1926–

al-Khuli, Lutfi, 1928–1999

Mahfuz, Najib, 1912–

Mahmud, Zaki Najib, 1905–1993

al-Manfaluti, Mustafa, 1876?–1924

Matar, Muhammad Afifi, 1935–

al-Mazini, Ibrahim 'Abd al-Qadir,
    1889–1949

Mirsal, Iman, 1966–

Muhammad 'Abduh, 1849–1905

Muhammad Farid, 1868–1919

Musa, Nabawiyah, 1886–1951

Musa, Salamah, 1887–1958

Nabarawi, Sayza, 1897–1985

Naji, Ibrahim, 1898–1953

Nasif, Malak Hifni, 1886–1918

Qasim Amin, 1863–1908

Qutb, Sayyid, 1903–1966

al-Rafi'i, Mustafa Sadiq, d. 1937

Rif'at, Alifah

Sabri, Isma'il, 1854–1923

al-Sa'dawi, Nawal, 1931–

al-Sa'id, Aminah, 1914–1995

Salim, 'Ali, 1936–

Sannu', Ya'qub ibn Rafa'il,
    1839–1912

Shafiq, Durriyah, 1908–1975

Sha'rawi, Huda, 1879–1947

al-Sharqawi, 'Abd al-Rahman,
    1920–1987

al-Sharuni, Yusuf, 1924–

Shawqi, Ahmad, 1868–1932

Shumayyil, Shibli, d. 1917

al-Siba'i, Yusuf, 1917–1978

Surur, Najib, 1932–1978

Taha, 'Ali Mahmud, 1903 or 1904–1949

al-Tahawi, Miral, 1968–

Tahir, Baha', 1935–

al-Tahtawi, Rifa'ah Rafi', 1801–1873

Taymur, Mahmud, 1894–1973

al-Taymuriyah, 'A'ishah, 1840 or
    41–1902 or 3

al-Zayyat, Latifah, 1923–1996

Emirati

al-Qasimi, Maysun Saqr

Iraqi

al-'Azzawi, Fadil, 1940–

al-Bayati, 'Abd al-Wahhab, 1926–1999

Bulus, Sarkun, 1943–

al-Haydari, Buland, 1926–1996

al-Jawahiri, Muhammad Mahdi,
    1900–1997

al-Juburi, Amal, 1967–

al-Mala'ikah, Nazik, 1923–

Mamduh, 'Aliyah, 1944–

Mikha'il, Dunya, 1965–

Naqqash, Samir

al-Nawwab, Muzaffar, 1934–

al-Sayyab, Badr Shakir, 1926–1964

al-Takarli, Fu'ad, 1927–

Yusuf, Sa'di, 1934–

Islamic

Abu al-'Ala' al-Ma'arri, 973–1057

Abu al-Fida' Isma'il ibn 'Ali, 1273–1331

Abu al-Qasim Khalaf ibn 'Abbas al-Zahrawi, d. 1013?

Abu Nuwas, ca. 756–ca. 810

Abu Tammam Habib ibn Aws al-Ta'i, fl. 808–842

Abu Ya'qub al-Sijistani, Ishaq ibn Ahmad, 10th century

al-Afghani, Jamal al-Din, 1838–1897

Alhazen, 965–1039

Arabian Nights, The

Avempace, d. 1138 or 1139

Averroes, 1126–1198

Avicenna, 980–1037

al-Baladhuri, Ahmad ibn Yahya, d. 892

al-Battani, Muhammad ibn Jabir, d. 929

al-Biruni, Muhammad ibn Ahmad, 973?–1048

al-Busiri, Sharaf al-Din Muhammad ibn Sa'id, 1213?–1296?

Buzurg ibn Shahriyar, 10th century

Dhu al-Rummah, Ghaylan ibn 'Uqbah, 696–735

al-Dinawari, Abu Hanifah Ahmad ibn Dawud, d. ca. 895

al-Farabi, ca. 872–950

al-Farazdaq, ca. 641–728

al-Farghani, fl. 861

al-Ghazzali, 1058–1111

al-Hallaj, al-Husayn ibn Mansur, 858 or 859–922

al-Hariri, 1054–1122

Hassan ibn Thabit, d. 674

Hunayn ibn Ishaq al-'Ibadi, 809?–873

Ibn 'Abd al-Hakam, d. 870 or 871

Ibn al-'Arabi, 1165–1240

Ibn al-Athir, 'Izz al-Din, 1160–1233

Ibn al-Nadim, Muhammad ibn Ishaq, fl. 987

Ibn al-Nafis, 'Ali ibn Abi al-Hazm, 1210 or 1211–1288

Ibn al-Qalanisi, Abu Ya'la Hamzah ibn Asad, d. 1160

Ibn al-Rumi, 836–896

Ibn 'Ata' Allah, Ahmad ibn Muhammad, d. 1309

Ibn Batuta, 1304–1377

Ibn Daniyal, Muhammad, 1249 or 1250–1310 or 1311

Ibn Fadlan, Ahmad, fl. 922

Ibn Hawqal, Muhammad, 10th century

Ibn Hazm, 'Ali ibn Ahmad, 994–1064

Ibn Ishaq, Muhammad, d. ca. 768

Ibn Jubayr, Muhammad ibn Ahmad, 1145–1217

Ibn Khaldun, 1332–1406

Ibn Masarrah, Muhammad ibn 'Abd Allah, 882 or 883–931

Ibn Miskawayh, Ahmad ibn Muhammad, d. 1030

Ibn Qayyim al-Jawziyah, Muhammad ibn Abi Bakr, 1292–1350

Ibn Sa'id, 'Ali ibn Musa, 1213–1286

Ibn Shaddad, Baha' al-Din Yusuf ibn Rafi', 1145–1234 or 1235

Ibn Sinan, Ibrahim, 908–946

Ibn Taymiyah, Ahmad ibn 'Abd al-Halim, 1263–1328

Ibn Tufayl, Muhammad ibn 'Abd al-Malik, d. 1185

al-Idrisi, ca. 1100–1166

Istakhri, Ibrahim ibn Muhammad, d. 957 or 958

Jabir ibn Hayyan, ca. 721–815?

al-Jahiz, d. 868 or 869

al-Katib al-Isfahani, 'Imad al-Din
    Muhammad ibn Muhammad,
    1125–1201

al-Khansa', d. ca. 645

al-Khuwarizmi, Muhammad ibn Musa,
    fl. 813–846

al-Kindi, d. ca. 873

Layla al-Akhyaliyah, d. ca. 700

Leo, *Africanus*, ca. 1492–ca. 1550

al-Maqrizi, Ahmad ibn 'Ali, 1364–1442

al-Mas'udi, d. 956?

al-Mawardi, 'Ali ibn Muhammad, 974?–
    1058

al-Muqaddasi, Muhammad ibn Ahmad,
    b. ca. 946

al-Mutanabbi, Abu al-Tayyib Ahmad ibn
    al-Husayn, 915 or 916–965

al-Nafzawi, 'Umar ibn Muhammad, fl.
    1410–1434

Rabi'ah al-'Adawiyah, d. 801?

al-Razi, Abu Bakr Muhammad ibn
    Zakariya, 865?–925?

al-Razi, Fakhr al-Din Muhammad ibn
    'Umar, 1149 or 50–1210

Sadr al-Din Shirazi, Muhammad ibn
    Ibrahim, d. 1641

Sirat Bani Hilal

Sirat Sayf ibn Dhi Yazan

al-Suhrawardi, Yahya ibn Habash, 1152
    or 1153–1191

al-Suyuti, 1445–1505

al-Tabari, 838?–923

al-Tabari, 'Ali ibn Sahl Rabban, 9th
    century

al-Tanukhi, al-Muhassin ibn 'Ali,
    940?–994

Thabit ibn Qurrah al-Harrani, d. 901

al-Tusi, Nasir al-Din Muhammad ibn
    Muhammad, 1201–1274

'Umar ibn Abi Rabi'ah, 643 or 644–711
    or 712

Usamah ibn Munqidh,
    1095–1188

Waddah al-Yaman, 'Abd al-Rahman ibn
    Isma'il, d. ca. 708

Walladah bint al-Mustakfi, d. 1091 or
    1092

Yaqut ibn 'Abd Allah al-Hamawi,
    1179?–1229

Israeli

Naqqash, Samir

Jordanian

Nasir, Amjad, 1955–

al-Sa'udi, Muna, 1945–

Kuwaiti

Al-Sabah, S.M., 1942–

al-'Uthman, Layla

Lebanese

'Awwad, Tawfiq Yusuf, 1911–1989

Barakat, Halim Isber, 1936–

Barakat, Huda, 1952–

Baydun, 'Abbas, 1945–

al-Da'if, Rashid, 1945–

Gibran, Kahlil, 1883–1931

Hawi, Khalil S., 1925–1982

al-Khal, Yusuf, 1917–1988

al-Khuri, Ilyas, 1948–

Nasr Allah, Imili, 1931–

Nu'aymah, Mikha'il,
    1889–1989

Rifqah, Fu'ad, 1930–
Rihani, Ameen Fares, 1876–1940
al-Shaykh, Hanan, 1945–

al-Shidyaq, Ahmad Faris, 1804?–1887
Ziyadah, Mayy, 1886–1941
Zurayq, Qustantin, 1909–2000

Libyan

al-Faqih, Ahmad Ibrahim, 1942–

Moroccan

Zafzaf, Muhammad, 1945–2001

Palestinian

Abu Shayib, Zuhayr, 1958–
al-'Aql, 'Abd al-Latif, 1942–
'Azzam, Samirah, 1925–1967
Badr, Liyanah, 1950–
al-Barghuthi, Murid, 1944–
Dahbur, Ahmad, 1946–
Darwish, Mahmud, 1941–
Habibi, Imil, 1921–1996
Jabra, Jabra Ibrahim, 1920–1994
Jayyusi, Salma Khadra, 1926–
Kanafani, Ghassan, 1936–1972
al-Karmi, Abu Salma 'Abd al-Karim,
     1907–1980
Khalifah, Sahar, 1941–
al-Khalili, 'Ali, 1943–

Khazindar, Walid, 1950–
Muhammad, Zakariya, 1951–
Nasir, Kamal, 1925–1973
Nasr Allah, Ibrahim, 1954–
al-Qasim, Samih, 1939–
al-Rimawi, Mahmud, 1948–
al-Sayigh, Mayy, 1940–
Sayigh, Tawfiq, 1924–1971
Shuqayr, Mahmud, 1941–
Tuqan, Fadwa, 1917–
Tuqan, Ibrahim 'Abd al-Fattah,
     1905–1941
Yakhlif, Yahya, 1944–
Zaqtan, Ghassan, 1954–
Zayyad, Tawfiq, 1932–1994

Pre-Islamic

'Abid ibn al-Abras, fl. 6th century
'Antarah ibn Shaddad, 6th century
Imru' al-Qays, 497–545

Tarafah ibn al-'Abd, 6th century
Zuhayr ibn Abi Sulma, d. 609

Saudi

Abu Khalid, Fawziyah
Kashghari, Badi'ah Dawud

Munif, 'Abd al-Rahman, 1933–
al-Qusaybi, Ghazi 'Abd al-Rahman,
     1940–

Sudanese

al-Fituri, Muhammad, 1936?–
al-Majdhub, Muhammad al-Mahdi,
     1919–1982

Salih, al-Tayyib, 1929–

Syrian

Adunis, 1930–
'Aridah, Nasib, 1887–1946
Arna'ut, 'A'ishah
Baghdadi, Shawqi, 1928–
Barakat, Halim Isber, 1936–
Haydar, Haydar, 1936–
al-Idlibi, Ulfat, 1912–
al-Khal, Yusuf, 1917–1988
al-Maghut, Muhammad, 1934–
Mardam, Khalil, 1895?–1959

Minah, Hanna, 1924–
Muhammad Rashid Rida, 1865–1935
al-Qabbani, Nizar, 1923–1998
Rifqah, Fu'ad, 1930–
Sa'adah, Antun, 1904–1949
al-Samman, Ghadah, 1942–
Shumayyil, Shibli, d. 1917
Wannus, Sa'd Allah, 1941–1997
Ziyadah, Mayy, 1886–1941
Zurayq, Qustantin, 1909–2000

Tunisian

al-Shabbi, Abu al-Qasim, 1909–1934

Yemeni

Ba Kathir, 'Ali Ahmad, 1910–1969

al-Baradduni, 'Abd Allah, 1926–1999

Authors by Time Period

Pre- and Early Islamic (to 661)

'Abid ibn al-Abras, fl. 6th century
'Antarah ibn Shaddad, 6th century
Hassan ibn Thabit, d. 674
Imru' al-Qays, 497–545

al-Khansa', d. ca. 645
Tarafah ibn al-'Abd, 6th century
Zuhayr ibn Abi Sulma, d. 609

Classical (661–1258)

Abu al-'Ala' al-Ma'arri, 973–1058
Abu al-Qasim Khalaf ibn 'Abbas al-
    Zahrawi, d. 1013?
Abu Nuwas, ca. 756–ca. 810
Abu Tammam Habib ibn Aws al-Ta'i, fl.
    808–842
Abu Ya'qub al-Sijistani, Ishaq ibn
    Ahmad, 10th century
Alhazen, 965–1039
Arabian Nights, The
Avempace, d. 1138 or 1139
Averroes, 1126–1198
Avicenna, 980–1037
al-Baladhuri, Ahmad ibn Yahya, d. 892
al-Battani, Muhammad ibn Jabir, d. 929
al-Biruni, Muhammad ibn Ahmad,
    973?–1048
Buzurg ibn Shahriyar, 10th century
Dhu al-Rummah, Ghaylan ibn 'Uqbah,
    696–735
al-Dinawari, Abu Hanifah Ahmad ibn
    Dawud, d. ca. 895
al-Farabi, ca. 872–950
al-Farazdaq, ca. 641–728
al-Farghani, fl. 861
al-Ghazzali, 1058–1111
al-Hallaj, al-Husayn ibn Mansur, 858 or
    859–922
al-Hariri, 1054–1122

Hunayn ibn Ishaq al-'Ibadi, 809?–873
Ibn 'Abd al-Hakam, d. 870 or 871
Ibn al-'Arabi, 1165–1240
Ibn al-Athir, 'Izz al-Din, 1160–1233
Ibn al-Nadim, Muhammad ibn Ishaq, fl.
    987
Ibn al-Qalanisi, Abu Ya'la Hamzah ibn
    Asad, d. 1160
Ibn al-Rumi, 836–896
Ibn Fadlan, Ahmad, fl. 922
Ibn Hawqal, Muhammad, 10th century
Ibn Hazm, 'Ali ibn Ahmad, 994–1064
Ibn Ishaq, Muhammad, d. ca. 768
Ibn Jubayr, Muhammad ibn Ahmad,
    1145–1217
Ibn Masarrah, Muhammad ibn 'Abd
    Allah, 882 or 883–931
Ibn Miskawayh, Ahmad ibn Muhammad,
    d. 1030
Ibn Shaddad, Baha' al-Din Yusuf ibn
    Rafi', 1145–1234 or 1235
Ibn Sinan, Ibrahim, 908–946
Ibn Tufayl, Muhammad ibn 'Abd
    al-Malik, d. 1185
al-Idrisi, ca. 1100–1166
Istakhri, Ibrahim ibn Muhammad, d. 957
    or 958
Jabir ibn Hayyan, ca. 721–815?
al-Jahiz, d. 868 or 869

al-Katib al-Isfahani, 'Imad al-Din Muhammad ibn Muhammad, 1125–1201

al-Khuwarizmi, Muhammad ibn Musa, fl. 813–846

al-Kindi, d. ca. 873

Layla al-Akhyaliyah, d. ca. 700

al-Mas'udi, d. 956?

al-Mawardi, 'Ali ibn Muhammad, 974?–1058

al-Muqaddasi, Muhammad ibn Ahmad, b. ca. 946

al-Mutanabbi, Abu al-Tayyib Ahmad ibn al-Husayn, 915 or 916–965

Rabi'ah al-'Adawiyah, d. 801?

al-Razi, Abu Bakr Muhammad ibn Zakariya, 865?–925?

al-Razi, Fakhr al-Din Muhammad ibn 'Umar, 1149 or 1150–1210

Sirat Bani Hilal

Sirat Sayf ibn Dhi Yazan

al-Suhrawardi, Yahya ibn Habash, 1152 or 1153–1191

al-Tabari, 838?–923

al-Tabari, 'Ali ibn Sahl Rabban, 9th century

al-Tanukhi, al-Muhassin ibn 'Ali, 940?–994

Thabit ibn Qurrah al-Harrani, d. 901

'Umar ibn Abi Rabi'ah, 643 or 644–711 or 712

Usamah ibn Munqidh, 1095–1188

Waddah al-Yaman, 'Abd al-Rahman ibn Isma'il, d. ca. 708

Walladah bint al-Mustakfi, d. 1091 or 1092

Yaqut ibn 'Abd Allah al-Hamawi, 1179?–1229

Mamluk and Turkish (1258–1800)

Abu al-Fida' Isma'il ibn 'Ali, 1273–1331

al-Busiri, Sharaf al-Din Muhammad ibn Sa'id, 1213?–1296?

Ibn al-Nafis, 'Ali ibn Abi al-Hazm, 1210 or 1211–1288

Ibn 'Ata' Allah, Ahmad ibn Muhammad, d. 1309

Ibn Batuta, 1304–1377

Ibn Daniyal, Muhammad, 1249 or 50–1310 or 11

Ibn Khaldun, 1332–1406

Ibn Qayyim al-Jawziyah, Muhammad ibn Abi Bakr, 1292–1350

Ibn Sa'id, 'Ali ibn Musa, 1213–1286

Ibn Taymiyah, Ahmad ibn 'Abd al-Halim, 1263–1328

Leo, *Africanus*, ca. 1492–ca.1550

al-Maqrizi, Ahmad ibn 'Ali, 1364–1442

al-Nafzawi, 'Umar ibn Muhammad, fl. 1410–1434

Sadr al-Din Shirazi, Muhammad ibn Ibrahim, d. 1641

al-Suyuti, 1445–1505

al-Tusi, Nasir al-Din Muhammad ibn Muhammad, 1201–1274

Modern (1800–Present)

Abazah, 'Aziz, 1898–1969

Abazah, Tharwat, 1927–2002

'Abd al-Hakim, Shawqi, 1936?–

'Abd Allah, Muhammad 'Abd al-Halim, 1913–1970

'Abd al-Qaddus, Ihsan, 1919–1990

'Abd al-Sabur, Salah, 1931–1981

Abu Hadid, Muhammad Farid, 1893–1968

Abu Khalid, Fawziyah

Abu Shadi, Ahmad Zaki, 1892–1955

Abu Shayib, Zuhayr, 1958–

Adunis, 1930–

al-Afghani, Jamal al-Din, 1839–1897

Ali Mubarak, *Basha*, 1823 or 1824–1893

Amin, Ahmad, 1886–1954
'Aql, 'Abd al-Latif, 1942–
al-'Aqqad, 'Abbas Mahmud, 1889–1964
'Aridah, Nasib, 1887–1946
Arna'ut, 'A'ishah
Aslan, Ibrahim, 1939–
'Awad, Luwis, 1915–1990
'Awwad, Tawfiq Yusuf, 1911–1989
'Azzam, Samirah, 1925–1967
al-'Azzawi, Fadil, 1940–
Badr, Liyanah, 1950–
Baghdadi, Shawqi, 1928–
Ba Kathir, 'Ali Ahmad, 1910–1969
Bakr, Salwa, 1949–
al-Banna', Hasan, 1906–1949
al-Baradduni, 'Abd Allah, 1926–1999
Barakat, Halim Isber, 1936–
Barakat, Huda, 1952–
Barghuthi, Murid, 1944–
al-Barudi, Mahmud Sami, 1839–1904
al-Bayati, 'Abd al-Wahhab, 1926–1999
Baydun, 'Abbas, 1945–
Bayram al-Tunisi, Mahmud, 1893–1961
Benhadouga, Abdelhamid, 1925–
Bint al-Shati', 1913–1998
al-Bisati, Muhammad, 1937–
Bulus, Sarkun, 1943–
Chahin, Salah, 1930–1986
Dahbur, Ahmad, 1946–
al-Da'if, Rashid, 1945–
Darwish, Mahmud, 1941–
Dunqul, Amal, d. 1983
al-Faqih, Ahmad Ibrahim, 1942–
al-Fituri, Muhammad, 1936?–
Ghanim, Fathi, 1924–1999
al-Ghazali, Zaynab, 1917–
al-Ghitani, Jamal, 1945–
Gibran, Kahlil, 1883–1931
Habibi, Imil, 1921–1996
Haddad, Qasim, 1948–
Hafiz Ibrahim, Muhammad, 1872?–1932
al-Hakim, Tawfiq, 1898–1987

Haqqi, Yahya, 1905–1993
Hatatah, Sharif, 1923–
Hawi, Khalil S., 1925–1982
Haydar, Haydar, 1936–
al-Haydari, Buland, 1926–1996
Haykal, Muhammad Husayn, 1888–1956
Husayn, Taha, 1889–1937
Ibrahim, Jamil 'Atiyah, 1937–
Ibrahim, Sun' Allah, 1937–
al-Idlibi, Ulfat, 1912–
Idris, Yusuf, 1927–1991
al-Jabarti, 'Abd al-Rahman, 1754–1822
Jabra, Jabra Ibrahim, 1920–1994
al-Jawahiri, Muhammad Mahdi, 1900–1997
Jayyusi, Salma Khadra, 1926–
al-Juburi, Amal
Kanafani, Ghassan, 1936–1972
al-Karmi, Abu Salma 'Abd al-Karim, 1907–1980
Kashghari, Badi'ah Dawud
al-Khal, Yusuf, 1917–1988
Khalifah, Sahar, 1941–
al-Khalili, 'Ali, 1943–
al-Kharrat, Idwar, 1926–
Khazindar, Walid, 1950–
al-Khuli, Lutfi, 1928–1999
al-Khuri, Ilyas, 1948–
al-Maghut, Muhammad, 1934–
Mahfuz, Najib, 1912–
Mahmud, Zaki Najib, 1905–1993
al-Majdhub, Muhammad al-Mahdi, 1919–1982
al-Mala'ikah, Nazik, 1923–
Mamduh, 'Aliyah, 1944–
al-Manfaluti, Mustafa, 1876?–1924
Mardam, Khalil, 1895?–1959
Matar, Muhammad Afifi, 1935–
al-Mazini, Ibrahim 'Abd al-Qadir, 1889–1949
Mikha'il, Dunya, 1965–
Minah, Hanna, 1924–

Mirsal, Iman, 1966–
Mosteghanemi, Ahlem, 1935–
Muhammad 'Abduh, 1849–1905
Muhammad Farid, 1868–1919
Muhammad Rashid Rida, 1865–1935
Muhammad, Zakariya, 1951–
Munif, 'Abd al-Rahman, 1933–
Musa, Nabawiyah, 1886–1951
Musa, Salamah, 1887–1958
Nabarawi, Saya, 1897–1985
Naji, Ibrahim, 1898–1953
Naqqash, Samir
Nasif, Malak Hifni, 1886–1918
Nasir, Amjad, 1955–
Nasir, Kamal, 1925–1973
Nasr Allah, Ibrahim, 1954–
Nasr Allah, Imili, 1931–
al-Nawwab, Muzaffar, 1934–
Nu'aymah, Mikha'il, 1889–1989
Qabbani, Nizar, 1923–1998
Qasim Amin, 1863–1908
al-Qasim, Samih, 1939–
al-Qasimi, Maysun Saqr
al-Qusaybi, Ghazi 'Abd al-Rahman,
    1940–
Qutb, Sayyid, 1903–1966
al-Rafi'i, Mustafa Sadiq, d. 1937
Rif'at, Alifah
Rifqah, Fu'ad, 1930–
Rihani, Ameen Fares, 1876–1940
al-Rimawi, Mahmud, 1948–
Sa'adah, Antun, 1904–1949
Al-Sabah, S. M., 1942–
Sabri, Isma'il, 1854–1923
al-Sa'dawi, Nawal, 1931–
al-Sa'id, Aminah, 1914–1995
Salih, al-Tayyib, 1929–
Salim, 'Ali, 1936–
al-Samman, Ghadah, 1942–
Sannu', Ya'qub ibn Rafa'il, 1839–1912

al-Sa'udi, Muna, 1945–
al-Sayigh, Mayy, 1940–
Sayigh, Tawfiq, 1924–1971
al-Sayyab, Badr Shakir, 1926–1964
al-Shabbi, Abu al-Qasim, 1909–1934
Shafiq, Durriyah, 1908–1975
Sha'rawi, Huda, 1879–1947
al-Sharqawi, 'Abd al-Rahman,
    1920–1987
al-Sharuni, Yusuf, 1924–
Shawqi, Ahmad, 1868–1932
al-Shaykh, Hanan, 1945–
al-Shidyaq, Ahmad Faris, 1804?–1887
Shumayyil, Shibli, d. 1917
Shuqayr, Mahmud, 1941–
al-Siba'i, Yusuf, 1917–1978
Surur, Najib, 1932–1978
Taha, 'Ali Mahmud, 1903 or
    1904–1949
al-Tahawi, Miral, 1968–
Tahir, Baha', 1935–
al-Tahtawi, Rifa'ah Rafi', 1801–1873
al-Takarli, Fu'ad, 1927–
Taymur, Mahmud, 1894–1973
al-Taymuriyah, 'A'ishah, 1840 or
    1841–1902 or 1903
Tuqan, Fadwa, 1917–
Tuqan, Ibrahim 'Abd al-Fattah,
    1905–1941
al-'Uthman, Layla
Wannus, Sa'd Allah, 1941–1997
Wattar, al-Tahir, 1936–
Yakhlif, Yahya, 1944–
Yusuf, Sa'di, 1934–
Zafzaf, Muhammad, 1945–2001
Zaqtan, Ghassan, 1954–
Zayyad, Tawfiq, 1932–1994
al-Zayyat, Latifah, 1925–
Ziyadah, Mayy, 1886–1941
Zurayq, Qustantin, 1909–2000

Frequently Cited
Web Sites

Al-Ahram Weekly On-Line. Ed. H. Guindy. Updated weekly. http://weekly.ahram.org.eg/ (accessed 17 Aug. 2003).

English weekly version of the famed Egyptian daily newspaper. Excellent coverage of arts, culture, and literature, easily searchable (but be sure to spell names several ways). Archives date back to May 1998.

Arab World Books. http://www.arabworldbooks.com/index.html (accessed 10 Aug. 2003).

Web site of an online bookstore and book club for Arabic literature. In addition to extensive information on modern authors, it includes authors' responses to book club discussions, an eclectic group of articles mainly on the topic of literature and politics, and an online bookstore. In English and Arabic.

Books and Writers. Ed. P. Liukkonen. http://www.kirjasto.sci.fi/calendar.htm (accessed 17 Aug. 2003).

Search by author's name alphabetically or by birthday. Short biographical sketches include works by and about the author, and links to other Web sites.

Center for Islam and Science. Ed. B.K. Iqbal. http://www.cis-ca.org/ (accessed 14 Aug. 2003).

Includes biographies of medieval and modern scholars, glossary of terms, bibliography on the relationship between Islam and science. Also serves as the home for *Islam & Science: Journal of Islamic Perspectives on Science.*

Egypt. Egyptian State Information Service. http://www.sis.gov.eg/ (accessed 10 Aug. 2003).

There are two mirror sites, one in the United States (http://www.us.sis.gov.eg/) and one in Britain (http://www.uk.sis.gov.eg/).

Gender Issues and Literature in the Middle East. http://www.u.arizona.edu/~talattof/women-lit/introduction.htm (accessed 13 Aug. 2003).

Created for a course taught at the University of Arizona. Choose "Arabic" from the left bar, then "Prose" or "Poetry." Note that several of the translations listed under "Poetry" should be under "Prose" and vice-versa.

Internet Medieval Sourcebook. Ed. P. Halsall. 8 Jan. 2000. Fordham University Center for Medieval Studies. http://www.fordham.edu/halsall/sbook.html (accessed 16 Aug. 2003).

Part of *ORB, Online Book for Medieval Studies* (http://www.the-orb.net/), and one unit of the *Internet History Sourcebooks Project* (http://www.fordham.edu/halsall/index.html), this site provides excerpted and full texts, together with multimedia images, for teaching purposes. The citations to this included in this book can also be accessed through *Internet Islamic History Sourcebook* (http://www.fordham.edu/halsall/islam/islamsbook.html), an augmented site which incorporates material from all the subsets of the *Internet History Sourcebooks Project*.

Islamic Philosophy Online. 5 Aug. 2003. Islamic Philosophy Online, Inc. http://www.muslimphilosophy.com/ (accessed 16 Aug. 2003).

Excellent site with books and articles in both English and Arabic on various aspects of Islamic Philosophy, including general overviews as well as pages and links devoted to individual philosophers. Home to the newly established *Journal of Islamic Philosophy*. Also hosts an e-discussion board.

Jehat.com. Ed. Y. Al Moharragi. http://www.jehat.com/en/ (accessed 9 Apr. 2004).

Originally a collaboration between al-Nadim Foundation in Bahrain and the Arab poet Qasim Haddad, this site is devoted to modern Arabic poetry. Includes biographies and translations, links to other poetry sites and to e-zines. In English, Arabic, and French.

Khalil Sakakini Cultural Centre. http://www.sakakini.org/first.html (accessed 4 Aug. 2003).

Home page of a Palestinian cultural arts organization. Includes biographies of artists and writers, with samples of their works, and online exhibits.

MacTutor History of Mathematics Archive. Ed. J.J. O'Connor and E.F. Robertson. Aug. 2003. School of Mathematics and Statistics, University of St. Andrews, Scotland. http://www-gap.dcs.st-and.ac.uk/~history/ or http://www-history.mcs.st-andrews.ac.uk/history/index.html (accessed 29 Aug. 2003).

Substantial biographies with references of mathematicians through the ages, essays on various topics in the history of mathematics, index of curves.

Malaspina Great Books. Ed. R. McNeil. http://www.malaspina.com/ (accessed 10 Aug. 2003).

Site devoted to presenting the ideas that have contributed to world culture, based on the framework of a great books list originally developed by Mortimer Adler. Includes biographies drawn from the fields of science, art, literature, music, and history. Each article includes a list of links to online booksellers and library catalogs.

Middle East and Islamic Studies Collection, Cornell University. Ed. A. Houissa. 24 Mar. 2003. http://www.library.cornell.edu/colldev/mideast/ (accessed 13 Aug. 2003).

Portal site for information on the Middle East, includes links to other Web pages as well as documents posted to this site.

MuslimHeritage.com. http://www.muslimheritage.com/default.cfm (accessed 10 Aug. 2003).

Provides source materials, 3-D models, and articles on the Muslim contribution to science, technology and civilization. Includes an interactive tour of the Muslim world, biographies of Muslim scholars, and articles on various topics. Biographies include a list of references and related articles on the same Web site.

Frequently Cited References

Allen, R., ed. *Modern Arabic Literature*. New York: Ungar, 1987.
  Includes reviews & analyses of works by individual authors, many translated from Arabic.

Arberry, A.J. *Arabic Poetry: A Primer for Students*. Cambridge: Cambridge UP, 1965.

Asfour, J.M., trans. and ed. *When the Words Burn: An Anthology of Modern Arabic Poetry, 1945–1987*. Dunvegan, Ontario: Cormorant, 1988.

Atiyeh, G.N., et al. *The Genius of Arab Civilization: Source of Renaissance*. 3rd ed. New York: New York UP, 1992.

Badran, M., and M. Cooke, eds. *Opening the Gates: A Century of Arab Feminist Writing*. Bloomington: Indiana UP, 1990.

Boullata, I. J., ed. and trans. *Modern Arab Poets, 1950–1975*. Washington, D.C.: Three Continents P, 1976.

Fairbairn, A., and G. al-Gosaibi, trans. *Feathers and the Horizon: A Selection of Modern Poetry from Across the Arab World*. 2nd ed. Canberra: Leros, 1989.

Ghazoul, F.J., and B. Harlow, eds. *The View from Within: Writers and Critics on Contemporary Arabic Literature*. Cairo: American U in Cairo P, 1994.

Gikandi, S., ed. *Encyclopedia of African Literature*. London: Routledge, 2003.

Gillispie, C.C., ed. *Dictionary of Scientific Biography*. 18 vols. New York: Scribner, 1970–1990.

Handal, N., ed. *The Poetry of Arab Women: A Contemporary Anthology*. New York: Interlink, 2001.

Jayyusi, S.K., ed. *Anthology of Modern Palestinian Literature*. New York: Columbia UP, 1992.

———, ed. *Modern Arabic Poetry: An Anthology*. New York: Columbia UP, 1987.

Johnson-Davies, D., trans. *Arabic Short Stories*. London: Quartet, 1983.

———, trans. *Arabic Short Stories*. London: Heinemann Educational; Washington, D.C.: Three Continents P, 1978.

———. *Under the Naked Sky: Short Stories from the Arab World*. Cairo: American U in Cairo P, 2000.

Khouri, M.A. and H. Algar, eds. and trans. *An Anthology of Modern Arabic Poetry*. Berkeley: U of California P, 1974.

Kirkpatrick, H. *The Modern Egyptian Novel: A Study in Social Criticism*. Oxford: Middle East Centre, St. Antony's College; London: Ithaca, 1974.
  Includes as an appendix, a synopsis of each novel discussed in the book.

Manzalaoui, Mahmoud, ed. *Arabic Short Stories 1945–1965*. Cairo: American U in Cairo P, 1985. Rpt. of *Arabic Writing Today: The Short Story*. 1968.

McGreal, I.P. *Great Thinkers of the Eastern World: The Major Thinkers and the Philosophical and Religious Classics of China, India, Japan, Korea, and the World of Islam*. New York: HarperCollins, 1995.

Meisami, J.S. and P. Starkey, eds. *Encyclopedia of Arabic Literature*. 2 vols. London: Routledge, 1998.

Nasr, S.H., and O. Leaman, eds. *History of Islamic Philosophy*. 2 vols. London: Routledge, 1996.

Ostle, R., E. de Moor, and S. Wild, eds. *Writing the Self: Autobiographical Writing in Modern Arabic Literature*. London: Saqi, 1998.

Pendergast, S., and T. Pendergast, eds. *Reference Guide to World Literature*. 3rd ed. 2 vols. Detroit: St. James-Thomson-Gale, 2003.

Serafin, S.R., ed. *Encyclopedia of World Literature in the 20th Century*. 3rd ed. 4 vols. Detroit: St. James Press, 1999.

Tuetey, C.G., trans. *Classical Arabic Poetry*. London: KPI, 1985.

al-Udhari, A., trans. and ed. *Modern Poetry of the Arab World*. Harmondsworth: Penguin, 1986.

Web Sites and References for Authors

Abazah, 'Aziz, 1898–1969

Web Sites

"'Aziz Abaza: A Prominent Modern Poet." *Egypt*. http://www.sis.gov.eg/calendar/html/cl100798.htm (accessed 10 Aug. 2003).

Biography and Criticism

Badawi, M.M. *Modern Arabic Drama in Egypt*. Cambridge: Cambridge UP, 1987. 215–217.

Mikhail, M. "Abaza, (Muhammad) 'Aziz." Meisami and Starkey, *Encyclopedia of Arabic Literature*. 1–2.

Abazah, Tharwat, 1927–2002

Web Sites

"Literary Circles Mourn a Prominent Novelist." *ArabicNews.com*. 25 March 2002. http://www.arabicnews.com/ansub/Daily/Day/020325/2002032527.html (accessed 10 Aug. 2003).

"Tharwat Abaza." *Egypt*. http://www.sis.gov.eg/calendar/html/o240322d.htm (accessed 10 Aug. 2003).

"Tharwat Abaza, Aristocratic Villager." *Egypt*. http://www.sis.gov.eg/calendar/html/cl150798.htm (accessed 10 Aug. 2003).

"Tharwat Abaza (1927–2002)." *al-Ahram Weekly On-line*. 21–27 March 2002. http://weekly.ahram.org.eg/2002/578/cu7.htm (accessed 10 Aug. 2003).

Translations

"Swimming in the Sand." *Egyptian Tales and Short Stories of the 1970s and 1980s*. Ed. W.M. Hutchins. Cairo: American U in Cairo P, 1987. 113–116.

Biography and Criticism

Mikhail, M. "Abaza, Tharwat." Meisami and Starkey, *Encyclopedia of Arabic Literature*. 2.

'Abd al-Hakim, Shawqi, 1936?–

Web Sites

"'Dhat al-Himma,' Masterpiece of Egyptian Author Shawki Abdel-Hakim." *Egypt*. http://www.sis.gov.eg/egyptinf/culture/html/hakim.htm (accessed 10 Aug. 2003).

Translations

"Hassan and Naima." Trans. M. Shaheen. Rev. A. Parkin and M. Manzalaoui. *Arabic Writing Today: Drama*. Ed. M. Manzalaoui. Cairo: American Research Center in Egypt, 1977. 297–334.

Biography and Criticism

Allen, *Modern Arabic Literature*. 1–5.

Badawi, M.M. *Modern Arabic Drama in Egypt*. Cambridge: Cambridge UP, 1987. 205–206.

Mikhail, M. "'Abd al-Hakim, Shawqi." Meisami and Starkey, *Encyclopedia of Arabic Literature*. 13.

'Abd Allah, Muhammad 'Abd al-Halim, 1913–1970

Web Sites

"Egyptian Novelist Muhammad Abd Al-Haleem Abduallah." *Egypt*. http://www.sis.gov.eg/calendar/html/cl300698.htm (accessed 10 Aug. 2003).

Biography and Criticism

Allen, R. "'Abd Allah, Muhammad 'Abd al-Halim." Meisami and Starkey, *Encyclopedia of Arabic Literature*. 12.

Sakkut, H. *The Egyptian Novel and Its Main Trends: From 1913 to 1952*. Cairo: American U in Cairo P, 1971. 41–45.

'Abd al-Qaddus, Ihsan, 1919–1990

Web Sites

"Ihsan Abdel Quddous." *Egypt*. http://www.sis.gov.eg/calendar/html/cl110198.htm (accessed Aug. 2003).

Includes a link to a short story, "Man in Heavens," at http://www.sis.gov.eg/public/magazine/iss009e/html/art11txt.htm.

Translations

"A Boy's Best Friend." Trans. W. Wassef. Rev. L. Hall. Manzalaoui, *Arabic Short Stories*. 156–169.

Arab Stories East and West. Leeds: Leeds U Oriental Soc., 1977. 35–45.

Includes translations of "The Genius" and "Revenge" by R.Y. Ebied and M.J.L. Young.

Biography and Criticism

"Abdel-Quddous, Ihsan (Mohammad)" *Contemporary Authors* 130 (1990): 1; 177 (1999): 2.

Starkey, P. "'Abd al-Quddus, Ihsan." Meisami and Starkey, *Encyclopedia of Arabic Literature*. 17–18.

'Abd al-Sabur, Salah, 1931–1981

Web Sites

"Salah 'Abd al-Sabur." *Jehat.com.* http://www.jehat.com/en/
default.asp?action=article&ID=93 (accessed 22 Apr. 2004).
Includes translations of the poems "Tale of the Sad Minstrel," "Expectation:
Night and Day," "The Gist of the Story," "The People of My Country," "Winter
Song," and "The Sun and the Woman."

"Salah Abdel-Sabour, Pioneer of Modern Poetry." *Egypt.* http://www.sis.gov.eg/
calendar/html/cl120897.htm (accessed 10 Aug. 2003).

Translations

"Dreams of the Ancient Knight." Khouri and Algar, *Anthology of Modern Arabic
Poetry.* 143–151.

Murder in Baghdad. Trans. K.I. Semaan. Leiden: Brill, 1972.

"The Night Traveler." Trans. M. Inani and A. Hollo. *Modern Arabic Drama: An
Anthology.* Ed. S.K. Jayyusi and R. Allen. Bloomington: Indiana UP, 1995.
289–304.

Boullata, *Modern Arab Poets.* 83–92.
Includes translations of "People in My Country," "The Shadow and the Cross,"
"A Song to God," and "The Tatars Attacked."

Biographies and Criticism

Allen, *Modern Arabic Literature.* 5–11.

Badawi, M.M. *Modern Arabic Drama in Egypt.* Cambridge: Cambridge UP, 1987.
220–228.

Husni, R. "'Abd al-Sabur, Salah." Meisami and Starkey, *Encyclopedia of Arabic
Literature.* 19–20.

Jayyusi, S.K. "'Abd al-Sabur, Salah." Serafin, *Encyclopedia of World Literature in the
20th Century.* 1: 1–2.

'Abid ibn al-Abras, fl. 6th century

Web Sites

'Abid ibn al-Abras. "A Lament for Fallen Friends." *Mosaic: Perspectives on Western
Civilization.* http://college.hmco.com/history/west/mosaic/chapter4/
module28.html (accessed 10 Aug. 2003).
Short introduction and translation of the poem.

Translations

*The Diwans of 'Abid ibn al-Abras, of Asad, and 'Amir ibn at-Tufail, of 'Amir ibn
Sa'sa'ah.* Trans. C. Lyall. Leyden: E.J. Brill; London: Luzac, 1913.

Biography and Criticism

Bauer, T. "'Abid ibn al-Abras." Meisami and Starkey, *Encyclopedia of Arabic
Literature.* 22.

Abu al-'Ala' al-Ma'arri, 973–1057

Web Sites

"Al Ma'arri." *Humanistic Texts*. Ed. R. Pay. 10 Aug. 2003, http://
    www.humanistictexts.org/al_ma'arri.htm (accessed 10 Aug. 2003).

Includes translations of 32 short poems. An abridged translation of a biography
of Abu al-'Ala' by Ibn Khallikan, a 13th century Arab writer, can be read at http://
www.humanistictexts.org/ibn_khallikan.htm.

Translations

The Diwan of Abul-Ala. Trans. H. Baerlein. London: Murray, 1948.

"Ma'arri." Tuetey, *Classical Arabic Poetry*. 269–282.

The Quatrains of Abu 'l-Ala. Trans. A.F. Rihani. London: Richards, 1904. (2nd ed.
    published as: *The Luzumiyat of Abul-Ala*. Trans. A. Rihani. New York: White,
    1920.)

Biography and Criticism

'Abd al-Rahman, A. "Abu 'l-'Ala' al-Ma'arri." *'Abbasid Belles-Lettres*. Ed. J.
    Ashtiany, et al. Cambridge History of Arabic Literature. Cambridge:
    Cambridge UP, 1990. 328–338.

Smoor, Pieter. *Kings and Bedouins in the Palace of Aleppo as Reflected in Ma'arri's
    Works*. Manchester: U of Manchester P, 1985.

van Gelder, G.J.H. "Abu al-'Ala' al-Ma'arri." Meisami and Starkey, *Encyclopedia of
    Arabic Literature*. 24–25.

Abu al-Fida' Isma'il ibn 'Ali, 1273–1331

Web Sites

"Abu al-Fida." *Damascus Online*. http://www.damascus-online.com/se/bio/
    abu_al.htm (accessed 10 Aug. 2003).

"Abu'l Fida [Abulfeda], Ismail." *Red Hill Observatory*. Ed. C.A. Plicht. http://
    www.plicht.de/chris/files/a/abulfidaismail.htm (accessed 10 Aug. 2003).

Autobiography

*The Memoirs of a Syrian Prince: Abu'l-Fida, Sultan of Hamah (672–732/
    1273–1331)*. Trans. P.M. Holt. Wiesbaden: Steiner, 1983.

Biography and Criticism

Irwin, R. "Abu al-Fida." Meisami and Starkey, *Encyclopedia of Arabic Literature*. 32.

Vernet, J. "Abu'l-Fida' Isma'il ibn 'Ali ibn Mahmud ibn . . . Ayyub, 'Imad al-Din."
    Gillispie, *Dictionary of Scientific Biography*. 1: 28–29.

Abu al-Qasim Khalaf ibn 'Abbas al-Zahrawi, d. 1013?

Web Sites

Ahmed, M. "El Zahrawi (Albucasis)—Father of Surgery." *Ummah.com*. http://
    www.ummah.net/history/scholars/el_zahrawi/ (accessed 10 Aug. 2003).

Shaikh, I. "Arab Surgeon Albucasis (Al-Zahrawi)" *MuslimHeritage.com*. http://
    www.muslimheritage.com/day_life/ (accessed 10 Aug. 2003).

Tschanz, D. "Az-Zahrawi: The Great Surgeon." *IslamOnline.net*. 10 Aug. 2003. http://www.islam-online.net/english/Science/2001/04/article5.shtml (accessed 10 Aug. 2003).

Zahoor, A. "Abu al-Qasim al-Zahravi (Albucasis)." Sadjad, R.S. Home page. http://www.unhas.ac.id/~rhiza/saintis/zahravi.html (accessed 10 Aug. 2003).

Biography and Criticism

Hamarneh, S.K. "Abu al-Qasim Khalaf bin 'Abbas az-Zahrawi (Albucasis)" Atiyeh, *The Genius of Arab Civilization*. 228–230.

———. "al-Zahrawi, Abu'l-Qasim Khalaf ibn 'Abbas." Gillispie, *Dictionary of Scientific Biography*. 14: 584–585.

———, and G. Sonnedecker. *A Pharmaceutical View of Abulcasis al-Zahrawi in Moorish Spain*. Leiden: Brill, 1963.

Abu Hadid, Muhammad Farid, 1893–1968

Web Sites

"Anniversary of Muhammad Farid Abu Hadeed, a Pioneer of Enlightenment." *Egypt*. http://www.sis.gov.eg/calendar/html/cl180598.htm (accessed 13 Aug. 2003).
 A slightly different version of his biography can be read at http://www.sis.gov.eg/eginfnew/culture/html/cul0112.htm.

"Mohamed Abuhadid." *Arab World Books*. http://www.arabworldbooks.com/authors/mohamed_abuhadid.html (accessed 13 Aug. 2003).

Biography and Criticism

Sakkut, H. *The Egyptian Novel and Its Main Trends: From 1913 to 1952*. Cairo: American U in Cairo P, 1971. 48–59.

Starkey, P. "Abu Hadid, Muhammad Farid." Meisami and Starkey, *Encyclopedia of Arabic Literature*. 33.

Abu Khalid, Fawziyah

Web Sites

Gender Issues and Literature in the Middle East. http://www.u.arizona.edu/~talattof/women-lit/introduction.htm (accessed 13 Aug. 2003).
 Includes translations of "Mother's Inheritance," "Tattoo Writing," and "To a Man."

Translations

Jayyusi, S.K., ed. *The Literature of Modern Arabia: An Anthology*. London: Kegan Paul International, 1988. 134–137.
 Includes translations of "Butterflies," "Distances of Longing," "My Friends," and "My Grandfather Attends the General Assembly" by M. Jayyusi and translations of "Departure," "A Pearl," and "Poem" by S. Jabsheh and J. Heath-Stubbs.

Handal, *The Poetry of Arab Women*. 70–72.
 Includes translations of "A Country," "Geometry of the Soul," "To Enjoy the Horror," and "Two Little Girls" by F. Mustafa.

Biography and Criticism

Arebi, S. *Women and Words in Saudi Arabia: The Politics of Literary Discourse*. New York: Columbia UP, 1994. 57–79.

Includes translations and analyses of the poems "Emerging from a Childbirth Fever," "An Unannounced Trial of an Overt Act of Love," and "Secret Diaries for Children."

Abu Nuwas, ca. 756–ca. 810

Web Sites

"Abu Nuwas." *The Knitting Circle*. 15 June 2003. Lesbian and Gay Staff Association, London South Bank University. http://www.sbu.ac.uk/stafflag/abunuwas.html (accessed 13 Aug. 2003).

"Abu Nuwas." *Out-Cyclopedia*. http://outcyclopedia.0catch.com/abunuwas.html (accessed 13 Aug. 2003).

"Abu Nuwas ibn Hani." *Humanistic Texts*. Ed. R. Pay. http:// www.humanistictexts.org/ibn_khallikan.htm (accessed 14 Aug. 2003). Abridged translation of a biography by Ibn Khallikan, a 13th century scholar.

"Abu Nuwas, the First and Foremost Islamic Gay Poet." *The World History of Male Love*. The Androphile Project. http://www.androphile.org/preview/Library/ Mythology/Arabian/AbuNuwas/AbuNuwasBio.html (accessed 13 Aug. 2003).

Includes biographical material and translations of poems, links to other sites, a short bibliography, and retellings of stories about Abu Nuwas from the *Arabian Nights*. Includes translations (some of which have been rewritten by an unnamed editor) of the poems "Wine of Paradise," "Credo," "Wa-Khaiymati Naturin," and "A Boy Is Worth More Than a Girl," which can be viewed at http://www.androphile.org/preview/Library/Poetry/.

"Princeton Online Arabic Poetry." *Princeton Online Poetry Project*. 27 Jan. 2003. Princeton University. http://www.princeton.edu/~arabic/poetry/index.html (accessed 13 Aug. 2003).

Short introductions, Arabic texts and audio recitations of "Don't Cry for Layla" and "The Wretch Paused."

Translations

"Abu Nuwas of Hakam-Madhhij." Tuetey, *Classical Arabic Poetry*. 197–211.

Bitar, F., ed. *Treasury of Arabic Love Poems, Quotations and Proverbs*. New York: Hippocrene, 1996. 37–41.

Includes translations of "Banan's Face," "The Bearer of Love," and "The Lover" by A. Wormhoudt.

Biography and Criticism

Kennedy, P.F. *The Wine Song in Classical Arabic Poetry: Abu Nuwas and the Literary Tradition*. Oxford: Clarendon, 1997.

Montgomery, J.E. "For the Love of a Christian Boy: A Song by Abu Nuwas." *Journal of Arabic Literature* 27 (1996): 115–124.

Schoeler, G. "Abu Nuwas." Trans. A. Giese. Meisami and Starkey, *Encyclopedia of Arabic Literature*. 41–43.

————. "Bashshar b. Burd, Abu 'l-'Atahiyah and Abu Nuwas." *'Abbasid Belles-Lettres*. Ed. J. Ashtiany, et al. Cambridge History of Arabic Literature. Cambridge: Cambridge UP, 1990. 275–299. See esp. 290–299.

Abu Shadi, Ahmad Zaki, 1892–1955

Web Sites

"Ahmad Zaki Abou Shadi." *Egypt*. http://www.sis.gov.eg/egyptianfigures/html/aboshadi.htm (accessed 13 Aug. 2003).

Translations

"From the Heaven." Trans. M.M. Badawi. *Journal of Arabic Literature* 6 (1975): 130–131.

Modern Arabic Poetry. Cambridge: Cambridge UP, 1967. 19–21.
    Includes translations of "Evening Prayer," "The Maiden of Bekhten," and "Union Eternal" by A.J. Arberry.

Biography and Criticism

Allen, *Modern Arabic Literature*. 21–29.

Ostle, R.C. "Abu Shadi, Ahmad Zaki." Meisami and Starkey, *Encyclopedia of Arabic Literature*. 45.

Abu Shayib, Zuhayr, 1958–

Web Sites

"Palestinian Poets, Zuheir Abu Shayeb." *Khalil Sakakini Cultural Centre*. http://www.sakakini.org/poets/zuheir-index.htm (accessed 14 Aug. 2003). Includes translation of "Martyr."

"Zuhayr Abou Chayeb." *Autodafe: The Censored Library*. July 2003. International Parliament of Writers. http://www.autodafe.org/bookshop/palestine/khaznadar.htm#3 (accessed 13 Aug. 2003).
    Translation of "Take This Sand Away from Me."

Translations

Jayyusi, *Anthology of Modern Palestinian Literature*. 98–101.
    Includes translations of "Fever of Questions," "Handsome and Tall," and "Probabilities" by M. Jayyusi and J. Reed and translations of "Martyr" and "Psalm" by M. Jayyusi and N.S. Nye.

Abu Tammam Habib ibn Aws al-Ta'i, fl. 808–842

Web Sites

"The Poets of Arabia, Selections." *Internet Medieval Sourcebook*. http://www.fordham.edu/halsall/source/arabianpoets1.html (accessed 13 Aug. 2003).
    Scroll down to see English translations of "The Ruin of the Barmecides," "To Taher Ben Hosien," and "To My Mistress."

Translations

"Abu Tammam." Arberry, *Arabic Poetry*. 50–62.

"Abu Tammam of Tayy." Tuetey, *Classical Arabic Poetry.* 235–240.

Biography and Criticism

Bauer, T. "Abu Tammam's Contribution to 'Abbasid Gazal Poetry." *Journal of Arabic Literature* 27 (1996): 13–21.

Meisami, J.S. "Abu Tammam." Meisami and Starkey, *Encyclopedia of Arabic Literature.* 47–49.

Stetkevych, S.P. *Abu Tammam and the Poetics of the 'Abbasid Age.* Leiden: Brill, 1991.

Abu Ya'qub al-Sijistani, Ishaq ibn Ahmad, 10th century

Web Sites

Walker, P.E. "Abu Ya'qub al-Sijistani." *The Internet Encyclopedia of Philosophy.* Ed. J. Fieser. http://www.utm.edu/research/iep/s/sijistan.htm (accessed 13 Aug. 2003).

Translations

"Abu Ya'qub Sijistani." *An Anthology of Philosophy in Persia.* Ed. S.H. Nasr with M. Aminrazavi. 2 vols. New York: Oxford UP, 1999. Vol. 2. 70–138.

The Wellsprings of Wisdom: a Study of Abu Ya'qub al-Sijistani's Kitab al-Yanabi'. Trans. P.E. Walker. Salt Lake City: U of UT P, 1994.

Biography and Criticism

Landolt, H. "Abu Ya'qub al-Sijzi, Ishaq ibn Ahmad." Meisami and Starkey, *Encyclopedia of Arabic Literature.* 50–51.

Walker, P.E. *Abu Ya'qub al-Sijistani: Intellectual Missionary.* London: Tauris in Association with the Institute of Ismaili Studies, 1996.

———. *Early Philosophical Shiism: The Ismaili Neoplatonism of Abu Ya'qub al-Sijistani.* Cambridge: Cambridge UP, 1993.

Adunis, 1930–

Web Sites

"Adonis." *Masthead* 7 (2003). http://au.geocities.com/masthead_2/issue7/adonis.html (accessed 13 Aug. 2003).

Includes translations of "Song to Counter Time," "I Heard Him Say—His Mouth Was a Stone," "Mirror of the Poor Man and the Sultan," "Prophecy," and "West and East."

"Adonis." *Middle East and Islamic Studies Collection, Cornell University.* Ed. A. Houissa. 24 Mar. 2003. http://www.library.cornell.edu/colldev/mideast/adonisc.htm (accessed 13 Aug. 2003).

Includes biographical information and 25 poems translated by Kamal Abu-Deeb from *Songs of Mihyar the Damascene.*

Other materials from the same Web site:

"Beyond the East/West: Towards a Culture of the Future." http://www.library.cornell.edu/colldev/mideast/btheast.htm—A lecture originally given by Adunis at Dartmouth College in 2001.

Chalal, E. "Adonis Indicts Arabic Poetry, Past and Present." http://
www.library.cornell.edu/colldev/mideast/chalalx.htm—An article that
originally appeared in *Aljadid* 3 (1996); Etel Adnan's reply to Adunis was
published in *Aljadid* 4 (1996) and can be accessed at http://
www.library.cornell.edu/colldev/mideast/adnan.htm.

Shatz, A. "An Arab Poet Who Dares to Differ." http://www.library.cornell.edu/
colldev/mideast/adunst.jpg.

"Adonis." *Selected International Poems.* 9 Mar. 2003. http://www.geocities.com/
marxist_lb/Adonis.htm (accessed 13 Aug. 2003).
Includes three poems in translation ("An Elegy for al-Hallaj," "The Language of
Sin," and "The Face of a Woman") as well as three poems in Arabic and biographical
information.

Adonis (Ali Ahmed Said) Ed. H. Hilmy. http://www.geocities.com/hhilmy_ma/
(accessed 13 Aug. 2003).
Includes Abu-Deeb article from *Encyclopedia of Arabic Literature*, several
dozen poems in translation. When last viewed, the links to the interview and the Arabic site did not work.

"Adonis (Ali Ahmad Said)" *Jehat.com.* http://www.jehat.com/en/
default.asp?action=article&ID=76 (accessed 22 Apr. 2004).
Includes entry from *Encyclopedia of Arabic Literature* and an article on changes
in his poetry over the years, both by Kamal Abu-Deeb. Also includes translations of
poems "The Face of the Sea," "A Grave for New York," "The Little Time," "A Mirror
for Khalidah," "The State of a Veil," "The Time," "Ishmael," and "This Is My Name."

The Ecstasy of Madness. Ed. C. Eichner. http://www.humboldt.edu/~me2/engl240/
student_projects/Adunis/adunis.html (accessed 13 Aug. 2003).
Compiled as a student project for an English class at Humboldt State University,
includes translations of poems with commentary, biography, and bibliography.

Translations

Asfour, *When the Words Burn.* 159–170.
Includes translations of "The Crow's Feather," "The Days of the Hawk," "A
Dialogue," "The Fall," "The Language of Sin," "A Mirror of the Stone," "The New
Noah," "The Road," "A Vision."

The Blood of Adonis. Trans. S. Hazo. Pittsburgh: U of Pittsburgh P, 1971.

If Only the Sea Could Sleep. Trans. K. Boullata, S. Einbinder, and M. Ghossein.
Kobenhavn: Green Integer; Saint Paul: Distributed by Consortium Book Sales,
2003.

An Introduction to Arab Poetics. Trans. C. Cobham. London: Saqi, 1990.

"Language, Culture, and Reality." Ghazoul and Harlow, *The View from Within.* 27–33.

The Pages of Day and Night. Trans. S. Hazo. Marlboro, Vt.: Marlboro, 1994.

Transformations of the Lover. Trans. S. Hazo. Athens, Ohio: Ohio UP, 1982.

Al-Udhari, *Modern Poetry of the Arab World.* 59–75.
Includes translations of "The Bird," "The Desert," "The Fire Tree," "Invasion,"
"The Minaret," "A Mirror for Autumn," "A Mirror for the Twentieth Century," "The
New Noah," "The Wound."

Victims of a Map. London: Al Saqi, 1984. 86–165.
Includes translations of "The Golden Age," "A Mirror for Beirut," "A Mirror for the Executioner," "A Mirror for the Twentieth Century," "Prophecy," "Psalm," "Song," "A Woman and a Man (Conversation, 1967)," and "Worries (A Dream)" by A. al-Udhari.

Biography and Criticism

Abu-Deeb, K. "Adunis." Meisami and Starkey, *Encyclopedia of Arabic Literature*. 57–59.

Allen, *Modern Arabic Literature*. 29–42.

Allen, R. "Adunis." Serafin, *Encyclopedia of World Literature in the 20th Century*. Vol. 1. 14–15.

Asfour, J. "Adonis and Muhammad al-Maghut: Two Voices in a Burning Land." *Journal of Arabic Literature* 20 (1989): 20–30.

Snir, R. "A Study of 'Elegy for al-Hallaj' by Adunis." *Journal of Arabic Literature* 25 (1994): 245–256.

Toorawa, S.M. "Adonis." Pendergast and Pendergast, *Reference Guide to World Literature*. 6–9.

Weidner, S. "A Guardian of Change? The Poetry of Adunis between Hermeticism and Commitment." *Conscious Voices: Concepts of Writing in the Middle East*. Eds. S. Guth, P. Furrer, and J. Christoph Burgel. Beiruter Texte und Studien 72. Stuttgart: Steiner, 1999. 277–292.

al-Afghani, Jamal al-Din, 1838–1897

Web Sites

al-Afghani, J. "Commentary on the Commentator." Khater, A. Home Page. 22 Jan. 2001. http://www2.chass.ncsu.edu/khater/personal/Jamal_al-Din.htm (accessed 14 Aug. 2003).
Translation of an essay by al-Afghani, posted as a reading for a history class at North Carolina State University.

Bashiri, I. "Jamal al-Din al-Afghani." *Bashiri Working Papers on Central Asia and Iran*. Ed. I. Bashiri. Feb. 2001. http://www.angelfire.com/rnb/bashiri/Afghani/Afghani.html (accessed 14 Aug. 2003).

Kalin, I. "Sayyid Jamal al-Din Muhammad b. Safdar al-Afghani." *Center for Islam and Science*. http://www.cis-ca.org/voices/a/afghni.htm (accessed 14 Aug. 2003).
Extensive article examining al-Afghani's beliefs and his influence.

Omran, Elsayed M.H., and O. Leaman. "al-Afghani, Jamal al-Din." *Islamic Philosophy Online*. http://www.muslimphilosophy.com/ip/rep/H048.htm (accessed 28 Aug. 2003).

Biography and Criticism

Keddie, N.R. "Afghani, Jamal al-Din al-." *Oxford Encyclopedia of the Modern Islamic World*. Ed. J.L. Esposito. New York: Oxford UP, 1995. Vol. 1. 23–27.
———. *An Islamic Response to Imperialism: Political and Religious Writings of Sayyid Jamal ad-Din "al-Afghani."* Berkeley: U of California P, 1983.

Includes translations of various writings.

―――. "Sayyid Jamal al-Din 'al-Afghani'." *Pioneers of Islamic Revival*. Ed. A. Rahnema. London: Zed, 1994. 11–29.

―――. *Sayyid Jamal ad-Din "al-Afghani": A Political Biography*. Berkeley: U of California P, 1972.

Kedourie, E. *Afghani and 'Abduh: An Essay on Religious Unbelief and Political Activism in Modern Islam*. New York: Humanities, 1966.

Kudsi-Zadeh, A.. *Sayyid Jamal al-Din al-Afghani: An Annotated Bibliography*. Leiden: Brill, 1970.

Zebiri, K. "al-Afghani, Jamal al-Din." Meisami and Starkey, *Encyclopedia of Arabic Literature*. 59–60.

Alhazen, 965–1039

Web Sites

"Alhazen." *The Window: Philosophy on the Internet*. Ed. C. Marvin and F. Sikernitsky. http://caribou.cc.trincoll.edu/depts_phil/philo/phils/muslim/alhazen.html (accessed 29 Aug. 2003).

"Ibn al-Haytham." *Center for Islam and Science*. http://www.cis-ca.org/voices/h/Al-Haytham.htm (accessed Aug. 2003).

O'Connor, J.J., and E.F. Robertson. "Abu Ali al-Hasan ibn al-Haytham." *The MacTutor History of Mathematics Archive*. http://www-gap.dcs.st-and.ac.uk/~history/Mathematicians/Al-Haytham.html (accessed 14 Aug. 2003).

"Physics." *The Free Arab Voice*. Ed. I. Alloush. http://www.freearabvoice.org/acPhysics_1.html (accessed 14 Aug. 2003).
A detailed study of Alhazen's work in optics.

Sopieva, N. "Ibn Al-Haitham the Muslim Physicist." *MuslimHeritage.com*. http://www.muslimheritage.com/day_life/ (accessed 14 Aug. 2003).

Translations

Alhacen's Theory of Visual Perception. Trans. A.M. Smith. Philadelphia: American Philosophical Soc., 2001.

Ibn al-Haytham's Completion of the Conics. Trans. J.P. Hogendijk. New York: Springer-Verlag, 1985.

Ibn al-Haytham's On the Configuration of the World. Trans. Y.T. Langermann. New York: Garland, 1990.

The Optics of Ibn al-Haytham. Trans. A.I. Sabra. London: Warburg Institute, U of London, 1989.

Biography and Criticism

Omar, S.B. *Ibn al-Haytham's Optics: A Study of the Origins of Experimental Science*. Minneapolis: Bibliotheca Islamica, 1977.

Sabra, A.I. "Abu 'Ali al-Hasan bin al-Hasan bin al-Haytham (Alhazen)" Atiyeh, *The Genius of Arab Civilization*. 196–197.

―――. "Ibn al-Haytham, Abu 'Ali al-Hasan ibn al-Hasan." Gillispie, *Dictionary of Scientific Biography*. Vol. 6. 189–210.

'Ali Mubarak, Basha, 1823 or 1824–1893

Web Sites

"Anniversary of Ali Pasha Mubarak, Pioneer of Education in Egypt." *Egypt*. http://www.sis.gov.eg/calendar/html/cl141197.htm (accessed 14 Aug. 2003).

Biography and Criticism

Crabbs, J. "Mubarak, 'Ali." Meisami and Starkey, *Encyclopedia of Arabic Literature*. 535–536.

Elkhadem, S. *History of the Egyptian Novel: Its Rise and Early Beginnings*. Fredericton, N.B.: York, 1985. 8.

Amin, Ahmad, 1886–1954

Web Sites

"Ahmad Amin." *Egypt*. http://www.us.sis.gov.eg/egyptianfigures/html/amin.htm (accessed 14 Aug. 2003).

Autobiography

My Life. Trans. I.J. Boullata. Leiden: Brill, 1978.

Translations

Orient and Occident. Trans. W.H. Behn. Berlin: Weinert, 1984.

Biography and Criticism

Boullata, I.J. "Amin, Ahmad." Meisami and Starkey, *Encyclopedia of Arabic Literature*. 86.

Mazyad, A.M.H.. *Ahmad Amin (Cairo 1886–1954): Advocate of Social and Literary Reform in Egypt*. Leiden: Brill, 1963.

'Antarah ibn Shaddad, 6th century

Web Sites

"Antara's Ode." *The Humanities Handbook*. Ed. W. Evans. Augusta State University. http://www.aug.edu/langlitcom/humanitiesHBK/handbook_htm/antara.htm (accessed 16 Aug. 2003).

This site was converted from the 7th edition of a printed handbook for use by students in a humanities course.

"Her Mouth." *Humanistic Texts*. Ed. R. Pay. http://www.humanistictexts.org/bedouin.htm#3%20%20%20Her%20Mouth (accessed 15 Aug. 2003).

"Pre-Islamic Arabia: The Hanged Poems." *Internet Medieval Sourcebook*. http://www.fordham.edu/halsall/source/640hangedpoems.html (accessed 15 Aug. 2003).

Translations

"'Antara." Arberry, *Arabic Poetry*. 34–37.

"'Antara of 'Abs." Tuetey, *Classical Arabic Poetry*. 115.

"The Mu'allaqa." *Desert Tracings*. Trans. M.A. Sells. Middletown, Connecticut: Wesleyan UP, 1989. 45–56.

Biography and Criticism

Arberry, A.J. *The Seven Odes*. London: Allen and Unwin; New York: Macmillan, 1957. 148–184.

Bauer, T. "'Antara ibn Shaddad al-'Absi." Meisami and Starkey, *Encyclopedia of Arabic Literature*. 94.

'Aql, 'Abd al-Latif, 1942–

Web Sites

"From 'An Elegy' by Abd al-Latif 'Aql." *Hanthala Palestine*. http:// hanthala.virtualave.net/poetry7.html (accessed 16 Aug. 2003).

"An Issue of Identity Nationalism." *Spotlight on the Muslim Middle East: Issues of Identity*. Ed. H.S. Greenberg and L. Mahony. 1995. American Forum for Global Education. http://www.globaled.org/muslimmideast/spage4.php (accessed 16 Aug. 2003).
   Scroll down for the translation of "Love Palestinian-Style."

Translations

Elmessiri, *The Palestinian Wedding*. 117–119, 137–141.
   Includes translations of "Love Palestinian-Style" and "On One Single Face."

Jayyusi, *Anthology of Modern Palestinian Literature*. 114–118.
   Includes translations of "From 'From Jerusalem to the Gulf'" and "On the Presence of Absence" by S. Elmusa and D. Davies.

al-'Aqqad, 'Abbas Mahmud, 1889–1964

Web Sites

"Abbas El-Aqqad." *Arab World Books*. http://www.arabworldbooks.com/authors/ abbas_elaqqad.html (accessed 16 Aug. 2003).

"The Arab's Impact on European Civilization." *Witness-Pioneer: A Virtual Islamic Organisation*. http://www.wponline.org/vil/Books/AM_AIEC/default.html (accessed 16 Aug. 2003).

"The Giant of Arab Thought, Abbas Mahmoud Al-Aqqad." *Egypt*. http:// www.sis.gov.eg/eginfnew/culture/html/cul0106.htm (accessed 16 Aug. 2003).

"Raising the Position of Women and Restoration of Their Rights." *Islam for All*. Mandurah Consulting Office. http://www.islam4all.com/new_page_62.htm (accessed 16 Aug. 2003).
   Translations of excerpts from al-'Aqqad's book, *Women in the Qur'an*.

Translations

Modern Arabic Poetry. Cambridge: Cambridge UP, 1967. 41–45.
   Includes translations of "Cheat Me!," "Competition," "Double Trouble,"
"Drinking Song," and "Love's Compound" by A.J. Arberry.

Biography and Criticism

Allen, *Modern Arabic Literature*. 49–55.

Allen, R. "al-'Aqqad, 'Abbas Mahmud." Meisami and Starkey, *Encyclopedia of Arabic Literature*. 97–99.

Dajani, Z.R. *Egypt and the Crisis of Islam*. New York: Lang, 1990.

Elkhadem, S. *History of the Egyptian Novel: Its Rise and Early Beginnings*. Fredericton, N.B.: York, 1985. 51–52.

Kirkpatrick, H. *The Modern Egyptian Novel: A Study in Social Criticism*. Oxford: Middle East Centre, St. Antony's College; London: Ithaca, 1974. 30–35.

Sakkut, H. *The Egyptian Novel and Its Main Trends: From 1913 to 1952*. Cairo: American U in Cairo P, 1971. 98–99.

Semah, D. *Four Egyptian Literary Critics*. Leiden: Brill, 1974.

Arabian Nights, The

Web Sites

Alf Layla wa Layla (A Thousand Nights and a Night) Ed. S. Gettman. Electronic Literature Foundation. http://www.arabiannights.org/index2.html (accessed 16 Aug. 2003).
    Selections from Lang and Burton translations, with illustrations by Goodenow and a critical essay on the development of the tales and their English translations.

Crocker, J. *Alf Layla wa Layla, The Book of the Thousand and One Nights*. http://www.crock11.freeserve.co.uk/arabian.htm (accessed 16 Aug. 2003).
    Vast site includes history of the tales and their translations, art and music inspired by the tales, movies based on various tales, artwork for printed editions, and short essays on various topics (e.g., Harun al-Rashid, flying carpets, genies). Extensive links to other sites.

Frost, G. "The Tale of the Puzzle of the Tales." *The Endicott Studio*. Ed. T. Windling. http://www.endicott-studio.com/forpuzl.html (accessed 16 Aug. 2003).
    Frost, an author of fantasy literature, gives a good introduction to the structure and history of the tales.

Stories from the Thousand and One Nights (The Arabian Nights' Entertainmant). Trans. E.W. Lane. Rev. S. Lane-Poole. Harvard Classics 16. New York: Collier, 1909–1914. *Bartleby.com Great Books Online*. 2001. http://www.bartleby.com/16/ (accessed 16 Aug. 2003).

The Thousand Nights and a Night. Ed. J.C. Byers. 10 Aug. 2003. http://www.wollamshram.ca/1001/index.htm (accessed 16 Aug. 2003).
    Full text of translations by Burton, Scott, Payne, Lang, Lane, and Dixon, as well as other books by Burton. Includes links to other sites.

Translations

The Arabian Nights. Trans. H. Haddawy. New York: Norton, 1990.

The Arabian Nights II: Sindbad and Other Popular Stories. Trans. H. Haddawy. New York: Norton, 1995.

Arabian Nights' Entertainments. Ed. R.L. Mack. Oxford: Oxford UP, 1995.
    Based on the English translation of Galland's French text.

Tales from the Thousand and One Nights. Trans. N.J. Dawood. Harmondsworth: Penguin, 1985.

Criticism

Alf Layla wa-Layla (*The Arabian Nights*) *Classical and Medieval Literature Criticism.* 2 (1988): 1–73.

Beaumont, D. *Slave of Desire: Sex, Love, and Death in the 1001 Nights.* Madison: Fairleigh Dickinson UP; London: Associated UP, 2002.

Blois, F. de. "Sindbad, Book of." Meisami and Starkey, *Encyclopedia of Arabic Literature.* 723–724.

Gerhardt, M.I. *The Art of Story-Telling: A Literary Study of the Thousand and One Nights.* Leiden: Brill, 1963.

Graham, Colin. "The Thousand and One Nights." Pendergast and Pendergast, *Reference Guide to World Literature.* 1533–1534.

Hovannisian, R.C., and G. Sabagh, eds. *The Thousand and One Nights in Arabic Literature and Society.* Cambridge: Cambridge UP, 1997.

Irwin, R. *The Arabian Nights: A Companion.* London: Allen Lane; London; New York: Penguin P, 1994.

Mahdi, M. *The Thousand and One Nights.* Leiden: Brill, 1995.

Pinault, D. "'Alf Layla wa-Layla." Meisami and Starkey, *Encyclopedia of Arabic Literature.* 69–77.

———. "Sindbad." Meisami and Starkey, *Encyclopedia of Arabic Literature.* 721–722.

———. *Story-Telling Techniques in the Arabian Nights.* Leiden: Brill, 1992.

Sallis, Eva. *Sheherazade Through the Looking Glass: The Metamorphosis of the Thousand and One Nights.* Richmond: Curzon, 1999.

'Aridah, Nasib, 1887–1946

Web Sites

"Nasib Aridah." *Al-Funun.* 13 Aug. 2003. Nasib Aridah Organization. http://www.al-funun.org/nasibaridah/ (accessed 16 Aug. 2003).
  Biography and bibliography, with some texts in Arabic.

Biography and Criticism

Allen, *Modern Arabic Literature.* 55–58.

Nijland, C. "'Arida, Nasib." Meisami and Starkey, *Encyclopedia of Arabic Literature.* 103.

Arna'ut, 'A'ishah

Web Sites

"Aisha Arnaout." *Jehat.com.* http://www.jehat.com/en/default.asp?action=article &ID=80 (accessed 22 Apr. 2004).
  Translation of the poem "Silently She Lived, Silently She Died."

Gender Issues and Literature in the Middle East. http://www.u.arizona.edu/~talattof/women-lit/introduction.htm (accessed 16 Aug. 2003).

Includes translations of "Untitled," "Untitled (2)," "Untitled 3," and "Untitled 4."

Translations

Handal, *The Poetry of Arab Women*. Trans. M. Fayad. 81–84.

Women of the Fertile Crescent. Washington, D.C.: Three Continents, 1978. 169–184.
Includes translations of "Before the Amputation," "Ever in Consciousness," "He Put on His Shirt," "I Arched My Body," "I Searched for the Wordless," "It Troubles Me," "Out of My Darkness," "Out of the Darkest Nadir," "Silently," "They Will Say I Imitate the Poets," "The Turtle Lifting Its Firm Head," "A Wing Carried Me" by K. Boullata.

Aslan, Ibrahim, 1939–

Web Sites

Anis, M. "Of Birds and Men." Rev. of *Malik al-Hazin* (*Heron*) and *Asafir al-Nil* (*Sparrows of the Nile*). *Al-Ahram Weekly On-Line* 8–14 June 2000. http://weekly.ahram.org.eg/2000/485/bks1.htm (accessed 16 Aug. 2003).

Aslan, I. "The Tactile Writer." *Cairo Times* 10–16 May 2001. http://www.cairotimes.com/content/archiv05/aslan.html.
Interview, photographs and summary of his book *Asafir al-Nil* (*Sparrows of the Nile*).

Translations

"A Dash of Light." Johnson-Davies, *Under the Naked Sky*. 60–64.

"The Little Girl in Green." Johnson-Davies, *Arabic Short Stories*. 154–157.

"The Performer." Johnson-Davies, *Egyptian Short Stories*. 30–36.

Biography and Criticism

Allen, R. "Aslan, Ibrahim." Meisami and Starkey, *Encyclopedia of Arabic Literature*. 109–110.

Al Masri, K. "Aslan, Ibrahim." Gikandi, *Encyclopedia of African Literature*. 33.

Avempace, d. 1138 or 1139

Web Sites

Inati, S.C. "Ibn Bajja, Abu Bakr Muhammad ibn Yahya ibn as-Say'igh." *Islamic Philosophy Online*. http://www.muslimphilosophy.com/ip/rep/H023.htm (accessed 28 Aug. 2003).

"Literary Excerpts on Art and Architecture in Andalusia." Trans. C. Robinson. *Andalusia: Virtual Classroom*. Ed. S. Balaghi. Hagop Kevorkian Center, New York University. http://www.nyu.edu/gsas/program/neareast/andalusia/pdf/13.pdf (accessed 16 Aug. 2003).
The second poem discussed is by Avempace.

Biography and Criticism

Goodman, L.E. "Ibn Bajjah." Nasr and Leaman, *History of Islamic Philosophy*. 294–312.

Pines, S. "Ibn Bajja, Abu Bakr Muhammad ibn Yahya ibn al-Sa'igh." Gillispie, *Dictionary of Scientific Biography.* Vol. 1. 408–410.

Wasserstein, D.J. "Ibn Bajja." Meisami and Starkey, *Encyclopedia of Arabic Literature.* 317.

Averroes, 1126–1198

Web Sites

"Abul-Waleed Muhammad Ibn Rushd." *Center for Islam and Science.* http://www.cisca.org/voices/r/ibn-rushd.htm (accessed 16 Aug. 2003).

Ead, H.A., ed. "Averroes as a Physician." *The Alchemy Web Site.* Ed. A. McLean. http://www.levity.com/alchemy/islam21.html (accessed 16 Aug. 2003).

Article that nicely summarizes his achievements in philosophy, medicine, and astronomy.

"Ibn Rushd." *Islamic Philosophy Online.* http://www.muslimphilosophy.com/ir/default.htm (accessed 16 Aug. 2003).

Includes links to texts of several works in Arabic; English translations of *Incoherence of the Incoherence*, *On the Harmony of Religion and Philosophy*, and others; critical articles, links, bibliography, videos of lectures about him, and even reviews of a movie based on his life.

"Ibn Rushd." *The Window: Philosophy on the Internet.* Ed. C. Marvin and F. Sikernitsky. http://www.trincoll.edu/depts/phil/philo/phils/muslim/rushd.html (accessed 16 Aug. 2003).

Leaman, O. "Ibn Rushd, Abu'l Walid Muhammad." *Islamic Philosophy Online.* http://www.muslimphilosophy.com/ip/rep/H025.htm (accessed 28 Aug. 2003).

Translations

Averroes' Middle Commentary on Aristotle's Poetics. Trans. C.E. Butterworth. Princeton: Princeton UP, 1986.

Averroes on Plato's Republic. Trans. R. Lerner. Ithaca: Cornell UP, 1974.

Averroes on the Harmony of Religion and Philosophy. Trans. G.F. Hourani. London: Printed for the Trustees of the E.J.W. Gibb Memorial and Published by Luzac, 1976.

Averroes' Questions in Physics. Trans. H. Tunik Goldstein. Dordrecht; Boston: Kluwer Academic Publishers, 1991.

Averroes' Tahafut al-Tahafut (The Incoherence of the Incoherence). Trans. S. Van den Bergh. London: Trustees of the E.J.W. Gibb Memorial, 1978.

Faith and Reason in Islam: Averroes' Exposition of Religious Arguments. Trans. I. Najjar. Oxford: Oneworld, 2001.

Ibn Rushd's Metaphysics. Trans. C. Genequand. Leiden: Brill, 1984.

Jihad in Mediaeval and Modern Islam. Trans. R. Peters. Leyden: Brill, 1977.

Biography and Criticism

Arnaldez, R. and A.Z. Iskandar. "Ibn Rushd, Abu'l-Walid Muhammad ibn Ahmad ibn Muhammad." Gillispie, *Dictionary of Scientific Biography.* Vol. 12. 1–9.

"Averroes." *Classical and Medieval Literature Criticism*. 7 (1991): 1–74.

"Averroes." *Medieval Philosophers* (*Dictionary of Literary Biography* 115). Ed. J. Hackett. Detroit: Gale, 1992. 68–79.

Butterworth, C.E. "Averroes (Ibn Rushd)" McGreal, *Great Thinkers of the Eastern World*. 465–468.

Davidson, H.A. *Alfarabi, Avicenna, and Averroes on Intellect: Their Cosmologies, Theories of the Active Intellect, and Theories of Human Intellect*. New York: Oxford UP, 1992.

Fakhry, M. *Averroes (Ibn Rushd): His Life, Works and Influence*. Oxford: Oneworld, 2001.

Leaman, O. *Averroes and His Philosophy*. Oxford: Clarendon, 1988.

———. "Ibn Rushd." Meisami and Starkey, *Encyclopedia of Arabic Literature*. 365–366.

Martin, M.A. "Abu al-Walid Muhammad bin Rushd (Averroes)" Atiyeh, *The Genius of Arab Civilization*. 100.

Urvoy, D. "Ibn Rushd." Nasr and Leaman, *History of Islamic Philosophy*. 330–345.

———. *Ibn Rushd, Averroes*. Trans. O. Stewart. London: Routledge, 1990.

Avicenna, 980–1037

Web Sites

"Abu'l 'Ali al-Husayn b. 'Abd Allah ibn Sina." *Center for Islam and Science*. http://www.cis-ca.org/voices/s/ibnsina.html (accessed 16 Aug. 2003).

"Avicenna." *Islamic Philosophy Online*. http://www.muslimphilosophy.com/sina/default.htm (accessed 16 Aug. 2003).

Includes links to texts of several works in Arabic or Persian; English translations of *On Medicine* (excerpts), *Remarks and Admonitions* (Parts 1 and 4), and others; critical articles, links, bibliography, video of a lecture about him.

Kemal, S. "Ibn Sina, Abu 'Ali al-Husayn." *Islamic Philosophy Online*. http://www.muslimphilosophy.com/ip/rep/H026.htm (accessed 28 Aug. 2003).

O'Connor, J.J. and E.F. Robertson. "Abu Ali al-Husain ibn Abdallah ibn Sina (Avicenna)" *The MacTutor History of Mathematics Archive*. http://www-gap.dcs.st-and.ac.uk/~history/Mathematicians/Avicenna.html (accessed 14 Aug. 2003).

Autobiography

The Life of Ibn Sina. Trans. W.E. Gohlman. Albany: State U of New York P, 1974.

Translations

Avicenna on Theology. Trans. A.J. Arberry. London: Murray, 1951.

Avicenna's Commentary on the Poetics of Aristotle. Trans. I.M. Dahiyat. Leiden: Brill, 1974.

Avicenna's Psychology. Trans. F. Rahman. London: Oxford UP, 1952.

"Ibn Sina." *An Anthology of Philosophy in Persia*. Ed. S.H. Nasr with M. Aminrazavi. 2 vols. New York: Oxford UP, 1999. Vol. 1. 195–273.

The Metaphysica of Avicenna (Ibn Sina). Trans. P. Morewedge. London: Routledge and Kegan Paul, 1973.

The Propositional Logic of Avicenna. Trans. N. Shehaby. Dordrecht; Boston: Reidel, 1973.

A Treatise on the Canon of Medicine of Avicenna. Trans. O.C. Gruner. London: Luzac, 1930.

Biography and Criticism

Afnan, S. M. *Avicenna: His Life and Works.* London: Allen and Unwin, 1958.

Aminrazavi, M. "Avicenna (Ibn Sina)" McGreal, *Great Thinkers of the Eastern World.* 449–452.

Anawati, G.C. and A.Z. Iskandar. "Ibn Sina, Abu 'Ali al-Husayn ibn 'Abdallah." Gillispie, *Dictionary of Scientific Biography.* Vol. 15. 494–501.

"Avicenna." *Classical and Medieval Literature Criticism.* 16 (1996): 132–181.

Fry, C.G. *Avicenna's Philosophy of Education: an Introduction.* Washington, D.C.: Three Continents, 1990.

Gomez Nogales, S. "Ibn Sina." *Religion, Learning, and Science in the 'Abbasid Period.* Ed. M.J.L. Young, J.D. Latham, and R.B. Serjeant. Cambridge History of Arabic Literature. Cambridge: Cambridge UP, 1990. 389–404.

Goodman, L.E. *Avicenna.* London: Routledge, 1992.

Gutas, D. *Avicenna and the Aristotelian Tradition: Introduction to Reading Avicenna's Philosophical Works.* Leiden: Brill, 1988.

Inati, S. "Ibn Sina." Nasr and Leaman, *History of Islamic Philosophy.* 231–246.

Landolt, H. "Ibn Sina." Meisami and Starkey, *Encyclopedia of Arabic Literature.* 373–375.

Martin, M.A. "Abu 'Ali al-Husayn bin 'Abdallah bin Sina (Avicenna)" Atiyeh, *The Genius of Arab Civilization.* 226–227.

Nasr, S.H. "Ibn Sina's 'Oriental Philosophy.'" Nasr and Leaman, *History of Islamic Philosophy.* 247–251.

———. *Three Muslim Sages: Avicenna, Suhrawardi, Ibn Arabi.* Cambridge: Harvard UP, 1964.

Siraisi, Nancy G. *Avicenna in Renaissance Italy: The Canon and Medical Teaching in Italian Universities after 1500.* Princeton: Princeton UP, 1987.

'Awad, Luwis, 1915–1990

Web Sites

"Louis Awadh." *Egypt.* http://www.us.sis.gov.eg/egyptianfigures/html/Awadh.htm (accessed 16 Aug. 2003).

Saleh, A.A. "Thinking Ahead." *Al-Ahram Weekly Online.* 4–10 Oct. 2001. http://weekly.ahram.org.eg/2001/554/cu1.htm (accessed 16 Aug. 2003).

Translations

Khouri and Algar, *Anthology of Modern Arabic Poetry.* 139–143.
    Includes translations of "Kiriyalayson" and "Love at St. Lazare."

Biography and Criticism

El-Enany, R. "The Promethean Quest in Louis 'Awad's 'Memoirs of an Overseas Student.'" Ostle, Moor, and Wild, *Writing the Self*. 61–71.

Khouri, M.A. "Lewis 'Awad: A Forgotten Pioneer of the Free Verse Movement." *Journal of Arabic Literature* 1 (1970): 137–144.

Kirkpatrick, Hilary. *The Modern Egyptian Novel: A Study in Social Criticism*. Oxford: Middle East Centre, St. Antony's College; London: Ithaca, 1974. 65–71.

Stagh, Marina. *The Limits of Freedom of Speech: Prose Literature and Prose Writers in Egypt under Nasser and Sadat*. Stockholm: Almqvist and Wiksell, 1993. 277–290.

Staif, A.-N. "'Awad, Luwis." Meisami and Starkey, *Encyclopedia of Arabic Literature*. 113–114.

'Awwad, Tawfiq Yusuf, 1911–1989

Web Sites

'Awwad, T.Y. "Recommended Fiction on Lebanon." *Middle East Booklover*. http://www.middleeastbooklover.nl/fiction_lebanon.htm (accessed 16 Aug. 2003). Summary of his novel, *Death in Beirut*.

Translations

"Covenant with Death." *Arab Stories East and West*. Trans. R.Y. Ebied and M.J.L. Young. Leeds: Leeds U Oriental Society, 1977. 23–34.

Death in Beirut. Trans. L. McLoughlin. London: Heinemann Educational, 1976.

Biography and Criticism

Allen, *Modern Arabic Literature*. 61–65.

Amyuni, M.T. "'Awwad, Tawfiq Yusuf." Meisami and Starkey, *Encyclopedia of Arabic Literature*. 115.

"Awwad, Tawfiq Yusuf." *Contemporary Authors* 154 (1997): 21–22.

Ghandour, S. "Awwad, Tawfiq Yusuf." Serafin, *Encyclopedia of World Literature in the 20th Century*. Vol. 1. 169.

———. "Contesting Languages: Tawfiq Yusuf 'Awwad's 'Tawahin Bayrut.'" *Tradition and Modernity in Arabic Literature*. Ed. I.J. Boullata and T. DeYoung. Fayetteville: U of Arkansas P, 1997. 135–150.

'Azzam, Samirah, 1925–1967

Web Sites

'Azzam, Samirah. "Bread of Sacrifice." *Gender Issues and Literature in the Middle East*. http://www.u.arizona.edu/~talattof/women-lit/arabicprose/breadofsacrifice.htm (accessed 16 Aug. 2003).

Translations

"'Fate' by Samira 'Azzam." Trans. Y. Suleiman. *Journal of Arabic Literature* 19 (1988): 142–148.

"'I Want Water' by Samira 'Azzam." Trans. M.Y.I.H. Suleiman. *Journal of Arabic Literature* 20 (1989): 163–167.

"On the Road to Solomon's Pools." Trans. M. Cooke. *Blood into Ink: South Asian and Middle Eastern Women Write War.* Ed. M. Cooke and R. Rustomji-Kerns. Boulder: Westview, 1994. 18–22.

"The Protected One." Trans. M. Ibrahim and M. Cooke. Badran and Cooke, *Opening the Gates.* 54–56.

"Still Another Year." Trans. S. Rabie. Rev. P. Callaghan. Manzalaoui, *Arabic Short Stories.* 297–303.

"Tears for Sale." *An Arabian Mosaic: Short Stories by Arab Women Writers.* Trans. D. Cohen-Mor. Potomac, Md.: Sheba, 1993. 33–39.

"'Until Such a Time' by Samira 'Azzam." Trans. M.Y.I.H. Suleiman. *Journal of Arabic Literature* 21 (1990): 183–189.

Biography and Criticism

Piselli, K. "Samira Azzam: Author's Works and Vision." *International Journal of Middle East Studies* 20 (1988): 93–108.

Suleiman, Y. "'Azzam, Samira." Meisami and Starkey, *Encyclopedia of Arabic Literature.* 119.

———. "Palestine and the Palestinians in the Short Stories of Samira 'Azzam." *Journal of Arabic Literature* 22 (1991): 154–165.

al-'Azzawi, Fadil, 1940–

Web Sites

al-'Azzawi, F. "In Every Well a Joseph is Weeping." *Quarterly Review of Literature Poetry Book Series.* 13 Nov. 2001. http://www.princeton.edu/~qrl/vol36.htm#AZZAWI (accessed 16 Aug. 2003).

———. "Six Poems." *Kikah.com: Middle East Literature & Arts.* http://www.kikah.com/indexenglish.asp?code=kk22 (accessed 16 Aug. 2003).

Translations of "Inside a Black Hole," "When the Sky Still Had No Name," A Statue in a Square," "Feast in Candlelight," "Events," and "Too Much Water Flowed in the Rivers."

"Fadhil Al-Azzawi." *Readings by Iraqi Poets.* 12 Mar. 2002. Faulconer Gallery, Grinnell College. http://web.grinnell.edu/faulconergallery/iraq/poetry/Al-Azzawi/index.htm (accessed 23 Aug. 2003).

Includes translations of "Bedouins," "I Confess That I Have Lived My Life," "Listen, Noah," and "The Lion," with audio and video of the poet reading.

"Iraqi Poems." *Guardian* 1 Mar. 2001. http://books.guardian.co.uk/Print/0,3858,4614907,00.html (accessed 16 Aug. 2003).

Translations of "In a Magic Land" and "The Last Iraq."

Schoonhoven, J. "Fadhil al-Azzawi." *Poetry International Web.* Ed. Corine Vloet. Poetry International Web Foundation. http://www.poetryinternational.org/cwolk/view/16017 (accessed 16 Aug. 2003).

Includes Arabic text and translation of "In My Spare Time," audio & video of the poet speaking about writing poetry.

Badr, Liyanah, 1950–

Web Sites

"Liana Badr." *Arab World Books*. http://www.arabworldbooks.com/authors/
liana_badr.html (accessed 16 Aug. 2003).

"Palestinian Novelists, Liana Badr." *Khalil Sakakini Cultural Centre*. http://
www.sakakini.org/novelists/liana.html (16 Aug. 2003).
Includes translation of an excerpt from her novel *Stars of Jericho*.

Autobiography

"The Story of a Novel or Reflections of Details in the Mirror: Between Awareness
and Madness." *In the House of Silence: Autobiographical Essays by Arab
Women Writers*. Ed. F. Faqir. Trans. S. Eber and F. Faqir. Reading: Garnet,
1998. 25–32.

Translations

A Balcony over the Fakihani. Trans. P. Clark with C. Tingley. New York: Interlink,
1993.

A Compass for the Sunflower. Trans. C. Cobham. London: Women's Press, 1989.

The Eye of the Mirror. Trans. S. Kawar. Reading: Garnet, 1994.

Biography and Criticism

Palestinian Writers. Dir. M. Bellinelli. Prod. RTSI-Televisione svizzera.
Videocassette. Filmakers Library, 2001.

Saliba, T. "A Country Beyond Reach: Liana Badr's Writings of the Palestinian
Diaspora." *Intersections: Gender, Nation, and Community in Arab Women's
Novels*. Ed. L.S. Majaj, P.W. Sunderman, and T. Saliba. Syracuse: Syracuse UP,
2002. 132–161.

Baghdadi, Shawqi, 1928–

Web Sites

Baghdadi, S. "Young Palestinian Lovers." Al-Sayeh, K. Home page. 13 June 1999.
http://www.hally.net/personal/khaled/palestine/intifada/poetry/young.htm
(accessed 16 Aug. 2003).

Translations

"Friendship." Fairbairn and al-Gosaibi, *Feathers and the Horizon*. 30.

Biography and Criticism

Young, M.J.L. "Baghdadi, Shawqi." Meisami and Starkey, *Encyclopedia of Arabic
Literature*. 126.

Ba Kathir, 'Ali Ahmad, 1910–1969

Web Sites

"'Ali Ahmad Bakathir." *Islamist Intellectuals and Literature*. Ed. C. Szyska. http://
members.aol.com/ChrSzyska/bakatir.htm (accessed 16 Aug. 2003).
Short biography and summaries of three of his works.

Al-Kamali, F. "Commemorating the Life of Bakathir." *Yemen Times,* 19–25 Nov. 2001. http://www.yementimes.com/01/iss47/culture.htm (accessed 16 Aug. 2003).

Translations

The Ring: Three Moral Plays. Trans. Y. Mohamed. London: Ta-Ha, 1995.

Biography and Criticism

Badawi, M.M. *Modern Arabic Drama in Egypt.* Cambridge: Cambridge UP, 1987. 112–129.

Sakkut, H. *The Egyptian Novel and Its Main Trends: From 1913 to 1952.* Cairo: American U in Cairo P, 1971. 67–71.

Starkey, P. "Bakathir, 'Ali Ahmad." Meisami and Starkey, *Encyclopedia of Arabic Literature.* 128–129.

Bakr, Salwa, 1949–

Web Sites

"Salwa Bakr." *Arab World Books.* http://www.arabworldbooks.com/authors/ salwa_bakr.html (accessed 16 Aug. 2003).

Autobiography

"Writing as a Way Out." *In the House of Silence: Autobiographical Essays by Arab Women Writers.* Ed. F. Faqir. Trans. S. Eber and F. Faqir. Reading: Garnet, 1998. 33–40.

Translations

"Corncobs." Johnson-Davies, *Under the Naked Sky.* 131–141.

The Golden Chariot. Trans. D. Manisty. Reading, UK: Garnet, 1995.

My Grandmother's Cactus: Stories by Egyptian Women. London: Quartet, 1991. 17–37.
    Includes translations of "Woman on the Grass" and "Zeenat Marches in the President's Funeral" by M. Booth.

The Wiles of Men and Other Stories. Trans. D. Johnson-Davies. London: Quartet Books, 1992.

Biography and Criticism

Hafez, S. "Bakr, Salwa." *Contemporary World Writers.* Ed. T. Chevalier. 2nd ed. Detroit: St. James, 1993. 43–44.

Mikhail, M.N. "Bakr, Salwa." Gikandi, *Encyclopedia of African Literature.* 48–49.

Al-Nowaihi, M.M. "Reenvisioning National Community in Salwa Bakr's 'Golden Chariot.'" *Intersections: Gender, Nation, and Community in Arab Women's Novels.* Ed. L.S. Majaj, P.W. Sunderman, and T. Saliba. Syracuse: Syracuse UP, 2002. 68–93.

al-Baladhuri, Ahmad ibn Yahya, d. 892

Web Sites

"Accounts of the Arab Conquest of Egypt, 642." *Internet Medieval Sourcebook.* http:// www.fordham.edu/halsall/source/642Egypt-conq2.html (accessed 16 Aug. 2003).
    Another selection, on the Battle of Yarmuk, in Syria, can be read at http:// www.fordham.edu/halsall/source/yarmuk.html.

al-Baladhuri, A. ibn Y. "Surrender of Damascus to the Arabs, 635." *Mosaic: Perspectives on Western Civilization.* http://college.hmco.com/history/west/ mosaic/chapter4/source210.html (accessed 16 Aug. 2003).

Translations

The Origins of the Islamic State. Trans. P.K. Hitti. Piscataway, N.J.: Gorgias, 2002.

Biography and Criticism

Athamina, K. "The Sources of al-Baladhuri's 'Ansab al-Ashraf'." *Jerusalem Studies in Arabic and Islam* 5 (1984): 237–262.

Conrad, L.I. "al-Baladhuri." Meisami and Starkey, *Encyclopedia of Arabic Literature.* 131–132.

al-Banna', Hasan, 1906–1949

Web Sites

Bah, A.M., and K.T. Bah. "Introducing a Muslim Activist: Hasan al-Banna." *Journal of Islamic Guidance* 2.1 (1998): 23–25. http://www.igs-alirshaad.net/rnt.htm (accessed 16 Aug. 2003).

al-Banna, H. "Jihad." *IslamistWatch.org.* http://www.islamistwatch.org/texts/banna/ banna.html (accessed 16 Aug. 2003).

———. "Peace in Islam." *Young Muslims, Maryland.* http://host06.ipowerweb.com/ ~ymofmdc/books/peace_in_islam/ (accessed 16 Aug. 2003).

Also includes the full-text translations of "The Islamic Creed," "Towards the Light," "The Message of the Teachings," "Our Message," and "Between Yesterday and Today."

Denoeux, G. "Hasan al-Banna." *Arabies Trends.* http://www.arabies.com/ Special%20Report/Hasan%20al-Banna.htm (accessed 16 Aug. 2003).

"Hasan al-Banna'." *Witness-Pioneer: A Virtual Islamic Organisation.* http:// www.wponline.org/vil/Articles/scholars/hasan_al_banna.htm (accessed 16 Aug. 2003).

Translations

Five Tracts of Hasan Al-Banna (1906–1949). Trans. C. Wendell. Berkeley: U of California P, 1978.

Biography and Criticism

Carre, O. "Banna', Hasan al-." *Oxford Encyclopedia of the Modern Islamic World.* Ed. J.L. Esposito. New York: Oxford UP, 1995. Vol. 1. 195–199.

Commins, D. "Hasan al-Banna (1906–1949)" *Pioneers of Islamic Revival.* Ed. A. Rahnema. London: Zed, 1994. 125–153.

El-Awaisi, A. al-F.M. "Emergence of a Militant Leader: A Study of the Life of Hasan al-Banna, 1906–1928." *Journal of South Asian and Middle Eastern Studies* 22.1 (1998): 46–63.

Zebiri, K. "al-Banna', Hasan." Meisami and Starkey, *Encyclopedia of Arabic Literature.* 132.

al-Baradduni, 'Abd Allah, 1926–1999

Web Sites

"Abdoullah al Baradouni." *Selected International Poems*. 9 Mar. 2003. http://
geocities.com/marxist_lb/abdoullah_al_baradouni.htm (accessed 17 Aug.
2003).
Translation of "From Exile to Exile."

"Al-Baradouni Died." *Yemen Times* 6–12 Sept. 1999. http://www.yementimes.com/
99/iss36/ (accessed 17 Aug. 2003).

"Yemen's Most Famous Poet Dies." *Middle East and Islamic Studies Collection,
Cornell University*. http://www.library.cornell.edu/colldev/mideast/barad.htm
(accessed 17 Aug. 2003).

Translations

"Her Hands." Fairbairn and al-Gosaibi, *Feathers and the Horizon*. 34.

Jayyusi, S.K., ed. *The Literature of Modern Arabia: An Anthology*. London: Kegan
Paul International, 1988. 56–61.
Includes translations of "Answers to One Question," "Between the Knife and
the Killer," "Between Two Voids," "The Kindness of the Enemy," "Longing," and
"Treachery of Words" by S. Boulus and J. Heath-Stubbs and translation of "End of
Death" by J. Heath-Stubbs and S.K. Jayyusi.

"A Rose from al-Mutanabbi's Blood." Trans. D. Der Hovanessian with S.E. Jayyusi,
Modern Arabic Poetry. 158–160.

Barakat, Halim Isber, 1936–

Web Sites

Arab Culture and Civilization. Ed. M. Toler. National Institute for Technology and
Liberal Education. http://www.nitle.org/arabworld/main_menu.php (accessed
16 Aug. 2003).
Use the Search box to find video interviews of and printed readings by Barakat
on Arab identity and the Arab family.

Barakat, H. "The Crane." Trans. H. Haddawy. *Jehat.com*. http://www.jehat.com/ar/
the-crane/english/crane-3e.htm (accessed 17 Aug. 2003).
Excerpts from his novel.

Translations

Days of Dust. Trans. T. Le Gassick. Washington, D.C.: Three Continents, 1983.

Six Days. Trans. B. Frangieh and S. McGehee. Washington, D.C.: Three Continents,
1990.

Biography and Criticism

Allen, *Modern Arabic Literature*. 73–77.

Allen, R. "'Awdat al-Ta'ir ila al-Bahr', Halim Barakat." *The Arabic Novel: An
Historical and Critical Introduction*. 2nd ed. Syracuse: Syracuse UP, 1995.
153–159.

Frangieh, B.K. "Barakat, Halim." Meisami and Starkey, *Encyclopedia of Arabic Literature*. 136.

Barakat, Huda, 1952–

Web Sites

Al Malky, R. "The Spin in the Tale." Rev. of *The Tiller of Waters*. In *Egypt Today*. Feb. 2002. http://www.egypttoday.com/ET_Feb_2002/main/wo_books.htm (accessed 17 Aug. 2003).

Marie, E. "Woven Archives of Beirut: A Conversation with Hoda Barakat." *Aljadid* 39 (2002). http://www.aljadid.com/interviews/0839marie.html (accessed 17 Aug. 2003).

Rakha, Y. "Hoda Barakat: Starting Over." *Al-Ahram Weekly On-Line* 25 Nov.–1 Dec. 1999. http://weekly.ahram.org.eg/1999/457/profile.htm (accessed 17 Aug. 2003).

Autobiography

"I Write Against My Hand." *In the House of Silence: Autobiographical Essays by Arab Women Writers*. Ed. F. Faqir. Trans. S. Eber and F. Faqir. Reading: Garnet, 1998. 41–48.

Translations

The Stone of Laughter. Trans. S. Bennett. New York: Interlink Books, 1995.

The Tiller of Waters. Trans. M. Booth. Cairo: American U in Cairo P, 2001.

Biography and Criticism

Aghacy, S. "Hoda Barakat's 'The Stone of Laughter': Androgyny or Polarization?" *Journal of Arabic Literature* 29.3–4 (1998): 185–201.

Fayad, M. "Barakat, Hoda." Serafin, *Encyclopedia of World Literature in the 20th Century*. Vol. 1. 196.

al-Barghuthi, Murid, 1944–

Web Sites

Galford, H. Rev. of *I Saw Ramallah*. *Washington Report on Middle East Affairs* 20.1 (2001). http://www.washington-report.org/backissues/010201/0101103.html (accessed 26 Aug. 2003).

"Palestinian Poets, Mureed Barghouti." *Khalil Sakakini Cultural Centre*. http:// www.sakakini.org/poets/mureed2-index.htm (17 Aug. 2003).
Includes translations of the poems "Certainty" and "Exception."

Autobiography and Interviews

I Saw Ramallah. Trans. A. Soueif. Cairo: American U in Cairo P, 2000.

Translations

Jayyusi, *Anthology of Modern Palestinian Literature*. 126–131.
Includes translations of "Certainty," "Desire," "Exception," "The Guards," "I Run toward You . . . I Run with You," "Liberation," "An Official," "The Tribes," "A Vision" by L. Jayyusi and W.S. Merwin.

al-Barudi, Mahmud Sami, 1839–1904

Web Sites

"Mahmoud Sami al-Baroudi." *Egypt*. http://www.us.sis.gov.eg/egyptianfigures/html/
sami.htm (accessed 17 Aug. 2003).

Translations

"al-Barudi." Arberry, *Arabic Poetry*. 148–154.

Biography and Criticism

Badawi, M.M. "Al-Barudi, Precursor of the Modern Arabic Poetic Revival." *Welt des
Islams* 12 (1969): 228–244.

Ostle, R.C. "al-Barudi, Mahmud Sami." Meisami and Starkey, *Encyclopedia of
Arabic Literature*. 137–138.

al-Battani, Muhammad ibn Jabir, d. 929

Web Sites

"Abus Abdallah Battani." *Malaspina Great Books*. http://www.malaspina.com/site/
person_170.asp (accessed 17 Aug. 2003).

O'Connor, J.J., and E.F. Robertson. "Abu Abdallah Mohammad ibn Jabir Al-Battani."
The MacTutor History of Mathematics Archive. http://www-gap.dcs.st-
and.ac.uk/~history/Mathematicians/Al-Battani.html (accessed 14 Aug. 2003).

Biography and Criticism

Hartner, W. "al-Battani, Abu 'Abd Allah Muhammad ibn Jabir ibn Sinan al-Raqqi al-
Harrani al-Sabi'." Gillispie, *Dictionary of Scientific Biography* Vol. 1. 507–516.

al-Bayati, 'Abd al-Wahhab, 1926–1999

Web Sites

"'Abd al-Wahhab al-Bayyati." *Books and Writers*. http://www.kirjasto.sci.fi/
bayyati.htm (accessed 17 Aug. 2003).

"Abd al Wahhab al Bayyati." *Selected International Poems*. 9 Mar. 2003. http://
geocities.com/marxist_lb/al_Bayyati.htm (accessed 17 Aug. 2003).
     Arabic text of many poems, but also includes translations of "Secret of Fire,"
"False Critics," and "The Birth of Unborn Cities."

"Abdul Wahab Al-Bayati." *Jehat.com*. http//:www.jehat.com/en/
default.asp?action=article&ID=78 (accessed 22 Apr. 2004).
     Includes translation of "About Waddah of Yemen-Love and Death."

Free Verse: A Journal of Contemporary Poetry & Poetics 3 (2002). http://
english.chass.ncsu.edu/freeverse/Archives/Winter_2002/Iraqi_Poems/A_al-
Bayati.htm (accessed 17 Aug. 2003).
     Includes translations of "The Nightmare" and "The Sea Is Far-Off: I Hear Its
Sigh" by S.J. Altoma.

Hegazi, A.A.M. "Points of Reference." *Al-Ahram Weekly On-Line*. 12–18 Aug. 1999.
http://weekly.ahram.org.eg/1999/442/cu1.htm (accessed 17 Aug. 2003).
     Memoir by an Arab poet and author.

The Poems of Abd al-Wahhab al-Bayyati. Ed. J. Boland, et al. *Contemporary Arabic Literature (Literature of North Africa and the Middle East).* http://www.humboldt.edu/~me2/engl240/student_projects/Al-Bayyati/ (17 Aug. 2003).

Created by students at Humboldt State University as a class project, site contains biography, bibliography, criticism, and translations of "The City," "The Fugitive," "Something about Happiness," "The Face," "The Gypsy Symphony," "The Magus," and "The Saint."

Rakha, Y. "Abdel-Wahab Al-Bayyati: Prometheus at the Sheraton." *Al-Ahram Weekly On-Line* 11–17 Feb. 1999. http://weekly.ahram.org.eg/1999/416/people.htm (accessed 17 Aug. 2003).

Translations

Boullata, *Modern Arab Poets.* 15–17.

Includes translations of "Apology for a Short Speech," "The Sorrows of Violets," and "The Village Market."

Jayyusi, *Modern Arabic Poetry.* 170–179.

Includes translations of "The Birth of Aisha and Her Death" and "Elegy for Aisha" by. S. Boulos and C. Middleton and translations of "The Impossible" and "Luzumiyya" by S.K. Jayyusi and C. Middleton.

Khouri and Algar, *Anthology of Modern Arabic Poetry.* 109–121.

Includes translations of "The Book of Poverty and Revolution," "Traveller without Baggage," "Two Poems to My Son 'Ali," and "The Village Market."

Love, Death, and Exile. Trans. B.K. Frangieh. Washington, D.C.: Georgetown UP, 1990.

Al-Udhari, *Modern Poetry of the Arab World.* 36–41.

Includes translations of "The Arab Refugee," "An Apology for a Short Speech," "The Fugitive," "Hamlet," "Profile of the Lover of the Great Bear," and "To Ernest Hemingway."

Biography and Criticism

Allen, *Modern Arabic Literature.* 78–84.

Boullata, I.J. "al-Bayati, 'Abd al-Wahhab." Meisami and Starkey, *Encyclopedia of Arabic Literature.* 142–143.

———. "Bayati, 'Abdal-Wahhab al-." *Contemporary World Writers.* Ed. Tracy Chevalier. 2nd ed. Detroit: St. James, 1993. 48–50.

———. "al-Bayyati, Abd al-Wahhab." Serafin, *Encyclopedia of World Literature in the 20th Century.* Vol. 1. 217–218.

Corrao, F.M. "'The Autobiography of the Thief of Fire' by 'Abd al-Wahhab al-Bayyati." Ostle, Moor, and Wild, *Writing the Self.* 241–248.

Kadhim, H.N. "'Abd al-Wahhab al-Bayati's 'Odes to Jaffa.'" *Journal of Arabic Literature* 32 (2001): 88–106.

Al-Musawi, M.J. "'Abd al-Wahhab al-Bayati's Poetics of Exile." *Journal of Arabic Literature* 32 (2001): 212–238.

Baydun, 'Abbas, 1945–

Web Sites

"Abbas Beydoun." *Masthead* 7 (2003). http://au.geocities.com/masthead_2/issue7/
    beydoun.html (17 Aug. 2003).
    Translations of "From 'Rooms,'" "Dreams and Potatoes," "A Wave," and "The
Mail of Steps."

Baydun, A. "Cultural Diversity." *Deutsche Stiftung fur Internationale Entwicklung*. 6
    Feb. 2003. http://www.dse.de/ef/cultures/beydoun.htm (accessed 17 Aug.
    2003).

———. "Six Poems by Lebanese Abbas Beydhoun." *Kikah.com: Middle Eastern
    Literature & Art*. http://www.kikah.com/
    indexenglish.asp?fname=kikahenglish\live\k2\2003-06-
    01\202.htm&storytitle=Rooms (accessed 17 Aug. 2003).
    Includes translations of "The Mail of Steps," "Silence and Blood," "Three Stan-
zas from 'Rooms,'" "The Flower of Life and My Father's Black Heart," "Murderers,"
and "A Man without Burdens."

"Biographical Information about Some Participants Poets in the XI International
    Poetry Festival of Medellin." *International Poetry Festival of Medellin*.
    Corporation of Art and Poetry Prometeo. http://www.epm.net.co/
    VIIfestivalpoesia/html/englishXI.html (accessed 17 Aug. 2003).

"War on Iraq: Dialogue about the War." *Qantara.de: Dialogue with the Islamic
    World*. Ed. L. Lorenz-Mayer. Bundeszentrale fur Politische Bildung, Deutsche
    Welle, Goethe-Institut Inter Nationes, and Institut fur Auslandsbeziehungen.
    http://www.qantara.de/webcom/show_article.php?wc_c=459 (accessed 17 Aug.
    2003).
    Correspondence with German author M. Kleeberg on the war in Iraq.

Autobiography and Interviews

"Abbas Beydhoun: Writing the Language of Absence." Interviewed by Camilo
    Gomez-Rivas. *Banipal* 10–11 (2001): 32–38.

Translations

"From 'The Poem of Tyre'." Trans. S.S. Elmusa. *Literary Review* 37 (1994):
    475–476.

Bayram al-Tunisi, Mahmud, 1893–1961

Web Sites

"Beiram Al-Tounsi: Pioneer of Vernacular Arabic Verse 'Zagal.'" *Egypt*. http://
    www.sis.gov.eg/calendar/html/cl040398.htm (accessed 17 Aug. 2003).
    Another article can be read at http://www.us.sis.gov.eg/egyptianfigures/html/
Tunsi.htm.

Biography and Criticism

Booth, Marilyn. *Bayram al-Tunisi's Egypt: Social Criticism and Narrative Strategies*.
    Exeter: Published for the Middle East Centre, St. Antony's College, Oxford, by
    Ithaca, 1990.

————. "Force and Transitivity: Bayram al-Tunisi and a Poetics of Anticolonialism."
   Ghazoul and Harlow, *The View from Within*. 149–176.

————. "al-Tunisi, Mahmud Bayram." Meisami and Starkey, *Encyclopedia of Arabic
   Literature*. 784-785.

Benhadouga, Abdelhamid, 1925–

Web Sites

"Culture." *WINNE*. http://www.winne.com/algeria2/english/bf-culture.htm (accessed
   17 Aug. 2003).

Translations

"The South Wind." Trans. H. Abdel-Jaouad. *Literary Review* 41 (1998): 258–260.

Biographies and Criticism

Bamia, A.A. "Ibn Haduqa, 'Abd al-Hamid." Serafin, *Encyclopedia of World
   Literature in the 20th Century*. Vol. 2. 454–455.

Bois, M. "Benhedouga, Abdelhamid." Meisami and Starkey, *Encyclopedia of Arabic
   Literature*. 149.

Hassan, W.S. "Ben Hadouga, 'Abdelhamid." Gikandi, *Encyclopedia of African
   Literature*. 55.

Bint al-Shati', 1913–1998

Web Sites

"Aisha Abd al-Rahman (pseudonym: Bint al-Shati)." Al-Neshawy, F. Home Page. http://
   /www.hut.fi/~fahim/damietta/pages/famous.html#aisha (accessed 17 Aug. 2003).

"Aisha, Abdelrahman." *Arab World Books*. http://www.arabworldbooks.com/authors/
   aisha_abdelrahman.html (accessed 17 Aug. 2003).

Bois, D. "Aishah Abd al-Rahman." *Distinguished Women of Past and Present*. Ed. D.
   Bois. http://www.distinguishedwomen.com/biographies/abdalrahman.html
   (accessed 17 Aug. 2003).

"Dr. Aisha Abdel Rahman, Bint el Shatei (Daughter of the Riverbank)." *Egypt*. http://
   www.sis.gov.eg/calendar/html/cl021298.htm (accessed 17 Aug. 2003).

Biography and Criticism

Starkey, P. "'Abd al-Rahman, 'A'isha [Bint al-Shati']." Meisami and Starkey,
   Encyclopedia of Arabic Literature. 18.

al-Biruni, Muhammad ibn Ahmad, 973?–1048

Web Sites

"Abu Raihan Muhammad al-Biruni." *Afghan Sweden Online*. Ed. W. Dariab. http://
   medlem.spray.se/afghan/aburayhan_eng_01.htm (accessed 17 Aug. 2003).

"Al-Biruni." *Islamic Paths*. http://www.islamic-paths.org/Home/English/History/
   Personalities/Content/Biruni.htm (accessed 17 Aug. 2003).

"al-Biruni." *The Window: Philosophy on the Internet*. Ed. C. Marvin and F.
   Sikernitsky. http://caribou.cc.trincoll.edu/depts_phil/philo/phils/muslim/
   biruni.html (accessed 17 Aug. 2003).

al-Biruni, M. ibn A. "The Existing Monuments or Chronology, c. 1030 CE." *Internet Medieval Sourcebook*. http://www.fordham.edu/halsall/source/1030al-biruni1.html (accessed 17 Aug. 2003).

Harvey, J.H. "al-Biruni on Plants." *Salaam: Muslim Information Resources*. http://www.salaam.co.uk/knowledge/al-biruni.php (accessed 17 Aug. 2003).

Hermi, L. "Abu Raihan Al-Biruni." *Araf* 7 (1996). http://www.araf.net/dergi/sayi07/lotfi962/lotfi962.shtml (accessed 17 Aug. 2003).

O'Connor, J.J., and E.F. Robertson. "Abu Arrayhan Muhammad ibn Ahmad al-Biruni." *The MacTutor History of Mathematics Archive*. http://www-gap.dcs.st-and.ac.uk/~history/Mathematicians/Al-Biruni.html (accessed 14 Aug. 2003).

Translations

"Abu Rayhan Biruni." *An Anthology of Philosophy in Persia*. Ed. S.H. Nasr with M. Aminrazavi. 2 vols. New York: Oxford UP, 1999. Vol. 1. 374–400.

Alberuni's India. Trans. E.C. Sachau. New York: Norton, 1971.

The Chronology of Ancient Nations. Trans. E.C. Sachau. Frankfurt/Main: Minerva, 1984.

Biography and Criticism

"Al-Biruni." *Classical and Medieval Literature Criticism*. 28 (1999): 111–189.

Blois, F. de. "al-Biruni, Abu Rayhan." Meisami and Starkey, *Encyclopedia of Arabic Literature*. 152–153.

Kennedy, E.S. "al-Biruni, Abu Rayhan Muhammad ibn Ahmad." Gillispie, *Dictionary of Scientific Biography*. Vol. 2. 147–158.

Saliba, G. "Al-Biruni and the Sciences of His Time." *Religion, Learning and Science in the 'Abbasid Period*. Ed. M.J.L. Young, J.D. Latham, and R.B. Serjeant. Cambridge History of Arabic Literature. Cambridge UP, 1990. 405–423.

al-Bisati, Muhammad, 1937–

Web Sites

"Mohamed El-Bisatie." *Arab World Books*. http://www.arabworldbooks.com/authors/mohamed_elbisatie.htm (accessed 17 Aug. 2003).

A translation of his short story "A Conversation from the Third Floor" can be read at http://www.arabworldbooks.com/Literature/story1.htm.

Translations

Houses behind the Trees. Trans. D. Johnson-Davies. Austin: U of Texas P, 1998.

A Last Glass of Tea and Other Stories. Trans. D. Johnson-Davies. Boulder: Rienner, 1998.

"The Money Order." Johnson-Davies, *Under the Naked Sky*. 149–152.

"My Brother." Johnson-Davies, *Arabic Short Stories*. 13–21.

Biography and Criticism

"Al-Bisatie, Mohamed." *Contemporary Authors* 181 (2000): 9–10.

Bulus, Sarkun, 1943–

Web Sites

Boulus, Sargon. "The Face." *Shine* 30 (2003). http://www.blesok.com.mk/
   tekst.asp?lang=eng&tekst=487 (accessed 17 Aug. 2003).
      Translations of "This Road Alone," "The Face," "A Song for the One Who Will
Walk," and "Annotations of a Traveller."

————. "It Just Grabbed Me, This Magic of Words, of Music." Interviewed by
   Margaret Obank. *Kikah.com: Middle Eastern Literature & Arts*. http://
   www.kikah.com/indexenglish.asp?code=kk22 (accessed 17 Aug.
   2003).
      Also included on this Web site are translations of "The Ziggurat Builders," "The
Story Will Be Told," "News About No One," "Remarks to Sindbad from the Old Man
of the Sea."

"Sargon Boulus." *Masthead* 7 (2003). http://au.geocities.com/masthead_2/issue7/
   boulus.html (accessed 17 Aug. 2003).
      Includes translations of "Remarks to Sindbad from the Old Man of the Sea,"
"The Story Will Be Told," "Tea with Mouayed al-Rawi in a Turkish Cafe in Berlin
after the Wall Came Down," and "Who Knows the Story."

Translations

Jayyusi, *Modern Arabic Poetry*. 183–187.
      Includes translations of "Lighter," "Poem," "My Father's Dream," and "Siege"
by S. Boulus and A. Elliot.

al-Busiri, Sharaf al-Din Muhammad ibn Sa'id, 1213?–1296?

Web Sites

al-Busiri, S. al-D.M. ibn S. "Qasidat al-Burda by al-Busairi." *Ahlul-Bayt Islamic
   Library*. http://www.geocities.com/ahlulbayt14/burda-10.html (accessed 17
   Aug. 2003).
      Translation of "al-Burdah," with links to the Arabic text and to commentary on
the poem.

"Mosque-Mausoleum of Sharaf al-Din al-Busiri (Alexandria)." *The Heritage of
   Islamic Egypt*. 6 Apr. 2001. Orientalisches Seminar der Universitat zu Koln.
   http://www.uni-koeln.de/phil-fak/orient/htm/islamic%20egypt/busiri.htm
   (accessed 17 Aug. 2003).
      Includes information on his life and his work.

"Qasida al-Burda and Qasida al-Mudariyya, of Imam al-Busiri." *Tazkiya.net*. http://
   www.tazkiya.net/Library/Multimedia/Audio/Qasidah/burda.htm (accessed 17
   Aug. 2003).
      Includes audio clips of recitations of these poems.

Biography and Criticism

Bosworth, C.E. "al-Busiri." Meisami and Starkey, *Encyclopedia of Arabic Literature*.
   163.

Buzurg ibn Shahriyar, 10th cent.

Web Sites

"A Ship Captain's Tale." Rael, P. *History/Africana Studies 256: Comparative Slavery.*
   http://www.bowdoin.edu/~prael/256/primaries.htm#A%20Ship's%20Captain's
   (accessed 17 Aug. 2003).
   Includes a translation of one of the tales, from a collection of primary sources
for a history class at Bowdoin College.

Translations

The Book of the Marvels of India. Trans. L.M. Devic. New York: Dial, 1929.

Biography and Criticism

Irwin, R. "Buzurg ibn Shahriyar." Meisami and Starkey, *Encyclopedia of Arabic
   Literature.* 166–167.

Chahin, Salah, 1930–1986

Web Sites

Chahin, S. "September Tunes." *Arab World Books.* http://www.arabworldbooks.com/
   authors/salah_jahin.htm (accessed 17 Aug. 2003).
   A translation of excerpts from his poem "September Tunes" can be read at http://
www.arabworldbooks.com/Readers2002/articles/jahin.html.

Biography and Criticism

Booth, M. "Jahin, Salah." Meisami and Starkey, *Encyclopedia of Arabic Literature.*
   407–408.

Dahbur, Ahmad, 1946–

Web Sites

"Palestinian Poets, Ahmed Dahbour." *Khalil Sakakini Cultural Centre.* http://
   www.sakakini.org/poets/ahmed-index.htm (accessed 17 Aug. 2003).
   Includes translation of "New Suggestions."

Translations

Jayyusi, *Anthology of Modern Palestinian Literature.* 139–144.
   Includes translations of "From 'I Do Not Renounce Madness,'" "The Hands
Again," "New Suggestions," "Our Country," "The Sparrow Told Me," and "The
Terms of Ambition" by L. Jayyusi and J. Reed.

———. *Modern Arabic Poetry.* 194–199.
   Includes translations of "The Death of the Shoemaker" and "In Memory of
'Iziddin al-Qalaq" by L. Jayyusi and C. Doria.

"The Prison." Elmessiri, *The Palestinian Wedding.* 187–189.

al-Da'if, Rashid, 1945–

Web Sites

Cheuse, A. Rev. of *Dear Mr. Kawabata. All Things Considered.* NPR. 14 Aug. 2000.
   http://www.npr.org/programs/atc/books_music/2000/aug/ (accessed 17 Aug. 2003).

Elinson, A.E. Rev. of *This Side of Innocence*. *Middle East Studies Association Bulletin* 35.2. http://w3fp.arizona.edu/mesassoc/Bulletin/35-2/35-21Literature.htm (accessed 18 Aug. 2003).

Autobiography and Interviews

"I Want Only That Readers Find Pleasure in Their Reading." Interviewed by Margaret Obank. *Banipal* 6 (1999): 48–49.

Translations

Dear Mr. Kawabata. Trans. P. Starkey. London: Quartet, 1999.

"From 'Trapped between Drowsiness and Sleep.'" Trans. M.T. Amyuni. *Literary Review* 37 (1994): 395–401.

This Side of Innocence. Trans. P. Haydar. New York: Interlink, 2001.

Biography and Criticism

Aghacy, S. "Rachid El Daif's 'An Exposed Space between Drowsiness and Sleep': Abortive Representation." *Journal of Arabic Literature* 27 (1996): 193–203.

———. "The Use of Autobiography in Rashid al-Daif's 'Dear Mr. Kawabata'." Ostle, Moor, and Wild, *Writing the Self*. 217–228.

Amyuni, M.T. "al-Da'if, Rashid." Meisami and Starkey, *Encyclopedia of Arabic Literature*. 180.

———. "Style as Politics in the Poems and Novels of Rashid al-Da'if." *International Journal of Middle East Studies* 28 (1996): 177–192.

Darwish, Mahmud, 1941–

Web Sites

Akash, M. "On Mahmoud Darwish." *Fence* 5.1 (2002). http://www.fencemag.com/v5n1/text/darwish.html (accessed 18 Aug. 2003).

Includes translations of "From 'Four Personal Addresses,'" "Neighing at the Slope," and "They Would Love to See Me Dead."

Badrah, S. "Mahmoud Darwish." *Poetic Touch*. http://www.poetictouch.net/ (accessed 18 Aug. 2003).

Includes translations of several poems, audio recitations by the poet, and links to other Web sites.

"Cultural Freedom, Mahmoud Darwish." *Lannan: A Foundation Dedicated to Cultural Freedom, Diversity, and Creativity*. http://www.lannan.org/CF/darwish.htm (accessed 18 Aug. 2003).

Announcement of 2001 Lannan Cultural Freedom Award to Darwish; includes audio of the poet reading as well as translations being read by others.

Darwish, M. "Confine Your Confinement." *Between the Lines* May 2002. http://www.between-lines.org/archives/2002/may/Mahmoud_Darwish.htm (accessed 18 Aug. 2003).

Originally published in Arabic in the newspaper *al-Ayyam* 22 Apr. 2002, this article is a reaction to the Israeli occupation of Ramallah on 28 Mar. 2002.

Handal, N. "Mahmoud Darwish: Palestine's Poet of Exile." *The Progressive* 66.5 (2002). http://www.progressive.org/May%202002/hand0502.html (accessed 18 Aug. 2003).

"Mahmoud Darwish." *Books and Writers*. http://www.kirjasto.sci.fi/darwish.htm
(accessed 18 Aug. 2003).

"Mahmoud Darwish." *Magda's Night Gallery*. Ed. Magda. Dec. 2002. http://
www.geocities.com/SoHo/Cafe/1324/darwish.htm (accessed 18 Aug. 2003).
    Translations of "My Mother," "Identity Card," "Diary of a Palestinian Wound,"
"Psalm 9," "Passport," "Pride and Fury," and "The Pigeons Fly."

"Palestinian Poets, M. Darwish." *Khalil Sakakini Cultural Centre*. http://
www.sakakini.org/poets/mahmoud-index.htm (accessed 18 Aug. 2003).
    Includes translations of "An Excerpt from 'Mural,'" "Without Exile," "Who Am
I?" "Intensive Care Unit," "Psalm 9," "I Am from There," and "Ahmad Al-Za'tar."
Also includes article by Adam Shatz, "A Poet's Palestine as Metaphor."

Sachs, S. "Poetry of Arab Pain: Are Israeli Students Ready?" *Middle East and
Islamic Studies Collection, Cornell University*. http://www.library.cornell.edu/
colldev/mideast/mdarwsh.htm (accessed 18 Aug. 2003).

Saleh, F. "Mahmoud Darwish: 'I Always Learn from Criticism.'" *The Star* 4 Aug. 2001.
http://star.arabia.com/article/0,5596,76_1490,00.html (accessed 18 Aug. 2003).

Autobiography and Interviews

"A Love Story between an Arab Poet and His Land: An Interview with Mahmud
Darwish." Interviewed by A. Shatz. *Journal of Palestine Studies* 31.3 (2002):
67–78.

"There Is No Meaning to My Life Outside Poetry." Interviewed by H. Mosbahi.
Trans. I. Muhawi. *Banipal* 4 (1999): 5–11.
    This issue also includes translations of poems and several articles about Dar-
wish.

Translations

The Adam of Two Edens: Selected Poems. Trans. H. Haddawi, et al. Ed. M. Akash and
D. Moore. Syracuse: Jusoor; Syracuse UP, 2000.

Akash, M., and C. Forche, eds. and trans. *Unfortunately, It Was Paradise: Selected
Poems*. Berkeley: U of California P, 2003.

Aruri, N. and E. Ghareeb, eds. *Enemy of the Sun*. Washington: Drum and Spear P,
1970.
    Includes translations of "About A Man," "Defiance," "A Dialogue with a Man
Who Hates Me!," "I Declare," "Identity Card," "Letter from Exile," "Lorca," "Lover
from Palestine," "My Homeland," "On Hope," "On Poetry," "Reflections in the
Street," "A Song for Men," "Thunderbird," and "Victim Number Forty-Eight."

Asfour, *When the Words Burn*. 194–200.
    Includes translations of "The Curtain Falls," "Identity Card," "Of Poetry," "The
Prison," "Promises from the Storm," "Soft Rain in a Distant Autumn," and "To the
Reader."

Bennani, B., ed. and trans. *Bread, Hashish, and Moon*. Greensboro: Unicorn Press,
Inc., 1982. 37–47.
    Includes translations of "Fall of the Moon," "A Naive Song on the Red Cross,"
"On Poetry," "A Painting on the Wall," "The Prison Cell," and "Soft Rain in Distant
Autumn."

Elmessiri, *The Palestinian Wedding*. 31+.

Includes translations of "Awaiting the Return," "Blessed Be That Which Has Not Come!," "Concerning Hopes," "A Lover from Palestine," "The Man with the Green Shadow," "Promises from al-'Asifah (The Storm)," "The Roses and the Dictionary," "To My Grandfather," "Victim Number 18."

Memory for Forgetfulness: Aug., Beirut, 1982. Trans. I. Muhawi. Berkeley: U of California P, 1995.

The Music of Human Flesh. Trans. D. Johnson-Davies. Washington D.C.: Three Continents, 1980.

Psalms: Poems. Trans. B. Bennani. Colorado Springs: Three Continents, 1994.

Sand, and Other Poems. Trans. R. Kabbani. London: KPI, 1986.

Al-Udhari, *Modern Poetry of the Arab World*. 125–142.

Includes translations of "Brief Reflections on an Ancient and Beautiful City on the Coast of the Mediterranean Sea," "Earth Poem," "The Flute Cried," "Horses Neighing at the Foot of the Mountain," "I Have Witnessed the Massacre," "The Passport," "Psalm 2," "Psalm 3," "A Sky for the Sea," "Victim No. 48," "We Lost but Love Gained Nothing," "We Love Life Whenever We Can," "We Travel Like Other People," and "When the Martyrs Go to Sleep."

Victims of a Map. Trans. A. al-Udhari. London: Al Saqi, 1984. 10–49.

"Athens Airport," "The Earth Is Closing on Us," "A Gentle Rain in a Distant Autumn," "Give Birth to Me Again That I May Know," "A Gypsy Melody," "If I Were to Start All Over Again," "Is It in Such a Song?," "They'd Love to See Me Dead," "The Wandering Guitar Player," "We Are Entitled to Love Autumn," "We Are Here Near There," "We Fear for a Dream," "We Go to a Country," "We Travel Like Other People," and "When the Martyrs Go to Sleep."

Biography and Criticism

Allen, *Modern Arabic Literature*. 84–89.

Caspi, M.M., and J.D. Weltsch. *From Slumber to Awakening: Culture and Identity of Arab Israeli Literati*. Lanham, Md.: UP of America, 1998. 47–51.

"Darwish, M." *Contemporary Authors* 164 (1998): 99–102.

Gonzalez-Quijano, Y. "The Territory of Autobiography: Mahmud Darwish's 'Memory for Forgetfulness'." Trans. H. Davis. Ostle, Moor, and Wild, *Writing the Self*. 183–191.

Hafez, S. "Darwish, Mahmud." *Contemporary World Writers*. Ed. T. Chevalier. 2nd ed. Detroit: St. James, 1993. 137–139.

Siddiq, M. "Darwish, Mahmud." Serafin, *Encyclopedia of World Literature in the 20th Century*. Vol. 1. 579–580.

Suleiman, Y. "Darwish, Mahmud." Meisami and Starkey, *Encyclopedia of Arabic Literature*. 183–184.

Dhu al-Rummah, Ghaylan ibn 'Uqbah, 696–735

Web Sites

"Zu 'r-Rumma." *Humanistic Texts*. Ed. R. Pay. http://www.humanistictexts.org/ibn_khallikan.htm (accessed 18 Aug. 2003).

Abridged translation of a biography by Ibn Khallikan, a 13th century author.

Translations

"To the Encampments of Mayya." *Desert Tracings*. Trans. M.A. Sells. Middletown, CT: Wesleyan UP, 1989.

Biography and Criticism

Jayyusi, S.K. "Umayyad Poetry." *Arabic Literature to the End of the Umayyad Period*. Ed. A.F.L. Beeston, et al. Cambridge History of Arabic Literature. Cambridge: Cambridge UP, 1983. 387–432. See esp. 427–432.

Montgomery, J.E. "Dhu al-Rumma." Meisami and Starkey, *Encyclopedia of Arabic Literature*. 188–189.

Sells, M. "Dhu al-Rumma's 'To the Two Abodes of Mayya.'" *Al-'Arabiyya* 15 (1982): 52–65.

al-Dinawari, Abu Hanifah Ahmad ibn Dawud, d. ca. 895

Web Sites

Izady, M.R. "Abu-Hanifa Ahmad Dinawari: The 1,100th Anniversary of a World-Class Kurdish Scholar." *Kurdish Worldwide Resources*. Ed. B.A. Eliasi. http://www.kurdish.com/kurdistan/history/dinawari.htm (accessed 18 Aug. 2003).

Zaimeche, S. "Al-Dinawari Advances Botany." *MuslimHeritage.com*. http://www.muslimheritage.com/day_life/ (accessed 18 Aug. 2003).

Biography and Criticism

Daniel, E.L. "al-Dinawari, Abu Hanifa Ahmad ibn Da'ud." Meisami and Starkey, *Encyclopedia of Arabic Literature*. 195.

Dunqul, Amal, d. 1983

Web Sites

Ghazoul, F.J. "Genesis and Exodus in the Poetry of Amal Dunqul." *Middle East Affairs*. 10 Apr. 1998. http://www.umassd.edu/specialprograms/mideastaffairs/dunqul.htm (accessed 18 Aug. 2003).

Tomoum, S. "Amal Dunqul: A Voice of an Epic." *Community Times Monthly* 19 June 2000. http://www.arabia.com/egypt/life/article/english/0,5127,2763,00.html (accessed 18 Aug. 2003).

Translations

"Against Whom?" Fairbairn and al-Gosaibi, *Feathers and the Horizon*. 42.

Bitar. F., ed. and trans. *Treasury of Arabic Love Poems, Quotations and Proverbs*. New York: Hippocrene, 1996. 105–109.
  Includes translations of "The Green Eyes" and "Oh . . . Her Face."

Jayyusi, *Modern Arabic Poetry*. 214–217.
  Includes translations of "The City a Wrecked Ship," "Corner," "The Scaffold," "Tomorrow," "Trains" by S. Elmusa and T.G. Ezzy.

"The Murder of the Moon." Asfour, *When the Words Burn*. 135.

Biographies and Criticism

Al Masri, K. "Dunqul, Amal." Gikandi, *Encyclopedia of African Literature*. 156–157.

Mehrez, Samia. "Dunqul, Amal." Serafin, *Encyclopedia of World Literature in the 20th Century*. Vol. 1. 646–647.

Starkey, P. "Dunqul, Amal." Meisami and Starkey, *Encyclopedia of Arabic Literature*. 198.

al-Faqih, Ahmad Ibrahim, 1942–

Web Sites

"Elfaqeeh." *Arab World Books*. http://www.arabworldbooks.com/authors/ elfaqeeh.html (accessed 18 Aug. 2003).

Autobiography and Interviews

"Ahmed Fagih, a Writer at Night." Interviewed by M. Obank. *Banipal* 4 (1999): 52–55.

Translations

Charles, Diana, and Me, and Other Stories. London: Kegan Paul International, 2000.

Gardens of the Night: A Trilogy. Trans. R. Harris, A. al-Ayouti, S. Allam. London: Quartet, 1995.

Gazelles, and Other Plays. London: Kegan Paul International; New York: Distributed by Columbia UP, 2000.

Valley of Ashes. London: Kegan Paul International; New York: Distributed by Columbia UP, 2000.

Who's Afraid of Agatha Christie? London: Kegan Paul International; New York: Distributed by Columbia UP, 2000.

Biography and Criticism

Bamia, A.A. "al-Faqih (Fagih), Ahamad Ibrahim." Gikandi, *Encyclopedia of African Literature*. 184.

al-Farabi, ca. 872–950

Web Sites

"Abu al-Nasr al-Farabi." *The Window: Philosophy on the Internet*. Ed. C. Marvin and F. Sikernitsky. http://caribou.cc.trincoll.edu/depts_phil/philo/phils/muslim/ farabi.html (accessed 18 Aug. 2003).

"Al-Farabi." *Islamic Philosophy Online*. http://www.muslimphilosophy.com/farabi/ default.htm (accessed 18 Aug. 2003).

Includes biographical information, full text of two works in Arabic, articles about his work, video lecture by Seyyed Hossein Nasr, and English translation of *The Philosophy of Plato and Aristotle*.

"Al-Farabi." *Theosophy Library Online*. http://theosophy.org/tlodocs/teachers/ AlFarabi.htm (accessed 18 Aug. 2003).

Netton, I.R. "al-Farabi, Abu Nasr." *Islamic Philosophy Online*. http:// www.muslimphilosophy.com/ip/rep/H021.htm (accessed 28 Aug. 2003).

al-Talbi, A. "Al-Farabi." *IBE: International Bureau of Education*. 29 July 2003. http://www.ibe.unesco.org/International/Publications/Thinkers/ThinkersPdf/ farabie.pdf (accessed 18 Aug. 2003).

On his contributions in education.

Translations

"Abu Nasr Farabi." *An Anthology of Philosophy in Persia*. Ed. S.H. Nasr with M. Aminrazavi. 2 vols. New York: Oxford UP, 1999. Vol. 1. 91–134.

Al-Farabi on the Perfect State. Trans. R. Walzer. Oxford: Oxford UP, 1985.

Alfarabi, the Political Writings. Trans. C.E. Butterworth. Ithaca: Cornell UP, 2001.

Alfarabi's Philosophy of Plato and Aristotle. Trans. M. Mahdi. New York: Free P of Glencoe-Macmillan, 1962.

Biography and Criticism

Aminrazavi, M. "Al-Farabi." McGreal, *Great Thinkers of the Eastern World*. 446–448.

Black, D.L. "al-Farabi." Nasr and Leaman, *History of Islamic Philosophy*. 178–197.

Fakhry, M. *al-Farabi: Founder of Islamic Neoplatonism: His Life, Works, and Influence*. Oxford: Oneworld, 2002.

"Al-Farabi." *Classical and Medieval Literature Criticism*. 58: 1–155.

"Al-Farabi." *Medieval Philosophers (Dictionary of Literary Biography 115)*. Ed. J. Hackett. Detroit: Gale, 1992. 184–195.

Galston, M. *Politics and Excellence: The Political Philosophy of Alfarabi*. Princeton: Princeton UP, 1990.

Ivry, A.L. "Al-Farabi." *Religion, Learning and Science in the 'Abbasid Period*. Ed. M.J.L. Young, J.D. Latham, and R.B. Serjeant. Cambridge History of Arabic Literature. Cambridge: Cambridge UP, 1990. 378–388.

Leaman, O. "al-Farabi, Abu Nasr Muhammad." Meisami and Starkey, *Encyclopedia of Arabic Literature*. 218.

Mahdi, M. *Alfarabi and the Foundation of Islamic Political Philosophy*. Chicago: U of Chicago P, 2001.

———. *al-Farabi and His School*. London: Routledge, 1992.

———, and O. Wright. "al-Farabi, Abu Nasr Muhammad ibn Muhammad ibn Tarkhan ibn Awzalagh." Gillispie, *Dictionary of Scientific Biography*. Vol. 4. 523–526.

al-Farazdaq, ca. 641–728

Web Sites

"al-Farazdak." *Humanistic Texts*. Ed. R. Pay. http://www.humanistictexts.org/ ibn_khallikan.htm (accessed 18 Aug. 2003).
   Translation of a biography by Ibn Khallikan, a 13th century author.

Translations

"Farazdak of Darim-Tamim." Tuetey, *Classical Arabic Poetry*. 169–174.

Biography and Criticism

Gelder, G.J.H. van. "al-Farazdaq, Hammam ibn Ghalib." Meisami and Starkey, *Encyclopedia of Arabic Literature*. 219–220.

Jayyusi, S.K. "Umayyad Poetry." *Arabic Literature to the End of the Umayyad Period*. Ed. A.F.L. Beeston, et al. Cambridge History of Arabic Literature. Cambridge: Cambridge UP, 1983. 387–432. See esp. 401–409.

Smoor, P. "Al-Farazdaq's Reception by Contemporaries and Later Generations."
Journal of Arabic Literature 20 (1989): 115–127.

al-Farghani, fl. 861

Web Sites

"Ahmad ibn Muhammad ibn Kath al-Farghani." *Malaspina Great Books*. http://
www.malaspina.com/site/person_517.asp (accessed 18 Aug. 2003).

"Al-Farghani." *The Window: Philosophy on the Internet*. Ed. C. Marvin and F.
Sikernitsky. http://www.trincoll.edu/depts/phil/philo/phils/muslim/
farghani.html (accessed 18 Aug. 2003).

Biography and Criticism

Abdukhalimov, B. "Ahmad al-Farghani and His Compendium of Astronomy."
Journal of Islamic Studies 10 (1999): 142–158.

Sabra, A.I. "al-Farghani, Abu'l-'Abbas Ahmad ibn Muhammad ibn Kathir." Gillispie,
Dictionary of Scientific Biography. Vol. 4. 541–545.

al-Fituri, Muhammad, 1936?–

Web Sites

Muhammad Al Fayturi. Ed. K. Madison, et al. 11 May 2001. http://
www.geocities.com/muhammad_al_fayturi/index.html (accessed 18 Aug. 2003).
Designed as a student project for a class at Humboldt State University, site
includes biography, bibliography, criticism, and translations of "To Two Unknown
Eyes," "Sorrow of the Black City," "A Scream," "The Darwish/Bidpai Collection,"
"Incident," and "The Dervish."

Salloum, H. "Muhammad Mftah Al-Fituri, the Arab-African Poet of Renewal."
Expressions of Soul. http://www.expressionsofsoul.com/id65.html (accessed 18
Aug 2003).

Translations

"He Died Tomorrow." Asfour, *When the Words Burn*. 104–106.

Jayyusi, *Modern Arabic Poetry*. 220, 222–223.
Includes translations of "The Closed Door," "The Story," and "The Vision." by
S. Boulus and P. Porter.

"The Moon and the Garden." Fairbairn and al-Gosaibi, *Feathers and the Horizon*. 50.

"Sad Saturday Night." Khouri and Algar, *Anthology of Modern Arabic Poetry*. 155–157.

Biography and Criticism

Berkley, C.E. "al-Fayturi, (Muhammad) Miftah." Meisami and Starkey, *Encyclopedia
of Arabic Literature*. 226–227.

Ghanim, Fathi, 1924–1999

Web Sites

"Fathi Ghanem." *Arab World Books*. http://www.arabworldbooks.com/authors/
fathi_ghanem.html (accessed 18 Aug. 2003).
Includes translation of a short article by Ghanim, "With Age My Sense of the
Sea Sharpens," in which he discusses several of his stories and novels.

"Fathi Ghanem." *Egypt*. http://www.sis.gov.eg/calendar/html/cl020299.htm (accessed 18 Aug. 2003).

Translations

"Dunya." Trans. F. Moussa. Rev. P. Ward-Green. Manzalaoui, *Arabic Short Stories*. 343–352.

The Man Who Lost His Shadow. Trans. D. Stewart. Boston: Houghton Mifflin, 1966.

"'Shelaby' by Fathi Ghanim." Trans. D. Waines. *Journal of Arabic Literature* 19 (1988): 49–54.

Biography and Criticism

Allen, R. "Ghanim, Fathi." Gikandi, *Encyclopedia of African Literature*. 203–204.

Elad, A. "Ideology and Structure in Fathi Ghanim's 'al-Jabal'." *Journal of Arabic Literature* 20 (1989): 168–186.

Mikhail, M. "Ghanim, Fathi." Meisami and Starkey, *Encyclopedia of Arabic Literature*. 248.

Stagh, M. *The Limits of Freedom of Speech: Prose Literature and Prose Writers in Egypt under Nasser and Sadat*. Stockholm: Almqvist and Wiksell, 1993. 309–320.

al-Ghazali, Zaynab, 1917–

Web Sites

"Subj: Zaynab al-Ghazali." *Jannah.org*. 5 May 2003. http://www.jannah.org/sisters/zaynab.html (accessed 18 Aug. 2003).

Autobiography and Interviews

Return of the Pharoah: Memoir in Nasir's Prison. Trans. M. Guezzou. Leicester: Islamic Foundation, 1994.

Biography and Criticism

Cooke, M. "'Ayyam Min Hayati': The Prison Memoirs of a Muslim Sister." *The Postcolonial Crescent: Islam's Impact on Contemporary Literature*. Ed. J.C. Hawley. New York: Lang, 1998. 121–139.

———. "Zaynab al-Ghazali, Saint or Subversive?" *Welt des Islams* 34 (1994): 1–20.

Hoffman, V.J. "An Islamic Activist, Zaynab al-Ghazali." *Women and the Family in the Middle East: New Voices of Change*. Ed. E.W. Fernea. Austin: U of Texas P, 1985. 233–254.

al-Ghazzali, 1058–1111

Web Sites

"Abu Hamid Al-Ghazali." *The Window: Philosophy on the Internet*. Ed. C. Marvin and F. Sikernitsky. http://caribou.cc.trincoll.edu/depts_phil/philo/phils/muslim/ghazali.html (18 Aug. 2003).

Abu Sway, M. "Muhammad al-Ghazali." *Center for Islam and Science*. http://www.cis-ca.org/voices/g/ghazali.htm (accessed 18 Aug. 2003).

"Al-Ghazali's Website." *Islamic Philosophy Online*. http://www.muslimphilosophy.com/gz/default.htm (accessed 18 Aug. 2003).

Extensive site with full text of many works in Arabic and English; biography, bibliography, original works, criticism and television and lecture transcripts.

al-Ghazzali. "Munkidh min al-Dalal ('Confessions,' or 'Deliverance from Error')." *Internet Medieval Sourcebook*. http://www.fordham.edu/halsall/basis/1100ghazali-truth.html (accessed 18 Aug. 2003).

"Imam al-Ghazzali." *Islamic Paths*. http://www.islamic-paths.org/Home/English/History/Personalities/Content/Ghazzali.htm (accessed 18 Aug. 2003).

Nakamura, K. "al-Ghazali, Abu Hamid." *Islamic Philosophy Online*. http://www.muslimphilosophy.com/ip/rep/H028.htm (accessed 28 Aug. 2003).

Translations

Abstinence in Islam. Trans. C.E. Farah. Minneapolis: Bibliotheca Islamica, 1992.

The Faith and Practice of al-Ghazzali. Trans. W.M. Watt. Oxford: Oneworld, 1994.

Al-Ghazali on the Manners Relating to Eating. Trans. D. Johnson-Davies. Cambridge: Islamic Texts Soc., 2000.

Ghazali's Book of Counsel for Kings (Nasihat al-Muluk). Trans. F.R.C. Bagley. London: Oxford UP, 1964.

Al-Ghazali's Book of Fear and Hope. Trans. W. McKane. Leiden: Brill, 1965.

The Incoherence of the Philosophers. Trans. M.E. Marmura. Provo, UT: Brigham Young UP, 1997.

Marriage and Sexuality in Islam. Trans. M. Farah. Salt Lake City: U of UT P, 1984.

The Ninety-Nine Beautiful Names of God. Trans. D.B. Burrell and N.. Cambridge: Islamic Texts Soc., 1992.

On the Duties of Brotherhood. Trans. M. Holland. London: Latimer, 1975.

The Recitation and Interpretation of the Qur'an. Trans. M. Abul Quasem. London: Kegan Paul International, 1982.

The Remembrance of Death and the Afterlife. Trans. T.J. Winter. Cambridge: Islamic Texts Soc., 1989.

Biography and Criticism

Aminrazavi, M. "Al-Ghazali." McGreal, *Great Thinkers of the Eastern World*. 457–460.

Campanini, M "al-Ghazzali." Nasr and Leaman, *History of Islamic Philosophy*. 258–274.

Diyab, A.N. "Al-Ghazali." *Religion, Learning and Science in the 'Abbasid Period*. Ed. M.J.L. Young, J.D. Latham, and R.B. Serjeant. Cambridge History of Arabic Literature. Cambridge: Cambridge UP, 1990. 424–445.

"al-Ghazali." *Classical and Medieval Literature Criticism*. 50 (2002): 1–95.

Hillenbrand, C. "al-Ghazali." Meisami and Starkey, *Encyclopedia of Arabic Literature*. 252–253.

Smith, M. *al-Ghazali, the Mystic: A Study of the Life and Personality of Abu Hamid Muhammad al-Tusi al-Ghazali*. London: Luzac, 1944.

Watt, W.M. *Muslim Intellectual: A Study of al-Ghazali*. Edinburgh: Edinburgh UP, 1963.

al-Ghitani, Jamal, 1945–

Web Sites

"Gamal el-Ghitani." *Arab World Books.* http://www.arabworldbooks.com/authors/gamal_elghitani.htm (accessed 18 Aug. 2003).

Autobiography and Interviews

"Intertextual Dialectics." Trans. S. Mehrez. Ghazoul and Harlow, *The View from Within.* 17–26.

"The Quest for the Authentic and Innovative." Interviewed by Nabil Sharaf el-Din. *Banipal* 13 (2002): 8–11.

This issue also contains translations of a short story and an excerpt from a novel.

Translations

"Buzzing." Trans. A. Nowaira. *Egyptian Tales and Short Stories of the 1970s and 1980s.* Ed. W.M. Hutchins. Cairo: American U in Cairo P, 1987. 151–157.

"An Invitation." Johnson-Davies, *Under the Naked Sky.* 46–56.

Zayni Barakat. Trans. F.A. Wahab. London: Viking; New York: King Penguin, 1988.

Biographies and Criticism

Allen, R. "'Al-Zayni Barakat', Jamal al-Ghitani." *The Arabic Novel: An Historical and Critical Introduction.* 2nd ed. Syracuse: Syracuse UP, 1995. 195–208.

Allen, *Modern Arabic Literature.* 100–104.

Hamarneh, W. "al-Ghitani, Jamal." Serafin, *Encyclopedia of World Literature in the 20th Century.* Vol. 2. 242–243.

Mehrez, S. *Egyptian Writers between History and Fiction: Essays on Naguib Mahfouz, Sonallah Ibrahim, and Gamal al-Ghitani.* Cairo: American U in Cairo P, 1994. 58–77, 96–118.

Sheble, R. "al-Ghitani, Gamal." Gikandi, *Encyclopedia of African Literature.* 204.

Starkey, P. "al-Ghitani, Jamal." Meisami and Starkey, *Encyclopedia of Arabic Literature.* 253–254.

Gibran, Kahlil, 1883–1931

Web Sites

Bushrui, S. "Kahlil Gibran of America." *Al-Hewar Center: The Center for Arab Culture and Dialogue.* Ed. S. Ghandour. http://www.alhewar.com/Gibran.html (accessed 18 Aug. 2003).

Gibran. Ed. Mira. http://leb.net/gibran/ (accessed 18 Aug. 2003).

Full text and selections from both Arabic (in English translation) and English works, art works, biography, bibliography, and illustrations. Includes *Spirits Rebellious, The Broken Wings, A Tear and a Smile, The Madman, The Forerunner, The Prophet, Sand and Foam, Jesus the Son of Man, The Earth Gods, The Wanderer, The Garden of the Prophet, Lazarus and His Beloved,* "The New Frontier," "I Believe in You," "My Countrymen," "Satan," "You Have Your Lebanon and I Have My Lebanon," "Your Thought and Mine."

Much of the same content, with a few added short pieces, is also available at *Gibran Khalil Gibran Virtual Library* (http://www.arab2.com/gibran/).

Juan Cole's Kahlil Gibran Page. Ed. J. Cole. http://www-personal.umich.edu/~jrcole/gibran/gibran1.htm (accessed 18 Aug. 2003).

"Kahlil Gibran." *al-Bab.com*. Ed. B. Whitaker. http://www.al-bab.com/arab/literature/gibran.htm (accessed 18 Aug. 2003).

Autobiography

Beloved Prophet: The Love Letters of Kahlil Gibran and Mary Haskell and Her Private Journal. Ed. V. Hilu. New York: Knopf, 1972.

Blue Flame: The Love Letters of Kahlil Gibran to May Ziadah. Ed. and trans. S. Bushrui and S. Kuzbari. New York: Longman, 1983.

Kahlil Gibran, a Self-Portrait. Trans. and ed. A.R. Ferris. New York: Citadel, 1959.

Translations and English Texts

The Beloved: Reflections on the Path of the Heart. Trans. J. Walbridge. Ashland, Ore.: White Cloud, 1994.

Dramas of Life. Philadelphia: Westminster, 1981.

Nymphs of the Valley. Trans. H.M. Nahmad. New York: Knopf, 1970.

The Treasured Writings of Kahlil Gibran. Secaucus, N.J.: Castle, 1985.

The Vision: Reflections on the Way of the Soul. Trans. J.R.I. Cole. Ashland, Ore.: White Cloud, 1994.

Biography and Criticism

Allen, *Modern Arabic Literature*. 169–176.

Gibran, J. *Kahlil Gibran: His Life and World*. Rev. and upd. ed. New York: Interlink 1998.

"Gibran, Kahlil." *Contemporary Authors* 150 (1996): 163–166.

"(Gibran) Kahlil Gibran." *Twentieth-Century Literary Criticism*. Ed. D. Poupard. Vol. 9. Detroit: Gale, 1983. 81–94.

"Kahlil Gibran." *Poetry Criticism*. Ed. D. Kelaskey. Vol. 9. Detroit: Gale, 1994. 68–83.

"Kahlil Gibran." *Twentieth-Century Literary Criticism*. Ed. D. Bryfonski and P.C. Mendelson. Vol. 1. Detroit: Gale, 1978. 325–330.

Naimy, N. "Gibran, Kahlil." Serafin, *Encyclopedia of World Literature in the 20th Century*. Vol. 2. 246–247.

———. *The Lebanese Prophets of New York*. Beirut: American U of Beirut, 1985. 35–56.

Nijland, C. "Jubran, Jubran Khalil." Meisami and Starkey, *Encyclopedia of Arabic Literature*. 415–416.

Naimy, M. *Kahlil Gibran: A Biography*. London: Quartet, 1988.

Shahid, I. "Gibran and the American Literary Canon: The Problem of 'The Prophet.'" *Tradition, Modernity, and Postmodernity in Arabic Literature: Essays in Honor of Professor Issa J. Boullata*. Ed. K. Abdel-Malek and W. Hallaq. Brill: Leiden, 2000. 321–334.

Waterfield, R. *Prophet: The Life and Times of Kahlil Gibran*. New York: St. Martin's, 1998.

Habibi, Imil, 1921–1996

Web Sites

"Emile Habibi." *Arab World Books*. http://www.arabworldbooks.com/authors/
emile_habibi.htm (accessed 18 Aug. 2003).

Zane, O. "Emile Habibi, the Pessoptimist Who Went Global." *Aljadid* 7 (1996). http:
//almashriq.hiof.no/general/000/070/079/al-jadid/aljadid-emileh.html (accessed
18 Aug. 2003).

Translations

"The Blue Charm and the Return of Jubaynah." *The Modern Arabic Short Story:
Shahrazad Returns*. Trans. M. Shaheen. 2nd ed. Rev. and exp. New York:
Palgrave Macmillan, 2002. 215–220.

"The Odds-and-Ends Woman." Trans. R. Allen and C. Tingley. Jayyusi, *Anthology of
Modern Palestinian Literature*. 454–459.

The Secret Life of Saeed, the Ill-Fated Pessoptimist. Trans. S.K. Jayyusi and T. Le
Gassick. New York: Vantage, 1982.

Biography and Criticism

Allen, R. "'Al-Waqa'i' al-Gharibah fi-Ikhtifa' Sa'id Abi al-Nahs al-Mustasha'il',
Emile Habibi." *The Arabic Novel: an Historical and Critical Introduction*. 2nd
ed. Syracuse: Syracuse UP, 1995. 209–222.

Allen, *Modern Arabic Literature*. 104–108.

Boullata, I.J. "Habibi, Imil (Habiby, Emile)" Meisami and Starkey, *Encyclopedia of
Arabic Literature*. 259.

Caspi, M.M. and J.D. Weltsch. *From Slumber to Awakening: Culture and Identity of
Arab Israeli Literati*. Lanham, Md.: UP of America, 1998. 71–81.

Hafez, S. "Habibi, Imil." *Contemporary World Writers*. Ed. T. Chevalier. 2nd ed.
Detroit: St. James, 1993. 224–226.

Heath, P. "Creativity in the Novels of Emile Habiby, with Special Reference to 'Sa'id
the Pessoptimist.'" *Tradition, Modernity, and Postmodernity in Arabic
Literature: Essays in Honor of Professor Issa J. Boullata*. Ed. K. Abdel-Malek
and W. Hallaq. Brill: Leiden, 2000. 158–172.

Shaheen, M. *The Modern Arabic Short Story: Shahrazad Returns*. 2nd ed. Rev. and
exp. New York: Palgrave Macmillan, 2002. 117–120.

Siddiq, M. "Habibi, Emile." Serafin, *Encyclopedia of World Literature in the 20th
Century*. Vol. 2. 331–332.

Taha, I. *The Palestinian Novel: a Communication Study*. London: Routledge Curzon,
2002. 55–86.

Haddad, Qasim, 1948–

Web Sites

Qassim Haddad. http://www.qhaddad.com/ (accessed 18 Aug. 2003).

Includes translations of 31 poems, biographical information, an autobiographical essay, an interview. The Arabic section of the site is much more extensive.

"Qassim Haddad." *Masthead* 7 (2003). http://au.geocities.com/masthead_2/issue7/
    haddad.html (accessed 18 Aug. 2003).
    Translations of "From 'Words from a Young Night'" and "The Friends There."

Translations

Asfour, *When the Words Burn.* 130–131.
    Includes translations of "Answer," "As They Say," and "The Feast of the Sea."

"The Pearl." Fairbairn and al-Gosaibi, *Feathers and the Horizon.* 56.

Biography and Criticism

Frangieh, B.K. "Qassim Haddad: Resignation and Revolution." *Banipal* 17 (2003):
    16–17.

Hafiz Ibrahim, Muhammad, 1872?–1932

Web Sites

"Hafez Ibrahim, Hafez Ibrahim." *Egypt.* http://www.sis.gov.eg/calendar/html/
    cl210798.htm (accessed 18 Aug. 2003).

"An Issue of Identity Nationalism." *Spotlight on the Muslim Middle East: Issues of
    Identity.* Ed. H.S. Greenberg and L. Mahony. 1995. American Forum for Global
    Education. http://www.globaled.org/muslimmideast/spage4.php.
    Scroll down to see the translation of "Egypt's Complaint Against the British
Occupation."

Translations

"Describing a Suit." Trans. C. Tingley with the help of S.K. Jayyusi, and C.
    Middleton. Jayyusi, *Modern Arabic Poetry.* 77–78.

Biography and Criticism

Elkhadem, S. *History of the Egyptian Novel: Its Rise and Early Beginnings.*
    Fredericton, N.B.: York, 1985. 12–15.

Starkey, P. "Ibrahim, (Muhammad) Hafiz." Meisami and Starkey, *Encyclopedia of
    Arabic Literature.* 386.

al-Hakim, Tawfiq, 1898–1987

Web Sites

"A Century's Judgement." *Al-Ahram Weekly Online* 8–14 Oct. 1998. http://
    weekly.ahram.org.eg/1998/398/cu1.htm (accessed 18 Aug. 2003).

Lavin, C. "The Sultan's Dilemma." *FreshAngles.* http://www.freshangles.com/
    xpressions/essays/articles/30.html (accessed 18 Aug. 2003).

"The Wise Sage of Arabic Literature." *Egypt.* http://www.sis.gov.eg/egyptinf/culture/
    html/tawfik.htm (accessed 18 Aug. 2003).
    Much of the same information can be read in "Tawfiq Al Hakim, Dean of Dra-
matic Literature" at http://www.sis.gov.eg/calendar/html/cl2607a.htm.

Autobiography

Maze of Justice: Diary of a Country Prosecutor. Trans. A. Eban. London: Saqi, 1989.

The Prison of Life: An Autobiographical Essay. Trans. P. Cachia. Cairo: American U
in Cairo P, 1992.

Translations

Fate of a Cockroach. Trans. D. Johnson-Davies. London: Heinemann, 1973.

In the Tavern of Life and Other Stories. Trans. W.M. Hutchins. Boulder, Colo.:
Rienner, 1998.

Jayyusi, S.K. ed. *Short Arabic Plays: An Anthology.* New York: Interlink, 2003.
177–205.
Includes translations of "Boss Kanduz's Apartment Building: A Commentary
on the Ethics of War" by R. Allen and C. Tingley and "War and Peace" by M. Jayyusi
and D. Wright.

Plays, Prefaces, and Postscripts of Tawfiq al-Hakim. 2 vols. Washington, D.C.: Three
Continents, 1981–1984.
Includes translations of "Angels' Prayer," 'Between War and Peace," "Food for
the Millions," "Incrimination," "King Oedipus," "Poet on the Moon," "Princess Sun-
shine," "Shahrazad," "Tender Hands," "Voyage to Tomorrow," and "The Wisdom of
Solomon" by W.M. Hutchins.

The Return of Consciousness. Trans. B. Winder. New York: New York UP, 1985.

Return of the Spirit. Trans. W.M. Hutchins. Washington, D.C.: Three Continents,
1990.

Manzalaoui, M. ed. *Arabic Writing Today: Drama.* Rev. A. Parkin and M.
Manzalaoui. Cairo: American Research Center in Egypt, 1977. 65–183.
Includes translations of "Song of Death" and "The Sultan's Dilemma" by M.
Badawi.

The Tree Climber. Trans. D. Johnson-Davies. London: Oxford UP, 1966.

Biographies and Criticism

Allen, *Modern Arabic Literature.* 111–124.

Badawi, M.M. *Modern Arabic Drama in Egypt.* Cambridge: Cambridge UP, 1987. 8–87.

Elkhadem, S. *History of the Egyptian Novel: Its Rise and Early Beginnings.*
Fredericton, N.B.: York, 1985. 44–50.

Hutchins, W.M. *Tawfiq al-Hakim: A Reader's Guide.* Boulder: Rienner, 2003.

Kirkpatrick, H. *The Modern Egyptian Novel: A Study in Social Criticism.* Oxford:
Middle East Centre, St. Antony's College; London: Ithaca, 1974. 41–51.

Long, R. *Tawfiq al Hakim, Playwright of Egypt.* London: Ithaca, 1979.

Sakkut, H. *The Egyptian Novel and Its Main Trends: From 1913 to 1952.* Cairo:
American U in Cairo P, 1971. 85–97.

Selim, S. "'The Maze of Justice' by Tawfiq al-Hakim." *African Literature and Its
Times.* Ed. J. Moss and L. Valestuk. World Literature and Its Times 2. Detroit:
Gale, 2000. 247–257.

Semah, D. "al-Hakim, Tawfiq." Serafin, *Encyclopedia of World Literature in the 20th
Century.* Vol. 2. 335.

Sheble, R. "al-Hakim, Tawfiq." Gikandi, *Encyclopedia of African Literature.*
215–216.

Starkey, P. "The Four Ages of Husayn Tawfiq: Love and Sexuality in the Novels of Tawfiq al-Hakim." *Love and Sexuality in Modern Arabic Literature.* Ed. R. Allen, H. Kilpatrick, and E. de Moor. London: Saqi, 1995. 56–64.

———. *From the Ivory Tower: A Critical Study of Tawfiq al-Hakim.* London: Published for the Middle East Centre, St. Antony's College, Oxford, by Ithaca, 1987.

———. "al-Hakim, Tawfiq." Meisami and Starkey, *Encyclopedia of Arabic Literature.* 263–265.

———. "Tawfiq al-Hakim." Pendergast and Pendergast, *Reference Guide to World Literature.* 993–995.

———. "Tawfiq al-Hakim, 1898–1987." *African Writers.* Ed. C.B. Cox. New York: Scribner's, 1997. 291–301.

al-Hallaj, al-Husayn ibn Mansur, 858 or 900–922

Web Sites

al-Hallaj, al-Husayn ibn Mansur. "Sayings." *Internet Medieval Sourcebook.* http://www.fordham.edu/halsall/source/all-hallaj-quotations.html (accessed 18 Aug. 2003).

"Husayn ibn Mansur al-Hallaj." *Sidi Muhammad Press.* Ed. I. al-Jamal. 3 Jan. 2003. http://www.sufimaster.org/husayn.htm (accessed 18 Aug. 2003).

Translations

"Four Poems of al-Hallaj." Trans. D.P. Brewster. *Journal of Arabic Literature* 9 (1978): 65–66.

"Seven Poems by al-Hallaj." Trans. M.M. Badawi. *Journal of Arabic Literature* 14 (1983): 46–47.

Biography and Criticism

Cooper, J. "al-Hallaj, Abu al-Mughith al-Husayn ibn Mansur." Meisami and Starkey, *Encyclopedia of Arabic Literature.* 266–267.

Mason, H.W. *Al-Hallaj.* Richmond: Curzon, 1995.

Massignon, L. *The Passion of al-Hallaj: Mystic and Martyr of Islam.* Trans. H. Mason. 4 vols. Princeton: Princeton UP, 1982.

———. *The Passion of al-Hallaj: Mystic and Martyr of Islam.* Trans. and ed. H. Mason. Abridged ed. Princeton: Princeton UP, 1994.

Selim, S. "Mansur al-Hallaj and the Poetry of Ecstasy." *Journal of Arabic Literature* 21 (1990): 26–42.

Haqqi, Yahya, 1905–1993

Web Sites

"Yehia Hakki." *Arab World Books.* http://www.arabworldbooks.com/authors/yehia_hakki.html (accessed 18 Aug. 2003).

"Yehya Haqqi, a Prominent Novelist with a Special Flavour." *Egypt.* http://www.sis.gov.eg/eginfnew/culture/html/cul0104.htm (accessed 18 Aug. 2003).

Translations

Blood and Mud. Trans. P. Cachia. Pueblo, Colo.: Passeggiata, 1999.

Manzalaoui, *Arabic Short Stories*. 76–107.

> Includes translations of "The Brass Four-Poster" by N. Sherif, revised by J. Wahba, and "An Empty Bed" by M. Manzalaoui, revised by L. Knight and L. Hall.

Good Morning! and Other Stories. Trans. M. Cooke. Washington, D.C.: Three Continents, 1987.

"Mother of the Destitute." *Modern Arabic Short Stories*. Trans. D. Johnson-Davies. London: Oxford UP, 1967. 97–105.

The Saint's Lamp and Other Stories. Trans. M.M. Badawi. Leiden: Brill, 1973.

"A Story from Prison." Johnson-Davies, *Egyptian Short Stories*. 118–132.

Biographies and Criticism

Allen, *Modern Arabic Literature*. 124–129.

Badawi, M.M. "'The Lamp of Umm Hashim': the Egyptian Intellectual between East and West." *Journal of Arabic Literature* 1 (1970): 145–161.

Cooke, M. *The Anatomy of an Egyptian Intellectual, Yahya Haqqi*. Washington, D.C.: Three Continents, 1984.

———. "Haqqi, Yahya." Meisami and Starkey, *Encyclopedia of Arabic Literature*. 271–272.

———. "Haqqi, Yahya." Serafin, *Encyclopedia of World Literature in the 20th Century*. Vol. 2. 345–346.

Elkhadem, S. *History of the Egyptian Novel: Its Rise and Early Beginnings*. Fredericton, N.B.: York, 1985. 52–53.

al-Hariri, 1054–1122

Web Sites

al-Hariri. "Maqamat ('The Assemblies')." *Internet Medieval Sourcebook*. http://www.fordham.edu/halsall/basis/1100Hariri.html (accessed 18 Aug. 2003). Translation of the first 12 of the 50 assemblies.

Translations

Makamat, or, Rhetorical Anecdotes of al-Hariri of Basra. Trans. T. Preston. Westmead, England: Gregg International, 1971.

Biography and Criticism

Beeston, A.F.L. "Al-Hamadhani, al-Hariri and the 'Maqamat' Genre." *'Abbasid Belles-Lettres*. Ed. J. Ashtiany, et al. Cambridge History of Arabic Literature. Cambridge: Cambridge UP, 1990. 125–135.

Drory, R. "al-Hariri." Meisami and Starkey, *Encyclopedia of Arabic Literature*. 272–273.

Sharlet, J. "Al-Hariri, al-Qasim ibn 'Ali Abu Muhammad al-Basri." Pendergast and Pendergast, *Reference Guide to World Literature*. 27–28.

Hassan ibn Thabit, d. 674

Web Sites

"Hassan ibn Thabit." *Answering Islam: A Christian-Muslim Dialog*. Aug. 2003. http://answering-islam.org/Index/H/hassan_b._thabit.html (accessed 18 Aug. 2003).

"Hassan ibn Thabit." *The True Creed*. http://www.geocities.com/Athens/6441/poemss1.html (accessed 18 Aug. 2003).
Translation of a poem to Khubaybah.

"Qasida in Praise of the Prophet Attributed to Hassan ibn Thabit." *Aisha Bewley's Home Page*. Ed. A. Bewley. 1 July 2003. http://ourworld.compuserve.com/homepages/ABewley/hassan.html (accessed 18 Aug. 2003).

Biography and Criticism

Gelder, G.J.H. van. "Hassan ibn Thabit." Meisami and Starkey, *Encyclopedia of Arabic Literature*. 275–276.

Hatatah, Sharif, 1923–

Web Sites

Arab Culture and Civilization. Ed. M. Toler. National Institute for Technology and Liberal Education. http://www.nitle.org/arabworld/main_menu.php (accessed 19 Aug. 2003).
Use the Search box to find a seven-part video interview of Hatatah and his wife Nawal al-Sa'dawi, on the status of women in the Arab world and the changes due to globalization.

Nawal El Saadawi, Sherif Hetata. 11 June 2003. http://www.nawalsaadawi.net/index.html (accessed 19 Aug. 2003).
Includes photos, biographies, and articles by and about the author and his wife, Nawal al-Sa'dawi.

See also sites listed under al-Sa'dawi, Nawal

Translations

The Net. Trans. S. Hatatah. London: Zed, 1986.

Biography and Criticism

Sheble, R. "Hetata, Sharif." Gikandi, *Encyclopedia of African Literature*. 221–222.

Hawi, Khalil S., 1925–1982

Web Sites

Haddad, F.S. "Khalil Hawi: A Graceful Poet from the Vineyards of Lebanon." *Middle East and Islamic Studies Collection, Cornell University*. http://www.library.cornell.edu/colldev/mideast/khalilh.htm (accessed 19 Aug. 2003).

"Khalil Hawi." *Jehat.com*. http://www.jehat.com/en/default.asp?action=article&ID=85 (accessed 21 May 2004).

Includes translations of "The Flute and Wind in the Hermit's Cell," "The Bridge," and "The Magi in Europe."

Translations

Asfour, *When the Words Burn*. 153–158.
  Includes translations of "The Cave," "The Magi in Europe," and "The Prisoner."

Hawi, K., and N. Naimy. *From the Vineyards of Lebanon*. Trans. F.S. Haddad. Beirut: American U of Beirut, 1991.

Literary Review 37 (1994): 491–497.
  Includes translations of "After the Ice" and "The Mariner and the Dervish" by A. Haydar and M. Beard.

Naked in Exile. Trans. A. Haydar and M. Beard. Washington, D.C.: Three Continents, 1984.

"Sindbad on His Eighth Voyage." *The Modern Arabic Short Story: Shahrazad Returns*. Trans. M. Shaheen. 2nd ed. rev. and exp. New York: Palgrave Macmillan, 2002. 179–190.

Biography and Criticism

Abu-Deeb, K. "Hawi, Khalil." Meisami and Starkey, *Encyclopedia of Arabic Literature*. 277.

Ali, Z.A.H. "The Aesthetics of Transgression: Khalil Hawi's 'The Sailor and the Dervish' and the European Grotesque." *Journal of Arabic Literature* 28 (1997): 219–241.

Allen, *Modern Arabic Literature*. 129–136.

Haydar, A. "Hawi, Khalil." Serafin, *Encyclopedia of World Literature in the 20th Century*. Vol. 2. 361–362.

Shaheen, M. *The Modern Arabic Short Story: Shahrazad Returns*. 2nd ed. Rev. and exp. New York: Palgrave Macmillan, 2002. 81–88.

Haydar, Haydar, 1936–

Web Sites

Abdel Moneim, A. "Book Reawakens Islamist Trend." *Middle East Times* 12 May 2000. http://www.metimes.com/2K/issue2000-19/eg/book_reawakens_islamist.htm (accessed 19 Aug. 2003).
  Discusses the controversy over his novel *A Banquet for Seaweed*.

Translations

"The Ants and the Qat." *Modern Syrian Short Stories*. Trans. M.G. Azrak. Rev. M.J.L. Young. Washington, D.C.: Three Continents, 1988. 28–30.

Biography and Criticism

Frangieh, Bassem K. "Haidar Haidar, Novelist of Social Change." *Banipal* 8 (2000): 32–34.

Young, M.J.L. "Haydar, Haydar." Meisami and Starkey, *Encyclopedia of Arabic Literature*. 277–278.

al-Haydari, Buland, 1926–1996

Web Sites

Buland al-Haydari. Ed. A. Berry, et al. http://www.humboldt.edu/~me2/engl240/
    student_projects/Al-Haydari/al-Haydari.html (accessed 19 Aug. 2003).
    Designed as a student project for a course in world literature, includes biography, bibliography, translations of poems with commentary ("Guilty Even If I Were Innocent," "Steps in Strange Lands," "A Call to Sleep.")

al-Haydari, Buland. *Magda's Night Gallery.* Ed. Magda. Dec. 2002. http://
    www.geocities.com/SoHo/Cafe/1324/haidari.htm (accessed 19 Aug. 2003).
    Includes translations of "Mailman" and "Old Age."

Translations

Asfour, *When the Words Burn.* 81–83.
    Includes "The Disappointment of an Ancient Man," "Journey of the Yellow Letters," and "Waiting Sails."

Boullata, *Modern Arab Poets.* 19–28.
    Includes "Barrenness," "The Lost Footstep," "The Postman," "Tomorrow Here," "Twenty Thousand Killed . . . Old News," and "Steps in Strange Lands."

Jayyusi, *Modern Arabic Poetry.* 242–246.
    Includes translations of "Age of the Rubber Seals," "The Dead Witness," "Dialogue," and "Genesis" by P.A. Byrne, with the help of S.K. Jayyusi.

Songs of the Tired Guard. Trans. A. al-Udhari. London: TR Press, 1977.

Al-Udhari, *Modern Poetry of the Arab World.* 42–47.
    Includes "Conversation at the Bend in the Road," "The Dead Witness," "Guilty Even If I Were Innocent," "My Apologies," and "The Postman."

Biography and Criticism

Allen, *Modern Arabic Literature.* 136–140.

Boullata, I.J. "al-Haydari, Buland." Meisami and Starkey, *Encyclopedia of Arabic Literature.* 278.

Loloi, P. "Haydari, Buland al-." *Contemporary World Writers.* Ed. T. Chevalier. 2nd ed. Detroit: St. James, 1993. 239–241.

Haykal, Muhammad Husayn, 1888–1956

Web Sites

Haykal, M.H. "Life of Muhammad." Trans. I.R.A. al-Faruqi. *Islamia.com.* http://
    www.islamia.com/Muhammad/biography_the_life_of_muhammad.htm
    (accessed 19 Aug. 2003).

"Mohammad Hussein Heikal." *Egypt.* http://www.us.sis.gov.eg/egyptianfigures/html/
    heikal.htm (accessed 19 Aug. 2003).

Translations

Mohammed Hussein Haikal's Zainab. Trans. J.M. Grinsted. London: Darf, 1989.

Biography and Criticism

Allen, R. "Haykal, Muhammad Husayn." Meisami and Starkey, *Encyclopedia of Arabic Literature*. 278–279.

Allen, *Modern Arabic Literature*. 140–143.

Dajani, Z.R. *Egypt and the Crisis of Islam*. New York: Lang, 1990.

Elkhadem, S. *History of the Egyptian Novel: Its Rise and Early Beginnings*. Fredericton, N.B.: York, 1985. 26–28.

Kirkpatrick, H. *The Modern Egyptian Novel: A Study in Social Criticism*. Oxford: Middle East Centre, St. Antony's College; London: Ithaca, 1974. 20–26.

Sakkut, H. *The Egyptian Novel and Its Main Trends: From 1913 to 1952*. Cairo: American U in Cairo P, 1971. 12–21.

Semah, D. *Four Egyptian Literary Critics*. Leiden: Brill, 1974.

Smith, C.D. *Islam and the Search for Social Order in Modern Egypt: A Biography of Muhammad Husayn Haykal*. Albany: State U of New York P, 1983.

Wessels, Antonie. *A Modern Arabic Biography of Muhammad: A Critical Study of Muhammad Husayn Haykal's Hayat Muhammad*. Leiden: Brill, 1972.

Hunayn ibn Ishaq al-'Ibadi, 809?–873

Web Sites

"Arab Translators." *Loq-Man Translations*. http://www.loqmantranslations.com/ArabicFacts/ArabTranslators.html (accessed 19 Aug. 2003).

O'Connor, J.J., and E.F. Robertson. "Abu Zayd Hunayn ibn Ishaq al-Ibadi." *The MacTutor History of Mathematics Archive*. http://www-gap.dcs.st-and.ac.uk/~history/Mathematicians/Hunayn.html (accessed 14 Aug. 2003).

Biography and Criticism

Anawati, G.C. and A.Z. Iskandar. "Hunayn ibn Ishaq al-'Ibadi, Abu Zayd." Gillispie, *Dictionary of Scientific Biography*. Vol. 15. 230–249.

Cooperson, M. "Hunayn ibn Ishaq al-'Ibadi." Meisami and Starkey, *Encyclopedia of Arabic Literature*. 295–296.

Goodman, L.E. "The Translation of Greek Materials into Arabic." *Religion, Learning, and Science in the 'Abbasid Period*. Ed. M.J.L. Young, J.D. Latham, and R.B. Serjeant. Cambridge History of Arabic Literature. Cambridge: Cambridge UP, 1990. 477–497. See especially 487–491.

Hamarneh, S.K. "Abu Zayd Hunayn bin Ishaq al-'Ibadi." Atiyeh, *The Genius of Arab Civilization*. 222–223.

Husayn, Taha, 1889–1937

Web Sites

Husayn, T. "From 'The Future of Culture in Egypt'." *Internet Modern History Sourcebook*. Ed. P. Halsall. 22 Sept. 2001. http://www.fordham.edu/halsall/mod/1954taha.html (accessed 19 Aug. 2003).

"November 14th, 1889, the Birth of Taha Hussein, an Egyptian Leader of the Englightenment." *Egypt.* http://www.uk.sis.gov.eg/calendar/html/cl141196.htm (accessed 19 Aug. 2003).

    Click on the link to read "The Water We Drink, the Air We Breathe" on Husayn and the museum established in his home. Another article on the museum can be read at http://www.uk.sis.gov.eg/egyptinf/culture/html/ta001.htm.

Rizk, Y.L. "Taha Hussein's Ordeal." *Al-Ahram Weekly On-Line* 24–30 May 2001. http://weekly.ahram.org.eg/2001/535/chrncls.htm (accessed 19 Aug. 2003). On the controversy surrounding the publication of his book, *On Jahiliyah Poetry.*

"Taha Hussein." *Arab World Books.* http://www.arabworldbooks.com/authors/taha_hussein.html (accessed 19 Aug. 2003).

"Taha Hussein: Remember You Doyen." *Egypt.* http://www.sis.gov.eg/egyptinf/culture/html/thussein.htm (accessed 19 Aug. 2003).

Autobiography

The Days. Trans. E.H. Paxton, H. Wayment, K. Cragg. Cairo: American U in Cairo P, 1997.

    Originally published as three separate works: *An Egyptian Childhood, The Stream of Days,* and *A Passage to France.*

Translations

The Call of the Curlew. Trans. A.B. As-Safi. Leiden: Brill, 1980.

The Sufferers. Trans. M. El-Zayyat. Cairo: American U in Cairo P, 1993.

Biographies and Criticism

Allen, *Modern Arabic Literature.* 146–153.

Cachia, P. "Husayn, Taha." Meisami and Starkey, *Encyclopedia of Arabic Literature.* 296–297.

———. "Taha Husayn, 1889–1973." *African Writers.* Ed. C.B. Cox. New York: Charles Scribner's Sons, 1997. 851–863.

———. *Taha Husayn, His Place in the Egyptian Literary Renaissance.* London: Luzac, 1956.

Dajani, Z.R. *Egypt and the Crisis of Islam.* New York: Lang, 1990.

Elkhadem, S. *History of the Egyptian Novel: Its Rise and Early Beginnings.* Fredericton, N.B.: York, 1985. 28–36.

Kirkpatrick, H. *The Modern Egyptian Novel: A Study in Social Criticism.* Oxford: Middle East Centre, St. Antony's College; London: Ithaca, 1974. 35–41.

Mahmoudi, A. *Taha Husain's Education: from the Azhar to the Sorbonne.* Richmond: Curzon, 1998.

Malti-Douglas, F. *Blindness and Autobiography: Al–Ayyam of Taha Husayn.* Princeton: Princeton UP, 1988.

Moor, E. de. "Autobiography, Theory and Practice: The Case of 'al-Ayyam'." Ostle, Moor, and Wild, *Writing the Self.* 128–138.

Nijland, Cornelis. "Instead of the Song of the Nightingale." *Tradition and Modernity in Arabic Literature.* Ed. I.J. Boullata and T. DeYoung. Fayetteville: U of Arkansas P, 1997. 161–172.

Reynolds, D.F. "'An Egyptian Childhood' by Taha Husayn." *African Literature and Its Times*. Ed. J. Moss and L. Valestuk. World Literature and Its Times 2. Detroit: Gale, 2000. 119–130.

Sakkut, H. *The Egyptian Novel and Its Main Trends: From 1913 to 1952*. Cairo: American U in Cairo P, 1971. 31–36, 100–103.

Semah, D. *Four Egyptian Literary Critics*. Leiden: Brill, 1974.

———. "Hussein, Taha." Serafin, *Encyclopedia of World Literature in the 20th Century*. Vol. 2. 446–447.

Sheble, R. "Husayn, Taha." Gikandi, *Encyclopedia of African Literature*. 228–230.

Ibn 'Abd al-Hakam, d. 870 or 871

Web Sites

Ibn 'Abd al-Hakam. "The Islamic Conquest of Spain." *Internet Medieval Sourcebook*. http://www.fordham.edu/halsall/source/conqspain.html (accessed 19 Aug. 2003).

———. "The Moorish Conquest of Spain." *Mosaic: Perspectives on Western Civilization*. http://college.hmco.com/history/west/mosaic/chapter4/source260.html (accessed 19 Aug. 2003).

Translations

The History of the Conquest of Spain. Trans. and ed. J.H. Jones. New York: B. Franklin, 1969.

"Narrative of the Conquest of al-Andalus." Trans. D.A. Cohen. *Medieval Iberia: Readings from Christian, Muslim, and Jewish Sources*. Ed. O.R. Constable. Philadelphia: U of Pennsylvania P, 1997. 32–36.

Biography and Criticism

Conrad, L.I. "Ibn 'Abd al-Hakam." Meisami and Starkey, *Encyclopedia of Arabic Literature*. 302.

Ibn al-'Arabi, 1165–1240

Web Sites

Chittick, W.C. "Ibn al-'Arabi." Godlas, Alan. *Islam, Islamic Studies, Arabic, Religion: Resources for Studying Islam*. http://www.uga.edu/islam/ibnarab.html (accessed 19 Aug. 2003).
Originally published in *Encyclopedia Iranica* as "Ebn al-'Arabi, Mohyi-al-Din."

———. "Muhyi al-Din Muhammad Ibn al-'Arabi al-Hatimi al-Ta'i." *Center for Islam and Science*. http://www.cis-ca.org/voices/a/ibnarabi.htm (accessed 28 Aug. 2003).

Ibn al-'Arabi. "The Seals of Wisdom ('Fusus al-Hikam')" *Aisha Bewley's Islamic Home Page (2)*. Ed. A. Bewley. 12 Aug. 2003. http://bewley.virtualave.net/fusus.html (accessed 19 Aug. 2003).

———. "Selections from al-Futuhat al-Makkiyya." *Aisha Bewley's Islamic Home Page*. Ed. A. Bewley. 1 July 2003. http://ourworld.compuserve.com/homepages/ABewley/ibnArabi.html (accessed 19 Aug. 2003).

The Muhyiddin Ibn 'Arabi Society. http://www.ibnarabisociety.org/ (accessed 19 Aug. 2003).

Home page of a scholarly organization devoted to the study of his works. Includes a short biography, critical articles, and list of publications (mainly translations of his works) sponsored by the society.

Robinson, N. "Ibn al-'Arabi, Muhyi al-Din." *Islamic Philosophy Online.* http://www.muslimphilosophy.com/ip/rep/H022.htm (accessed 28 Aug. 2003).

Translations

The Bezels of Wisdom. Trans. R.W.J. Austin. New York: Paulist, 1980.

Contemplation of the Holy Mysteries and the Rising of the Divine Lights. Trans. C. Twinch and P. Beneito. Oxford: Anqa, 2001.

Divine Governance of the Human Kingdom. Int. T.B. al-Jerrahi al-Halveti. Louisville, Ky.: Fons Vitae, 1997.

"Gentle Now, Doves of the Thornberry and Moringa Thicket." Trans. M.A. Sells. *The HarperCollins World Reader: Antiquity to the Early Modern World.* Ed. M.A. Caws and C. Prendergast. New York: HarperCollins College Publishers, 1994. 1009–1011.

Mysteries of Purity. Trans. E. Winkel. Notre Dame, Ind.: Cross Cultural Publications, 1994.

The Seven Days of the Heart. Trans. P. Beneito and S. Hirtenstein. Oxford: Anqa, 2000.

Sufis of Andalusia. Trans. R.W.J. Austin. Berkeley: U of California P, 1972.

Biography and Criticism

Addas, C. *The Quest for the Red Sulphur: The Life of Ibn 'Arabi.* Trans. P. Kingsley. Cambridge: Islamic Texts Soc., 1993.

Chittick, W.C. "Ibn 'Arabi." Nasr and Leaman, *History of Islamic Philosophy.* 497–509.

Knysh, Alexander. "Ibn 'Arabi." *The Literature of al-Andalus.* Ed. M.R. Menocal, R.P. Scheindlin, and M. Sells. Cambridge: Cambridge UP, 2000. 331–344.

———. *Ibn 'Arabi in the Later Islamic Tradition: The Making of a Polemical Image in Medieval Islam.* Albany: State U of New York P, 1999.

Landau, R. *The Philosophy of Ibn Arabi.* New York: Macmillan, 1959.

McGregor, R.J.A. "Ibn al-Arabi, Muhyi al-Din." Pendergast and Pendergast, *Reference Guide to World Literature.* 493–494.

Nasr, S.H. *Three Muslim Sages: Avicenna, Suhrawardi, Ibn 'Arabi.* Cambridge: Harvard UP, 1964.

Nettler, R.L. "Ibn al-'Arabi." Meisami and Starkey, *Encyclopedia of Arabic Literature.* 311–312.

Sells, M.A. "Ibn 'Arabi." McGreal, *Great Thinkers of the Eastern World.* 475–479.

Ibn al-Athir, 'Izz al-Din, 1160–1233

Web Sites

Ibn al-Athir, 'I. al-D. "The Franks Seize Antioch." *The Crusades: Voices and Perspectives*. Ed. George McDowell. http://www.umich.edu/~iinet/ worldreach/assets/docs/crusades/IbnalAthir.html (accessed 19 Aug. 2003).
    A selection on the conquest of Jerusalem by the Crusaders can be read at http:// www.umich.edu/~iinet/worldreach/assets/docs/crusades/IbnalAthir2.html, and on the reconquest by Saladin at http://www.umich.edu/~iinet/worldreach/assets/docs/ crusades/SaladinJerusalem.html.

———. "On the Tatars." *Internet Medieval Sourcebook*. http://www.fordham.edu/ halsall/source/1220al-Athir-mongols.html (accessed 19 Aug. 2003).

"Umayyads." *Islamic Coins Collection*. Ed. F. Barrage. http://islamiccoins.50g.com/ umayyads/readingumayyadcoins.htm (accessed 19 Aug. 2003).
    Includes translation of section on the minting of coins by the caliph 'Abd al-Malik ibn Marwan.

Translations

The Annals of the Saljuq Turks. Trans. D.S. Richards. London: RoutledgeCurzon, 2002.

"The Battle of Hittin." Trans. E.J. Costello. *The Art of War in World History: from Antiquity to the Nuclear Age*. Comp. G. Chaliand. Berkeley: U of California P, 1994. 400–404.

Biography and Criticism

Richards, D.S. "Ibn al-Athir, 'Izz al-Din." Meisami and Starkey, *Encyclopedia of Arabic Literature*. 316.

Ibn al-Nadim, Muhammad ibn Ishaq, fl. 987

Web Sites

"Islamic Encyclopedia." *All Things Considered*. NPR. 23 Jan. 1999. http:// discover.npr.org/features/feature.jhtml?wfId=1006769 (accessed 20 Aug. 2003).
    Audio Interviewed by Seyyed Hossein Nasr on the *Fihrist*.

Translations

The Fihrist of Ibn al-Nadim. Ed. and trans. B. Dodge. New York: Columbia UP, 1970.

Biography and Criticism

Kimber, R.A. "Ibn al-Nadim." Meisami and Starkey, *Encyclopedia of Arabic Literature*. 355–356.

Ibn al-Nafis, 'Ali ibn Abi al-Hazm, 1210 or 1211–1288

Web Sites

Al-Ghazal, S.K. "Ibn Al-Nafis and the Discovery of the Pulmonary Circulation."
IslamOnline.net. 20 Aug. 2003. http://www.islamonline.net/English/Science/
2002/08/article06.shtml (accessed 20 Aug. 2003).

"Ibn al-Nafis." *Islamset: Islam, Science, Environment & Technology*. Islamic
Organization for Medical Sciences. http://www.islamset.com/isc/nafis/
main.html (accessed 20 Aug. 2003).
    Includes five articles on his contribution as a scientist and a philosopher, and a
translation of *Comprehensive Book on the Art of Medicine*.

"Ibn al-Nafis." *The Window: Philosophy on the Internet*. Ed. C. Marvin and F.
Sikernitsky. http://www.trincoll.edu/depts/phil/philo/phils/muslim/nafis.html
(accessed 28 Aug. 2003).

"Ibn Nafis (al-)" *Malaspina Great Books*. http://www.malaspina.com/site/
person_880.asp (accessed 20 Aug. 2003).

Translations

The Theologus Autodidactus of Ibn al-Nafis. Ed. and trans. M. Meyerhof and J.
Schacht. Oxford: Clarendon P, 1968.

Biography and Criticism

Iskandar, A.Z. "Ibn al-Nafis, 'Ala' al-Din Abu 'l-Hasan 'Ali ibn Abi 'l-Hazm al-
Qurashi." Gillispie, *Dictionary of Scientific Biography*. Vol. 9. 602–606.

Netton, I.R. "Ibn al-Nafis." Meisami and Starkey, *Encyclopedia of Arabic Literature*.
356.

Ibn al-Qalanisi, Abu Ya'la Hamzah ibn Asad, d. 1160

Web Sites

Christie, N.G.F. "The Presentation of the Franks in Selected Muslim Sources from the
Crusades of the 12th Century." *De Re Militari*. Ed. P. Konieczny. 6 Aug. 2003.
Society for Medieval Military History. http://www.deremilitari.org/
RESOURCES/ARTICLES/christie.htm (accessed 20 Aug. 2003).
    An unpublished master's thesis, includes a chapter on Ibn al-Qalanisi.

"The Franks Conquer Jerusalem." *The Crusades: Voices and Perspectives*. Ed. G.
McDowell. http://www.umich.edu/~iinet/worldreach/assets/docs/crusades/
IbnalAthir2.html (accessed 20 Aug. 2003).
    The second account is a short extract on the Crusaders' capture of Jerusalem in
1096. A translation of his account of the siege of Damascus in 1148 can be read at
http://www.umich.edu/~iinet/worldreach/assets/docs/crusades/Damascus.html.

Translations

The Damascus Chronicle of the Crusades. Trans. H.A.R. Gibb. London: Luzac, 1967.

Biography and Criticism

Richards, D.S. "Ibn al-Qalanisi." Meisami and Starkey, *Encyclopedia of Arabic
Literature*. 358–359.

Ibn al-Rumi, 836–896

Web Sites

"The Poets of Arabia, Selections." *Internet Medieval Sourcebook*. http://
www.fordham.edu/halsall/source/arabianpoets1.html (accessed 20 Aug. 2003).
Scroll down to translations of "To a Lady Weeping," "On a Valetudinarian," and
"On a Miser."

Translations

"Ibn al-Rumi." Arberry, *Arabic Poetry*. 62–72.

Biography and Criticism

Gelder, G.J.H. van. "Ibn al-Rumi." Meisami and Starkey, *Encyclopedia of Arabic
Literature*. 364–365.

Gruendler, B. *Medieval Arabic Praise Poetry: Ibn al-Rumi and the Patron's
Redemption*. London: RoutledgeCurzon, 2003.

Smoor, P. "Elegies and Other Poems on Death by Ibn al-Rumi." *Journal of Arabic
Literature* 27 (1996): 49–85.

Ibn 'Ata' Allah, Ahmad ibn Muhammad, d. 1309

Web Sites

"About Ahmad Ibn 'Ata'Allah." *Mysticism in World Religions*. Ed. D. Platt. http://
www.digiserve.com/mystic/Muslim/Ibn_Ata_Allah/ (accessed 20 Aug. 2003).

"The Hikam of Ibn 'Ata'llah." *Witness-Pioneer: A Virtual Islamic Organisation*.
http://www.wponline.org/vil/Books/IA_Hikmah/Default.html (accessed 20
Aug. 2003).
Includes translation of commentary on the book by Ibn 'Ajibah.

"On Dhikr, from Mifath al-Falah (The Key to Success) by Ibn 'Ata'llah al-Iskandari."
Aisha Bewley's Islamic Home Page. Ed. A. Bewley. 1 July 2003. http://
ourworld.compuserve.com/homepages/ABewley/Page5.html (accessed 20 Aug.
2003).
Translation of one chapter from this book.

Translations

The Key to Salvation and the Lamp of Souls. Trans. M.A.K. Danner. Cambridge:
Islamic Texts Soc., 1996.

Biography and Criticism

Meisami, J.S. "Ibn 'Ata' Allah." Meisami and Starkey, *Encyclopedia of Arabic
Literature*. 313–314.

Ibn Batuta, 1304–1377

Web Sites

"The Arabian Marco Polo." *Al Shindagh* Aug.–Sept. 1996. http://
www.alshindagah.com/august/ibn_batt.htm (accessed 20 Aug. 2003).

Buchan, James. "Even to the Borders of China." Rev. of *The Travels of Ibn Battutah*,
ed. T. Mackintosh-Smith. *Guardian* 21 Dec. 2002. http://books.guardian.co.uk/
reviews/classics/0,6121,863105,00.html (accessed 20 Aug. 2003).

Chughtai, A.S. "Ibn Battuta, the Great Traveler." *Islamic Paths*. http://www.islamic-
    paths.org/Home/English/History/Personalities/Content/Battuta.htm (accessed
    20 Aug. 2003).

Ibn Batuta. "Ibn Battuta Sets Forth." *Theatrum Mediterraneum*. Ed. T.F. Arnold.
    http://classes.yale.edu/99-00/hist325b/Ibn/BattFez1.htm (accessed 20 Aug.
    2003).
    Follow the links for extensive selections from the *Travels*.

———. "Selections from 'The Travels of Ibn Batuta.'" *Project South Asia*. Ed. K.J.
    Schmidt. 27 May 2003. Missouri Southern State College. http://www.mssc.edu/
    projectsouthasia/history/primarydocs/Foreign_Views/IbnBattuta/ (accessed 20
    Aug. 2003).
    Chapters on South Asia, from the 1829 Lee translation.

———. "Travels in Asia and Africa 1325–1354." *Internet Medieval Sourcebook*. http://
    www.fordham.edu/halsall/source/1354-ibnbattuta.html (accessed 20 Aug. 2003).
    Selections from the Gibb translation, which serve to summarize the entire book.
Other selections can be read at http://www.fordham.edu/halsall/source/batuta.html.

"Islamic Travel Narratives: The 'Rihla' of Ibn Battuta." *Contexts and Comparisons: A
    Student Guide to the Great Works Course*. Baruch College. http://
    newman.baruch.cuny.edu/digital/2000/c_n_c/c_04_medieval/
    islamic_travel.htm (accessed 20 Aug. 2003).
    Includes translation of the section on the pilgrimage to Mecca and Medina. Part
of a student handbook for Great Works of Literature course at Baruch College, City
University of New York.

Taylor, J.M. "Ibn Battuta and His Saharan Travels." Home Page. http://
    www.manntaylor.com/battuta.html (accessed 20 Aug. 2003).

"The Travels of Ibn Battuta." *Old World Contacts*. Ed. D. Campbell, J. Dingle, and K.
    Morris. 3 July 2001. The Applied History Research Group, University of
    Calgary. http://www.ucalgary.ca/applied_history/tutor/oldwrld/diplomats/
    battuta.html (accessed 20 Aug. 2003).

"Travels of Ibn Batuta." *Najaco*. http://www.najaco.com/adventure/articles/muslim/
    ibn_batuta/1.htm (accessed 20 Aug. 2003).

Translations

Ibn Battuta in Black Africa. Trans. and ed. S. Hamdun and N. King. London:
    Collings, 1975.

The Travels of Ibn Batuta. Trans. S. Lee. New York: B. Franklin, 1971.

The Travels of Ibn Battuta, A.D. 1325–1354. Trans. and ed. H.A.R. Gibb. Cambridge:
    Hakluyt Soc., 1971.

Biography and Criticism

Conrad, L.I. "Ibn Battuta." Meisami and Starkey, *Encyclopedia of Arabic Literature*.
    318–319.

Douglass, S., and J. Littleton. "'Ibn Battuta in Black Africa' by Abu Abdalla ibn
    Batutta." *African Literature and Its Times*. J. Moss, and L. Valestuk. World
    Literature and Its Times 2. Detroit: Gale, 2000. 203–213.

Dunn, R.E. *The Adventures of Ibn Battuta, a Muslim Traveler of the 14th Century*. Berkeley: U of California P, 1986.

"Ibn Battuta." *Classical and Medieval Literature Criticism*. 57 (2003): 1–75.

Rosenthal, F. "Ibn Battuta." Gillispie, *Dictionary of Scientific Biography*. Vol. 1. 516–517.

Winder, R.B. "Muhammad bin 'Abdallah bin Battutah." Atiyeh, *The Genius of Arab Civilization*. 268.

Ibn Daniyal, Muhammad, 1249 or 1250–1310 or 1311

Web Sites

Feeny, J. "Shadows of Fancy." *Karaghiozis.net*. Ed. Alexis. http://www.karaghiozis.net/articles/shadows.html (accessed 20 Aug. 2003).
    Gives information on an Egyptian theater troupe, al-Warsha, which performs shadow plays, including those by Ibn Daniyal, who is profiled in "A Shadow Theater Playwright."

Biography and Criticism

Badawi, M.M. "Medieval Arabic Drama: Ibn Daniyal." *Journal of Arabic Literature* 13 (1982): 83–107.

Corrao, F.M. "Laughter Festival and Rebirth: Ibn Daniyal's Shadow Plays, an Example of Cultural Tolerance in the Early Mamluk Ages." *Proceedings of the Colloquium on Logos, Ethos, Mythos in the Middle East & North Africa (LEM): Budapest, 18–22 September 1995*. Ed. K. Devenyi. The Arabist 17–18. 2 vols. Budapest: Eotvos Lorand University Chair for Arabic Studies: Csoma de Koros Soc. Section of Islamic Studies, 1996. 13–28.

Rowson, E.K. "Ibn Daniyal." Meisami and Starkey, *Encyclopedia of Arabic Literature*. 319–320.

Ibn Fadlan, Ahmad, fl. 922

Web Sites

Montgomery, J.E. "Ibn Fadlan and the Rusiyyah." *Journal of Arabic and Islamic Studies* 3 (2000). http://www.uib.no/jais/v003ht/montgo1.htm (accessed 20 Aug. 2003).
    Includes a translation of the relevant section.

"The Travels of Ibn Fadlan." *MuslimHeritage*.com. http://www.muslimheritage.com/day_life/ (accessed 20 Aug. 2003).

Biography and Criticism

Bosworth, C.E. "Ibn Fadlan, Ahmad." Meisami and Starkey, *Encyclopedia of Arabic Literature*. 323.

Gabriel, J. "Among the Norse Tribes: The Remarkable Account of Ibn Fadlan." *Aramco World* 50.6 (1999): 36–42.

Ibn Hawqal, Muhammad, 10th century

Web Sites

"Ibn Hauqal's World Map." *Cartographic Images*. Ed. J. Siebold. 12 Feb. 1998.
Henry Davis Consulting. http://gate.henry-davis.com/MAPS/EMwebpages/
213B.html (accessed 20 Aug. 2003).
Facsimile of the map, with an interpretative redrawing.

Biography and Criticism

Beckingham, C.F. "Ibn Hauqal's Map of Italy." *Iran and Islam: In Memory of the
Late Vladimir Minorsky*. Ed. C.E. Bosworth. Edinburgh: Edinburgh UP, 1971.
73–78.

Richter-Bernburg, L. "Ibn Hawqal." Meisami and Starkey, *Encyclopedia of Arabic
Literature*. 332.

Vernet, J. "Ibn Hawqal, Abu'l-Qasim Muhammad." Gillispie, *Dictionary of Scientific
Biography*. Vol. 6. 186.

Ibn Hazm, 'Ali ibn Ahmad, 994–1064

Web Sites

Arnaldez, R. "Ibn Hazm." *Islamic Philosophy Online*. http://
www.muslimphilosophy.com/ip/ibnhazm.htm (accessed 20 Aug. 2003).

Ibn Hazm, 'A. ibn A. "On the Nature of Love." *Islamic Psychology Online*. Ed. Abu
S.I. ibn I. Malik. 5 Jan. 2001. http://www.angelfire.com/al/islamicpsychology/
general/nature_of_love.html (accessed 21 Aug. 2003).
Translated excerpt from *The Ring of the Dove*. Another excerpt, "The Signs of
Love," can be read at http://www.angelfire.com/al/islamicpsychology/general/
signs_of_love.html.

Leaman, O., and S. Albdour. "Ibn Hazm, Abu Muhammad 'Ali." *Islamic Philosophy
Online*. http://www.muslimphilosophy.com/ip/rep/H047.htm (accessed 28 Aug.
2003).

"The Philosophy and Thoughts of Ibn Hazm on Science." *MuslimHeritage.com*. http:/
/www.muslimheritage.com/day_life/ (accessed 20 Aug. 2003).

Witkam, J.J. "Ibn Hazm's Tawq al-Hamama ('The Ring of the Dove')"
Universiteitsbibliotheek. Universiteit Leiden. http://ub.leidenuniv.nl/bc/olg/
selec/Tawq/index2.html (accessed 19 Apr. 2004).
Facsimile of the unique manuscript of this book, with an introduction in
English.

Translations

"On the Inconsistencies of the Four Gospels." Trans. T.E. Burman. *Medieval Iberia:
Readings from Christian, Muslim, and Jewish Sources*. Ed. O.R. Constable.
Philadelphia: U of Pennsylvania P, 1997. 81–83.

The Ring of the Dove. Trans. A.J. Arberry. London: Luzac, 1953.

Andalusian Poems. Boston: Godine, 1993. 9–10.
Includes translations of the poems "With a Knife" and "The Visit" by C. Middleton and L. Garza-Falcon.

Biography and Criticism

Chejne, A.G. *Ibn Hazm*. Chicago: Kazi, 1982.

Ormsby, E. "Ibn Hazm." *The Literature of al-Andalus*. Ed. M.R. Menocal, R.P. Scheindlin, and M. Sells. Cambridge History of Arabic Literature. Cambridge: Cambridge UP, 2000. 237–251.

Scheindlin, R.P. "Ibn Hazm." Meisami and Starkey, *Encyclopedia of Arabic Literature*. 333–334.

Ibn Ishaq, Muhammad, d. ca. 768

Web Sites

"The Earliest Biography of Muhammad, by Ibn Ishaq." *Left Shoe News + Human Rights Abuses in Islamic Countries*. Ed. R.E. Burns. http://www.hraic.org/ hadith/ibn_ishaq.html (accessed 20 Aug. 2003).
From the translation by Edward Rehatsek.

Ibn Ishaq, M. "Selections from the 'Life of Muhammad.'" *Internet Medieval Sourcebook*. http://www.fordham.edu/halsall/source/muhammadi-sira.html (accessed 20 Aug. 2003).

Translations

The Life of Muhammad. Trans. A. Guillaume. London; New York: Oxford UP, 1955.

The Making of the Last Prophet. Reconstructed by G.D. Newby. Columbia: U of South Carolina P, 1989.

Biography and Criticism

Conrad, L.I. "Ibn Ishaq." Meisami and Starkey, *Encyclopedia of Arabic Literature*. 336–337.

Ibn Jubayr, Muhammad ibn Ahmad, 1145–1217

Web Sites

"Ahmad ibn Jubayr." *Najaco*. http://www.najaco.com/adventure/articles/muslim/ jubayr/1.htm (accessed 20 Aug. 2003).

Ibn Jubayr, M. ibn A. "Ibn Jubayr Arrives in Mecca." *Theatrum Mediterraneum*. Ed. T.F. Arnold. http://classes.yale.edu/99-00/hist325b/Jubayr/JubaMecc1.html (accessed 20 Aug. 2003).
Follow the links for more selections.

———. "The Travels of Ibn Jubayr." P. Hyams. *History 259, the Crusades*. Aug. 2000. College of Arts and Sciences, Cornell University. http:// www.arts.cornell.edu/prh3/259/texts/jubayr.htm (accessed 20 Aug. 2003).

"The Travels of Ibn Jubair." *MuslimHeritage*.com. http://www.muslimheritage.com/ day_life/ (accessed 20 Aug. 2003).

Translations

The Travels of Ibn Jubayr. Ed. W. Wright. 2nd ed., rev. Ed. M.J. de Goeje. New York: AMS, 1973.

The Travels of Ibn Jubayr. Trans. R.J.C. Broadhurst. London: Cape, 1952.

Biography and Criticism

Netton, I.R. "Basic Structures and Signs of Alienation in the 'Rihla' of Ibn Jubayr."
    Journal of Arabic Literature 22 (1991): 21–37.

Wasserstein, D.J. "Ibn Jubayr." Meisami and Starkey, *Encyclopedia of Arabic
    Literature.* 340.

Ibn Khaldun, 1332–1406

Web Sites

Al-Araki, A.M. *Ibn Khaldun, a Forerunner for Modern Sociology: Discourse of the
    Method and Concept of Economic Sociology.* May 1998. http://home.hio.no/
    ~araki/arabase/ibn/khaldun.html (accessed 20 Aug. 2003).
    Introductory pages of the author's book, on Ibn Khaldun's life and work.

Ibn Khaldun on the Web. Ed. T. Spalding. http://www.isidore-of-seville.com/
    ibnkhaldun/ (accessed 20 Aug. 2003).
    Well-arranged portal site, including links to biographies, scholarly papers, and
English translations of selections.

Issawi, C., and O. Leaman. "Ibn Khaldun, 'Abd al-Rahman." *Islamic Philosophy
    Online.* http://www.muslimphilosophy.com/ip/rep/H024.htm (accessed 28 Aug.
    2003).

Autobiography

Ibn Khaldun and Tamerlane. Trans. W.J. Fischel. Berkeley: U of California P,
    1952.

Translations

An Arab Philosophy of History. Trans. C. Issawi. Princeton, N.J.: Darwin P,
    1987.

The Muqaddimah, an Introduction to History. Trans. F. Rosenthal. 3 vols. New York:
    Pantheon Books, 1958.

Biography and Criticism

Al-Azmeh, A. "Ibn Khaldun." Meisami and Starkey, *Encyclopedia of Arabic
    Literature.* 343–344.

———. *Ibn Khaldun, an Essay in Reinterpretation.* London: Cass, 1982.

Lacoste, Y. *Ibn Khaldun: The Birth of History and the Past of the Third World.*
    London: Verso, 1984.

Lakhsassi, A. "Ibn Khaldun." Nasr and Leaman, *History of Islamic Philosophy.* 350–
    364.

Martin, M.A. "'Abd ar-Rahman bin Muhammad bin Khaldun." Atiyeh, *The Genius of
    Arab Civilization.* 102–103.

Rabi, M.M. *The Political Theory of Ibn Khaldun.* Leiden: E.J. Brill,
    1967.

Rosenthal, F. "Ibn Khaldun." Gillispie, *Dictionary of Scientific Biography.* Vol. 7.
    320–323.

Ibn Masarrah, Muhammad ibn 'Abd Allah, 882 or 883–931

Web Sites

Atiyeh, G.N. "Ibn Masarra, Muhammad ibn 'Abd Allah." *Islamic Philosophy Online.*
http://www.muslimphilosophy.com/ip/rep/H032.htm (accessed 28 Aug. 2003).

"Ibn Masarra." *Theosophy Library Online.* http://theosophy.org/tlodocs/teachers/
IbnMasarra.htm (accessed 21 Aug. 2003).

"Ibn-Masarra: His 'Risala al-I'tibar'." Kenny, J. Home Page. http://www.op.org/
nigeriaop/kenny/Masarra.htm (accessed 21 Aug. 2003).
Introduction to the Arabic text and translation.

Biography and Criticism

Asin Palacios, M. *The Mystical Philosophy of Ibn Masarra and His Followers.* Trans.
E.H. Douglas and H.W. Yoder. Leiden: Brill, 1978.

Goodman, L.E. "Ibn Masarrah." Nasr and Leaman, *History of Islamic Philosophy.*
277–293.

Ibn Miskawayh, Ahmad ibn Muhammad, d. 1030

Web Sites

"Ahmad Ibn Muhammad (Ibn) Miskawayh." *Center for Islam and Science.* http://
www.cis-ca.org/voices/m/miskawayh.htm (accessed 21 Aug. 2003).

Ibn Miskawayh, A. ibn M. "The Experiences of the Nations." *Internet Medieval
Sourcebook.* http://www.fordham.edu/halsall/source/980Ibn-Miskawaih.html
(accessed 21 Aug. 2003).

Jamal al-Din, N. "Miskawayh." http://www.ibe.unesco.org/International/
Publications/Thinkers/ThinkersPdf/miskawae.pdf.
His contributions in the field of education.

Leaman, O. "Ibn Miskawayh, Ahmad ibn Muhammad." *Islamic Philosophy Online.*
http://www.muslimphilosophy.com/ip/rep/H042.htm (accessed 21 Aug. 2003).

Omar, M.N. "Man and Society in Miskawayh's Ethics." *Historiska Institutionen.*
Lunds Universitet. http://www.hist.lu.se/middleeast/full_texts/
man_and_society.pdf (accessed 21 Aug. 2003).

Translations

"Abu 'Ali Ahmad ibn Muhammad Miskawayh." *An Anthology of Philosophy in
Persia.* Ed. S.H. Nasr with M. Aminrazavi. 2 vols. New York: Oxford UP, 1999.
Vol. 1. 274–332.

An Unpublished Treatise of Miskawaih on Justice. Ed. and trans. M.S. Khan. Leiden:
Brill, 1964.

Biography and Criticism

Endress, G. "Miskawayh." Meisami and Starkey, *Encyclopedia of Arabic Literature.*
529–530.

Leaman, O. "Ibn Miskawayh." Nasr and Leaman, *History of Islamic Philosophy.*
252–257.

Ibn Qayyim al-Jawziyah, Muhammad ibn Abi Bakr, 1292–1350

Web Sites

Ibn Qayyim al-Jawziyah, M. ibn A.B. "The Prophet's Guidance on Recovery from
the Affliction of Distress and Grief." *Islamic Psychology Online.* Ed. Abu S.I.
ibn I. Malik. 5 Jan. 2001. http://www.angelfire.com/al/islamicpsychology/
general/distress_and_grief.html (accessed 21 Aug. 2003).

    Several more translations are available on the same site. Choose them from the
index http://www.angelfire.com/al/islamicpsychology/general.html.

Translations

Ibn Qayyim al-Jawziyya on the Invocation of God. Trans. M.A. Fitzgerald and M.Y.
Slitine. Cambridge: Islamic Texts Soc., 2000.

Medicine of the Prophet. Trans. P. Johnstone. Cambridge: Islamic Texts Soc.,
1998.

Natural Healing with the Medicine of the Prophet. Philadelphia, Penn.: Pearl,
1993.

Patience and Gratitude. Trans. N. al-Khattab. London: Ta-Ha, 1997.

The Soul's Journey after Death. Trans. A. Bewley. Commentary by L. Mabrouk. 2nd
ed. London: Dar al-Taqwa, 1990.

Biography and Criticism

Zakeri, M. "Ibn Qayyim al-Jawziyya." Meisami and Starkey, *Encyclopedia of Arabic
Literature.* 359–360.

Ibn Sa'id, 'Ali ibn Musa, 1213–1286

Web Sites

Ibn Sa'id, 'A. ibn M. "Book of the Maghrib." *Internet Medieval Sourcebook.* http://
www.fordham.edu/halsall/source/maghrib.html (accessed 21 Aug.
2003).

"World Map of Ibn Sa'id." *Cartographic Images.* Ed. J. Siebold. 12 Feb. 1998. Henry
Davis Consulting. http://gate.henry-davis.com/MAPS/EMwebpages/
221mono.html (accessed 21 Aug. 2003).

    Introduction to the map, which can be seen at http://gate.henry-davis.com/
MAPS/EMwebpages/221.html.

Translations

The Banners of the Champions. Trans. J.A. Bellamy and P.O. Steiner. Madison:
Hispanic Seminary of Medieval Studies, 1989.

*Moorish Poetry: A Translation of The Pennants, an Anthology Compiled in 1243 by
the Andalusian Ibn Said.* Trans. A.J. Arberry. Cambridge: Cambridge UP, 1953.

Biography and Criticism

Wasserstein, D.J. "Ibn Sa'id al-Maghribi." Meisami and Starkey, *Encyclopedia of
Arabic Literature.* 368.

Ibn Shaddad, Baha' al-Din Yusuf ibn Rafi', 1145–1234 or 1235

Web Sites

Ibn Shaddad, B. al-D.Y. ibn R. "Salah al-Din." *The Crusades: Voices and Perspectives.* Ed. G. McDowell. http://www.umich.edu/~iinet/worldreach/ assets/docs/crusades/Saladinarab.html (accessed 21 Aug. 2003).

Translations

The Life of Saladin. Trans. H. Gibb. Oxford: Clarendon P, 1973.

The Rare and Excellent History of Saladin. Trans. D.S. Richards. Aldershot: Ashgate, 2001.

Biography and Criticism

Richards, D.S. "Ibn Shaddad." Meisami and Starkey, *Encyclopedia of Arabic Literature.* 370.

Ibn Sinan, Ibrahim, 908–946

Web Sites

O'Connor, J.J., and E.R. Robertson. "Ibrahim ibn Sinan ibn Thabit ibn Qurra." *The MacTutor History of Mathematics Archive.* http://www-gap.dcs.st-and.ac.uk/ ~history/Mathematicians/Ibrahim.html (accessed 21 Aug. 2003).

Biography and Criticism

Bellosta, H. "Ibrahim ibn Sinan on Analysis and Synthesis." *Arabic Sciences and Philosophy* 1 (1991): 163–165, 211–232.

Rashed, R. "Ibrahim ibn Sinan ibn Thabit ibn Qurra." Gillispie, *Dictionary of Scientific Biography.* Vol. 7. 2–3.

Ibn Taymiyah, Ahmad ibn 'Abd al-Halim, 1263–1328

Web Sites

"Ibn Taymiyah." *Islamic Philosophy Online.* http://www.muslimphilosophy.com/it/ default.htm (accessed 21 Aug. 2003).

Portal site, with links to biographies, texts in Arabic, translations in English and French, articles, and other sites.

Pavlin, J. "Ibn Taymiyya, Taqi al-Din." *Islamic Philosophy Online.* http:// www.muslimphilosophy.com/ip/rep/H039.htm (accessed 28 Aug. 2003).

Translations

Ibn Taymiyya against the Greek Logicians. Trans. W.B. Hallaq. New York: Oxford UP, 1993.

A Muslim Theologian's Response to Christianity. Ed. and trans. T.F. Michel. Delmar, NY: Caravan Books, 1984.

Al-'Ubudiyyah, being a True Slave of Islam. Trans. N. al-Khattab. London: Ta-Ha, 1999.

Biography and Criticism

Bosworth, C.E. "Ibn Taymiyya." Meisami and Starkey, *Encyclopedia of Arabic Literature*. 377–378.

Ibn Tufayl, Muhammad ibn 'Abd al-Malik, d. 1185

Web Sites

Inati, S.C. "Ibn Tufayl, Abu Bakr Muhammad." *Islamic Philosophy Online*. http://www.muslimphilosophy.com/rep/H030.htm (accessed 21 Aug. 2003).

Translations

Ibn Tufayl's Hayy ibn Yaqzan. Trans. L.E. Goodman. New York: Twayne Publishers, 1972.

The Improvement of Human Reason. Trans. S. Ockley. Hildesheim: Georg Olms Verlag, 1983.

The Journey of the Soul. Trans. R. Kocache. London: Octagon P, 1982.

"The Story of Hayy ibn Yaqzan." *Two Andalusian Philosophers*. Trans. J. Colville. London: Kegan Paul, 1999.

Biography and Criticism

Conrad, L.I., ed. *The World of Ibn Tufayl: Interdisciplinary Perspectives on Hayy ibn Yaqzan*. Leiden: Brill, 1996.

Goodman, L. "Ibn Tufayl." Nasr and Leaman, *History of Islamic Philosophy*. 313–329.

———. "Ibn Tufayl." *The Literature of al-Andalus*. Ed. M.R. Menocal, R.P. Scheindlin, and M. Sells. Cambridge History of Arabic Literature. Cambridge: Cambridge UP, 2000. 318–330.

Hasanali, P. "Ibn Tufayl." Meisami and Starkey, *Encyclopedia of Arabic Literature*. 378–379.

Hawi, S.S. *Islamic Naturalism and Mysticism: A Philosophical Study of Ibn Tufayl's Hayy Yaqsan*. Leiden: Brill, 1974.

Hourani, G.F. "Ibn Tufayl, Abu Bakr Muhammad." Gillispie, *Dictionary of Scientific Biography*. Vol. 13. 488–489.

Ibrahim, Jamil 'Atiyah, 1937–

Web Sites

"Gamil Ateya Ibrahim." *Arab World Books*. http://www.arabworldbooks.com/authors/gamil_ibrahim.html (accessed 21 Aug. 2003).

Translations

"The Child and the King." Johnson-Davies, *Egyptian Short Stories*. 133–135.

Down to the Sea. Trans. F. Liardet. London: Quartet, 1991.

"The Old Man." Johnson-Davies, *Arabic Short Stories*. 149–150.

Ibrahim, Sun' Allah, 1937–

Web Sites

Bibawy, A. "Warda—Chronicle of the Political and the Personal." *Middle East Times* 8 Sept. 2000. http://www3.estart.com/arab/entertainment/warda.html (accessed 21 Aug. 2003).

Irwin, R. "Briefing for an Inquisition." Rev. of *The Committee*. *New York Times Book Review* 16 Dec. 2001. http://query.nytimes.com/gst/fullpage.html?res=9A02E6DE123CF935A25751C1A9679C8B63 (accessed 21 Aug. 2003).

"Sonallah Ibrahim." *Arab World Books*. http://www.arabworldbooks.com/authors/sonallah_ibrahim.htm (accessed 21 Aug. 2003).

Translations

The Committee. Trans. M. St. Germain and C. Constable. Syracuse: Syracuse UP, 2001.

The Smell of It, and Other Stories. Trans. D. Johnson-Davies. London: Heinemann Educational, 1971.

"The Snake." Johnson-Davies, *Egyptian Short Stories*. 93–102.

Zaat. Trans. A. Calderbank. Cairo: American U in Cairo P, 2001.

Biography and Criticism

Al Masri, K. "Ibrahim, Sun' Allah." Gikandi, *Encyclopedia of African Literature*. 232.

Draz, C.K. "Opaque and Transparent Discourse in Sonallah Ibrahim's Works." Ghazoul and Harlow, *The View from Within*. 134–148.

Mehrez, S. "Dr. Ramzi and Mr. Sharaf: Sun'allah Ibrahim and the Duplicity of the Literary Field." *Tradition, Modernity, and Postmodernity in Arabic Literature: Essays in Honor of Professor Issa J. Boullata*. Ed. K. Abdel-Malek and W. Hallaq. Brill: Leiden, 2000. 262–283.

———. *Egyptian Writers between History and Fiction: Essays on Naguib Mahfouz, Sonallah Ibrahim, and Gamal al-Ghitani*. Cairo: American U in Cairo P, 1994. 39–57, 119–145.

Mikhail, M.N. "Structure and Ideology in Sun'allah Ibrahim's Novella 'al-Lajna'." *World Literature Today* 60.2 (1986): 221–223.

Moor, E.C.M. de. "Ibrahim, Sun' Allah." Meisami and Starkey, *Encyclopedia of Arabic Literature*. 386–387.

Stagh, M. *The Limits of Freedom of Speech: Prose Literature and Prose Writers in Egypt under Nasser and Sadat*. Stockholm: Almqvist and Wiksell, 1993. 184–210.

al-Idlibi, Ulfat, 1912–

Web Sites

al-Idlibi, U. "The Women's Baths." *Gender Issues & Literature in the Middle East*. http://www.u.arizona.edu/~talattof/women-lit/introduction.htm (accessed 21 Aug. 2003).

Translations

"The Breeze of Youth." *An Arabian Mosaic: Short Stories by Arab Women Writers*. Trans. D. Cohen-Mor. Potomac, Md.: Sheba, 1993. 1–9.

"The Charm: A Short Story." Trans. B. Bezirgan and E. Fernea. *Women and the Family in the Middle East: New Voices of Change*. Ed. E.W. Fernea. Austin: U of Texas P, 1985. 49–55.

Grandfather's Tale. Trans. P. Clark. London: Quartet, 1998.

Sabriya: Damascus Bitter Sweet. Trans. P. Clark. London: Quartet, 1995.

"Seventy Years Later." Trans. S. Fattal. Badran and Cooke, *Opening the Gates*. 57–62.

Biography and Criticism

Clark, P. "al-Idlibi, Ulfat 'Umar." Meisami and Starkey, *Encyclopedia of Arabic Literature*. 388.

Idris, Yusuf, 1927–1991

Web Sites

Rizal, C.M., et al. "Yusuf Idris." *Iqra': A Compilation of Critical Assessment of Muslim Writers Around the Globe*. Coord. N.F.A. Manaf. Dept. of English Language and Literature and Dept. of Arabic Language and Literature, Kulliyyah of Islamic and Revealed Knowledge and Human Sciences, International Islamic University Malaysia. http://www.iiu.edu.my/irkhs/eng/iqra/yi.htm (accessed 21 Aug 2003).

   Biography, critical commentary, and translation of the short story "The Cheapest Night."

"Youssef Idrees, Pioneer of Arabic Short Story." *Egypt*. http://www.sis.gov.eg/calendar/html/cl010897.htm (accessed 21 Aug. 2003).

Translations

The Cheapest Nights and Other Stories. Trans. W. Wassef. London: Heinemann; Washington, D.C.: Three Continents, 1978.

City of Love and Ashes. Trans. R.N. Hewison. Cairo: American U in Cairo P, 1999.

"Farahat's Republic." *Modern Arabic Short Stories*. Trans. D. Johnson-Davies. London: Oxford UP, 1967. 1–18.

"The Farfoors." Abdel Wahab, Farouk. *Modern Egyptian Drama: An Anthology*. Minneapolis: Bibliotheca Islamica, 1974. 351–493.

"Flipflap and His Master." Trans. T. LeGassick. Rev. A. Parkin and Manzalaoui. *Arabic Writing Today: Drama*. Ed. M. Manzalaoui. Cairo: American Research Center in Egypt, 1977. 335–454.

In the Eye of the Beholder: Tales of Egyptian Life from the Writings of Yusuf Idris. Ed. R. Allen. Minneapolis: Bibliotheca Islamica, 1978.

A Leader of Men. Trans. Saad Elkhadem. Fredericton, N.B.: York, 1988.

The Piper Dies and Other Short Stories. Trans. D. Cohen-Mor. Potomac, Md.: Sheba, 1992.

Rings of Burnished Brass. Trans. C. Cobham. London: Heinemann; Washington, D.C.: Three Continents, 1984.

The Sinners. Trans. K. Peterson-Ishaq. Washington: Three Continents, 1984.

Three Egyptian Short Stories. Trans. S. El-Gabalawy. Fredericton, N.B.: York, 1991.

Biographies and Criticism

Allen, R. "The Artistry of Yusuf Idris." *World Literature Today* 55.1 (1981): 43–47.

———, ed. *Critical Perspectives on Yusuf Idris*. Washington, D.C.: Three Continents, 1994.

———. "Idris, Yusuf." Gikandi, *Encyclopedia of African Literature*. 233.

———. "Idris, Yusuf." Meisami and Starkey, *Encyclopedia of Arabic Literature*. 388–389.

———. "Idris, Yusuf." Serafin, *Encyclopedia of World Literature in the 20th Century*. Vol. 2. 460.

Allen, *Modern Arabic Literature*. 153–160.

Badawi, M.M. *Modern Arabic Drama in Egypt*. Cambridge: Cambridge UP, 1987. 153–164.

Burt, C., and J. Moss. "'Farahat's Republic' by Yusuf Idris." *African Literature and Its Times*. Ed. J. Moss and L. Valestuk. World Literature and Its Times 2. Detroit: Gale, 2000. 173–182.

Cohen, D. "'The Journey' by Yusuf Idris: Psycho-Analysis and Interpretation." *Journal of Arabic Literature* 15 (1984): 135–138.

Coppola, C. "The Cheapest Nights." *Reference Guide to Short Fiction*. Ed. N. Watson. Detroit: St. James, 1994. 662–663.

———. "Idris, Yusuf." *Reference Guide to Short Fiction*. Ed. N. Watson. Detroit: St. James, 1994. 260–261.

Elkhadem, S. "Youssef Idris and His Gay Leader of Men." Elkhadem, S. *On Egyptian Fiction: Five Essays*. Fredericton, N.B.: York, 2001. 13–16.

Hafez, S. "Yusuf Idris, 1927–1991." *African Writers*. Ed. C.B. Cox. New York: Charles Scribner's Sons, 1997. 345–365.

Kilany, H. "Idris, Yusuf." Pendergast and Pendergast, *Reference Guide to World Literature*. 502–504.

Kirkpatrick, H. *The Modern Egyptian Novel: A Study in Social Criticism*. Oxford: Middle East Centre, St. Antony's College; London: Ithaca, 1974. 113–126.

Kupershoeck, P.M. *The Short Stories of Yusuf Idris: A Modern Egyptian Author*. Leiden: Brill, 1981.

Mikhail, M.N. *Studies in the Short Fiction of Mahfouz and Idris*. New York: New York UP, 1992.

Salti, R. "A Different Leader of Men: Yusuf Idris against Arab Concepts of Male Homosexuality." *World Literature Today* 75.2 (2001): 246–256.

Stagh, M. *The Limits of Freedom of Speech: Prose Literature and Prose Writers in Egypt under Nasser and Sadat*. Stockholm: Almqvist and Wiksell, 1993. 262–276.

Wise, R. "Subverting Holy Scriptures: The Short Stories of Yusuf Idris." *The Postcolonial Crescent: Islam's Impact on Contemporary Literature*. Ed. J.C. Hawley. New York: Lang, 1998. 140–154.

al-Idrisi, ca. 1100–1166

Web Sites

"Idrisi (al-)" *Malaspina Great Books*. http://www.malaspina.com/site/person_667.asp (accessed 21 Aug. 2003).

"Al-Idrisi." *The Window: Philosophy on the Internet*. Ed. C. Marvin and F. Sikernitsky. http://www.trincoll.edu/depts/phil/philo/phils/muslim/idrisi.html (accessed 21 Aug. 2003).

Quick, A.H., and A. Shabbas. "Early Muslim Exploration Worldwide: Evidence of Muslims in the New World before Columbus." *Middle East Policy Council*. http://www.mepc.org/public_asp/workshops/musexpl.asp (accessed 21 Aug. 2003).
> From *Arab World Studies Notebook*, ed. A. Shabbas.

"World Maps of Idrisi." *Cartographic Images*. Ed. J. Siebold. 12 Feb. 1998. Henry Davis Consulting. http://www.henry-davis.com/MAPS/EMwebpages/ 219mono.html (accessed 21 Aug. 2003).
> An explanation of his maps can be viewed at http://www.henry-davis.com/ MAPS/EMwebpages/219.html and http://www.henry-davis.com/MAPS/ EMwebpages/219A.html.

Biography and Criticism

Ahmad, S. "al-Idrisi, Abu 'Abd Allah Muhammad ibn Muhammad ibn 'Abd Allah ibn Idris, al-Sharif al-Idrisi." Gillispie, *Dictionary of Scientific Biography*. Vol. 7. 7–9.

Irwin, R. "al-Idrisi, Muhammad ibn Muhammad." Meisami and Starkey, *Encyclopedia of Arabic Literature*. 389–390.

Tatistcheff, F.A. "Abu 'Abdallah Muhammad bin Muhammad 'Abdallah bin Idris al-Hammudi al-Hasani." Atiyeh, *The Genius of Arab Civilization*. 266.

Imru' al-Qays, 497–545

Web Sites

"Pre-Islamic Arabia: The Hanged Poems." *Internet Medieval Sourcebook*. http:// www.fordham.edu/halsall/source/640hangedpoems.html (accessed 21 Aug. 2003).
> Translation of his famous poem. The Arabic text can be viewed at http:// qalam.org/poetry/medieval/imru-al-qays/. A recitation in Arabic of the first part of the poem can be heard at http://www.princeton.edu/~arabic/poetry/index.html.

Translations

"Imrulkais of Kinda." Tuetey, *Classical Arabic Poetry*. 93–96.

Biography and Criticism

Arberry, A.J. *The Seven Odes*. London: George Allen and Unwin; New York: The Macmillan Company, 1957. 31–66.

Cross, C. "Al-Qays, Imru'." Pendergast and Pendergast, *Reference Guide to World Literature*. 30–31.

Jacobi, R. "Imru' al-Qays." Meisami and Starkey, *Encyclopedia of Arabic Literature*. 394–395.

Shahid, I. "The Last Days of Imru' al-Qays: Anatolia." *Tradition and Modernity in Arabic Literature*. Ed. I.J. Boullata and T. DeYoung. Fayetteville: U of Arkansas P, 1997. 207–222.

Tuetey, C.G. *Imrulkais of Kinda, Poet, circa A.D. 500–535: The Poems, the Life, the Background.* London: Diploma, 1977.

Istakhri, Ibrahim ibn Muhammad, d. 957 or 8

Web Sites

"World Map of Istakhri." *Cartographic Images.* Ed. J. Siebold. 12 Feb. 1998. Henry Davis Consulting. http://www.henry-davis.com/MAPS/EMwebpages/211mono.html (accessed 21 Aug. 2003).

Explanation of his world map, which can be seen at http://www.henry-davis.com/MAPS/EMwebpages/211.html and http://www.henry-davis.com/MAPS/EMwebpages/211A.html

Biography and Criticism

Conrad, L.I. "al-Istakhri." Meisami and Starkey, *Encyclopedia of Arabic Literature.* 401.

al-Jabarti, 'Abd al-Rahman, 1754–1822

Web Sites

"Egyptian Historian Abdul-Rahman al-Ghaberti, Herodotus of Egypt." *Egypt.* http://www.sis.gov.eg/calendar/html/cl180698.htm#sc1 (accessed 28 Aug. 2003).

"Al-Gabarti, Exclusive Source of 17th and 18th-Century Egypt." *Egypt* 25 (2001). http://www.sis.gov.eg/public/magazine/iss025e/html/mag07.htm (accessed 28 Aug. 2003).

al-Jabarti, 'Abd al-R. "Muhammad 'Ali's Tax Inspectors." *African Unification Front.* http://www.africanfront.com/auhistory2.php (accessed 21 Aug. 2003).

Translations

Abd al-Rahman al-Jabarti's History of Egypt. Ed. T. Philipp and M. Perlmann. Stuttgart: Franz Steiner Verlag, 1994.

Napoleon in Egypt: al-Jabarti's Chronicle of the French Occupation, 1798. Trans. S. Moreh. Princeton: M. Wiener, 1993.

Biography and Criticism

Moreh, S. "al-Jabarti, 'Abd al-Rahman." Meisami and Starkey, *Encyclopedia of Arabic Literature.* 403–404.

Philipp, T. and G. Schwald. *A Guide to 'Abd al-Rahman al-Jabarti's History of Egypt: 'Aja'ib al-Athar fi'l-Tarajim wa'l-Akhbar.* Stuttgart: Steiner, 1994.

Jabir ibn Hayyan, ca. 721–815?

Web Sites

Haq, S.N. "Abu 'Abd Allah/Abu Musa Jabir ibn Hayyan al-Sufi al-Azdi/Al-Tusi." *Center for Islam and Science.* http://cis-ca.org/voices/j/jabir.htm (accessed 21 Aug. 2003).

"Jabir ibn Haiyan." *Islamic Paths.* http://www.islamic-paths.org/Home/English/History/Personalities/Content/Haiyan.htm (accessed 21 Aug. 2003).

"Jabir ibn Haiyan (Geber)." *The Window: Philosophy on the Internet.* Ed. C. Marvin and F. Sikernitsky. http://www.trincoll.edu/depts/phil/philo/phils/muslim/haiyan.html (accessed 21 Aug. 2003).

"Jabir ibn Hayyan, Abu Musa." *Iranian Journal of Chemistry & Chemical Engineering.* Ed. M.N. Sarbolouki (2000). http://213.176.24.20/chemist/ Jabir.htm (accessed 21 Aug. 2003).

Translations

The Alchemical Works of Geber. Trans. R. Russell. York Beach, ME: Samuel Weiser, 1994.

"Jabir ibn Hayyan." *An Anthology of Philosophy in Persia.* Ed. S.H. Nasr with M. Aminrazavi. 2 vols. New York: Oxford UP, 1999. Vol. 2. 33–69.

Biography and Criticism

Haq, S.N. *Names, Natures and Things: The Alchemist Jabir ibn Hayyan and His Kitab al-Ahjar (Book of Stones).* Dordrecht: Kluwer, 1994.

Netton, I.R., and J.S. Meisami. "Jabir ibn Hayyan." Meisami and Starkey, *Encyclopedia of Arabic Literature.* 404.

Plessner, M. "Jabir ibn Hayyan." Gillispie, *Dictionary of Scientific Biography.* Vol. 7. 39–43.

Jabra, Jabra Ibrahim, 1920–1994

Web Sites

Jabra, J.I. "Mystery in Mesopotamia." *Al-Ahram Weekly On-Line* 17–23 Apr. 2003. http://weekly.ahram.org.eg/2003/634/bsc8.htm (accessed 21 Aug. 2003). Translation of a selection from his autobiography, *Shari' al-Amirat (Princesses' Street).*

Selim, S. "Fiction Mimics Reality." Rev. of *In Search of Walid Masoud. Journal of Palestine Studies* 31.2 (2002). http://www.ciaonet.org/olj/jps/ses01.html (accessed 21 Aug. 2003).

Autobiography and Interviews

The First Well: A Bethlehem Boyhood. Trans. I.J. Boullata. Fayetteville: U of Arkansas P, 1995.

"On Interpoetics." Interviewed by N. Yasin. Trans. A. El Gibali and B. Harlow. Ghazoul and Harlow, *The View from Within.* 207–212.

Translations

Asfour, *When the Words Burn.* 171–177.
    Includes translations of "Beyond Galilee," "The City," and "The Poet and Women."

Boullata, *Modern Arab Poets.* 125–133.
    Includes translations of "The Diary of the Epidemic Year (Fragment)," "Run Run My Pony," "A Stranger at the Fountain," and "The Trumpet."

"The Gramaphone." *Modern Arabic Short Stories.* Trans. D.Johnson-Davies. London: Oxford UP, 1967. 148–161.

Hunters in a Narrow Street. London: Heinemann, 1960.

In Search of Walid Masoud. Trans. R. Allen and A. Haydar. Syracuse: Syracuse UP, 2000.

Jayyusi, *Anthology of Modern Palestinian Literature.* 176–181.
Includes translations of "From 'Zero Hour,'" "For Socrates," and "Love Poem" by S. Elmusa and J. Reed.

Khouri and Algar, *Anthology of Modern Arabic Poetry.* 223–229.
Includes translations of "From a Poem Sequence" and "In the Deserts of Exile."

"My Demon and I." Trans. J.I. Jabra (the author). *Tradition and Modernity in Arabic Literature.* Ed. I.J. Boullata and T. DeYoung. Fayetteville: U of Arkansas P, 1997. 21–27.

The Ship. Trans. A. Haydar and R. Allen. Washington, D.C.: Three Continents, 1985.

Biography and Criticism

Allen, *Modern Arabic Literature.* 164–169.

Allen, R. "'Al-Safinah', Jabra Ibrahim Jabra." *The Arabic Novel: An Historical and Critical Introduction.* 2nd ed. Syracuse: Syracuse UP, 1995. 177–183.

Badawi, M.M. "Two Novelists from Iraq: Jabra and Munif." *Journal of Arabic Literature* 23 (1992): 140–154.

Boullata, I.J. "Jabra, Jabra Ibrahim." *Contemporary World Writers.* Ed. T. Chevalier. 2nd ed. Detroit: St. James, 1993. 269–270.

———. "Jabra, Jabra Ibrahim." Meisami and Starkey, *Encyclopedia of Arabic Literature.* 405.

———. "Jabra, Jabra Ibrahim." Serafin, *Encyclopedia of World Literature in the 20th Century.* Vol. 2. 525–526.

Neuwirth, A. "Jabra Ibrahim Jabra's Autobiography, 'al-Bi'r al-Ula,' and His Concept of a Celebration of Life." Ostle, Moor, and Wild, *Writing the Self.* 115–127.

Peled, M. "Sexuality in Jabra's Novel, 'The Search for Walid Mas'ud.'" *Love and Sexuality in Modern Arabic Literature.* Ed. R. Allen, H. Kilpatrick, and E. de Moor. London: Saqi, 1995. 140–153.

al-Jahiz, d. 868 or 869

Web Sites

"Abu Uthman Amr bin Basr al-Fuqaymi al-Basri al-Jahiz." *Center for Islam and Science.* http://www.cis-ca.org/voices/j/jahiz.htm (accessed 21 Aug. 2003).

"Abu 'Uthman 'Amr ibn Bahr al-Basri al-Jahiz." *The Enlightenment.* Ed. A. Naqvi. http://www.thenlightenment.com/history/ms3.html (accessed 21 Aug. 2003).

Bayrakdar, M. "Al-Jahiz and the Rise of Biological Evolutionism." *Salaam: Muslim Information Resources.* http://www.salaam.co.uk/knowledge/al-jahiz.php (accessed 21 Aug. 2003).

al-Jahiz, "The Merits of the Turks and the Imperial Army as a Whole." Richards, J.D. Home Page. Baker University. http://www.bakeru.edu/faculty/jrichards/World%20Civ%20II/E-Sources/E27AlJahiz.htm (accessed 21 Aug. 2003). Translation, with study questions for a course in world civilizations.

"Lord of the Golden Age of Arab Literature." *Marcus Garvey.* Ed. A.A.D. Wilson. http://www.marcusgarvey.com/gm18.htm (accessed 21 Aug. 2003).

Largely about al-Jahiz's essay "The Superiority of the Black Race over the White."

Tschanz, D.W. "Al-Jahiz, the First Islamic Zoologist." *IslamOnline.net*. 21 Aug. 2003. http://www.islamonline.net/english/Science/2001/10/article2.shtml (accessed 21 Aug. 2003).

Translations

Avarice and the Avaricious. Trans. J. Colville. London: Kegan Paul, 1999.

The Book of the Misers. Trans. R.B. Serjeant. Rev. by E. Ibrahim. Reading: Center for Muslim Contribution to Civilization: Garnet, 1997.

The Epistle on Singing-Girls of Jahiz. Ed. and trans. A.F.L. Beeston. Warminster: Aris and Phillips, 1980.

The Life and Works of Jahiz. Trans. C. Pellat. Trans. from French D.M. Hawke. Berkeley: U of California P, 1969.

Nine Essays of al-Jahiz. Trans. W.M. Hutchins. New York: P. Lang, 1989.

Sobriety and Mirth: A Selection of the Shorter Writings of al-Jahiz. Trans. J. Colville. London: Kegan Paul; New York: Distributed by Columbia UP, 2002.

Biography and Criticism

"Al-Jahiz." *Classical and Medieval Literature Criticism*. 25 (1998) 268–335.

Malti-Douglas, F. *Structures of Avarice: The Bukhala in Medieval Arabic Literature*. Leiden: Brill, 1985.

Pellat, C. "Al-Jahiz." *'Abbasid Belles-Lettres*. Ed. J. Ashtiany, et al. Cambridge History of Arabic Literature. Cambridge: Cambridge UP, 1990. 78–95.

Plessner, M. "al-Jahiz, Abu 'Uthman 'Amr ibn Bahr." Gillispie, *Dictionary of Scientific Biography*. Vol. 7. 63–65.

Richards, D.S. "al-Jahiz." Meisami and Starkey, *Encyclopedia of Arabic Literature*. 408–409.

Zwettler, M. "Abu 'Uthman 'Amr bin Bahr al-Jahiz." Atiyeh, *The Genius of Arab Civilization*. 76–79.

al-Jawahiri, Muhammad Mahdi, 1900–1997

Web Sites

"Iraqi Art and Literature Around the World." *Faulconer Gallery, Grinnell College*. 11 June 2003. http://web.grinnell.edu/faulconergallery/iraq/includes/files/one.html (accessed 21 Aug. 2003).
Poem "O Blessed Tigris" in English and Arabic. From an exhibit at Grinnell College in 2002.

al-Jawahiri, M.M. "Lullaby for the Hungry." *Selected International Poems*. 9 Mar. 2003. http://geocities.com/marxist_lb/ (accessed 21 Aug. 2003).
Also includes the text of two poems in Arabic.

"Poetry." *Iraq4u.com*. http://www.iraq4u.com/Poetry_search.asp (accessed 21 Aug. 2003).
Listen to the author read his poem (choose poem 2).

Translations

"Come Down, Darkness." Trans. C. Tingley with the help of S.K. Jayyusi, and C. Middleton. Jayyusi, *Modern Arabic Poetry*. 79–80.

"Transplant of Conscience." Fairbairn and al-Gosaibi, *Feathers and the Horizon*. 80.

Biography and Criticism

Husni, R. "al-Jawahiri, Muhammad Mahdi." Meisami and Starkey, *Encyclopedia of Arabic Literature*. 413.

Walther, W. "'My Hands Assisted the Hands of Events': The Memoirs of the Iraqi Poet Muhammad Mahdi al-Jawahiri." Ostle, Moor, and Wild, *Writing the Self*. 249–259.

Jayyusi, Salma Khadra, 1926–

Web Sites

Jayyusi, S.K. *Gender Issues & Literature in the Middle East*. http://www.u.arizona.edu/~talattof/women-lit/introduction.htm (accessed 21 Aug. 2003).

   Includes translations of "Dearest III," "Economics," "Encounter," "Shudan," and "A Tale."

Translations

"Awakening: Song of a Girl Awaiting Her First Love." Fairbairn and al-Gosaibi, *Feathers and the Horizon*. 82.

"Dearest Love II." Elmessiri, *The Palestinian Wedding*. 77–81.

"Elegy to the Martyrs." Khouri and Algar, *Anthology of Modern Arabic Poetry*. 207–209.

Handal, *The Poetry of Arab Women*. 130–133.

   Includes translations of "Dearest Love" and "In the Casbah" by C. Doria and translation of "The Sunken Ship" by S. Chopra with S.K. Jayyusi.

Women of the Fertile Crescent. Washington, D.C.: Three Continents, 1978. 121–136.

   Includes translations of "Dearest Love-I," "Dearest Love-III," "In the Casbah," "Scraping Limit," "Shudan," "The Sky the Moon Lost," "Storm in Kabyl Land," and "A Tale" by K. Boullata.

Jayyusi, *Anthology of Modern Palestinian Literature*. 182–189.

   Includes translations of "Khartoum," "Songs for an Arab City," "The Three of Us Alone," and "The Woman" by S.K. Jayyusi and J. Heath-Stubbs.

Jayyusi, *Modern Arabic Poetry*. 277–285.

   Includes translations of "April Woman," "Scrapping Limits," and "The Ship of Love" by S.K. Jayyusi and C. Doria and "On Visiting the M.D. Anderson" by A. Royal and C. Doria.

"Poem." Trans. P. Alanah with S.K. Jayyusi and C. Middleton. *Women and the Family in the Middle East: New Voices of Change*. Ed. E.W. Fernea. Austin: U of Texas P, 1985. xi–xii.

"Without Roots." Boullata, *Modern Arab Poets*. 149–152.

al-Juburi, Amal, 1967–

Web Sites

al-Juburi, A. "Reflections: A Personal Vision of Poetry." *Aljadid* 31 (2000). http://
www.aljadid.com/essays/0631jubburi.html (accessed 21 Aug. 2003).

Nijland, K. "Amal al-Jubouri." *Poetry International Web*. Ed. C. Vloet. Poetry
International Web Foundation. http://www.poetryinternational.org/cwolk/view/
16187 (accessed 21 Aug. 2003).
Biographical notes, link to translation and text of poem "Veil of Religions."

Translations

Handal, *The Poetry of Arab Women*. 134–135.
Includes translations of "Enheduanna and Goethe" and "Protest" by S.J.
Altoma.

Kanafani, Ghassan, 1936–1972

Web Sites

Dayal, S. Rev. of *All That's Left to You*. *Middle East Affairs* 9 (1990–1991): 72. http://
www.washington-report.org/backissues/0591/9105072.htm (accessed 21 Aug.
2003).

"Ghassan Kanafani." *Books and Writers*. http://www.kirjasto.sci.fi/kanaf.htm
(accessed 21 Aug. 2003).

Kanafani, G. "Jaffa: Land of Oranges." *Al-Ahram Weekly On-Line* 31 Dec. 1998.
http://weekly.ahram.org.eg/1998/1948/kanafani.htm (accessed 21 Aug. 2003).

Translations

All That's Left to You. Trans. M. Jayyusi and J. Reed. Austin: Center for Middle
Eastern Studies, U of Texas at Austin, 1990.

"The Death of Bed Number 12." *Modern Arabic Short Stories*. Trans. D.Johnson-
Davies. London: Oxford UP, 1967. 28–42.

"The Little One Goes to the Camp." Trans. M. Jayyusi and C. Tingley. Jayyusi,
Anthology of Modern Palestinian Literature. 474–480.

Men in the Sun and Other Palestinian Stories. Trans. H. Kilpatrick. Boulder, Co.:
Rienner, 1999.

Palestine's Children. Trans. B. Harlow and K.E. Riley. Boulder, Co.: Rienner
Publishers, 2000.

"The Slave Fort." Johnson-Davies, *Arabic Short Stories*. 164–168.

"Thoughts on Change and the 'Blind Language.'" Trans. B. Harlow and N. Yaziji.
Ghazoul and Harlow, *The View from Within*. 34–52.

Biography and Criticism

Allen, R. "'Ma tabaqqa la-kum', Ghassan Kanafani." *The Arabic Novel: An
Historical and Critical Introduction*. 2nd ed. Syracuse: Syracuse UP, 1995.
147–153.

———. *Modern Arabic Literature*. 176–180.

Audebert, C.F. "Choice and Responsibility in 'Rijal fi al-Shams.'" *Journal of Arabic Literature* 15 (1984): 76–93.

Campbell, I. "Blindness to Blindness: Trauma, Vision, and Political Consciousness in Ghassan Kanafani's 'Returning to Haifa.'" *Journal of Arabic Literature* 32 (2001): 53–73.

Harlow, B. *After Lives: Legacies of Revolutionary Writing*. London: Verso, 1996.

Kilpatrick, H. "Kanafani, Ghassan." Meisami and Starkey, *Encyclopedia of Arabic Literature*. 426.

———. "Tradition and Innovation in the Fiction of Ghassan Kanafani." *Journal of Arabic Literature* 7 (1976): 53–64.

Siddiq, M. "Kanafani, Ghassan." Serafin, *Encyclopedia of World Literature in the 20th Century*. Vol. 2. 597–598.

al-Karmi, Abu Salma 'Abd al-Karim, 1907–1980

Web Sites

"Abdelkarim Al-Karmi (Abu Salma)." *Barghouti.com*. http://www.barghouti.com/poets/abusalma/ (accessed 21 Aug. 2003).
   Includes translation and text of poem "We Will Return."

"Abu Salma." *Selected International Poems*. 9 Mar. 2003. http://www.geocities.com/marxist_lb/abou_salma.htm (accessed 21 Aug. 2003).
   One poem in English and Arabic.

Translations

Jayyusi, *Anthology of Modern Palestinian Literature*. 95–97.
   Includes translations of "I Love You More," "My Country on Partition Day," and "We Shall Return" by S. Elmusa and N.S. Nye.

Biography and Criticism

"Karmi, Abdul Karim." *Contemporary Authors* 102 (1981): 300.

Kashghari, Badi'ah Dawud

Web Sites

Ibrahim, D. "A Poetess Caught between Modernity and Tradition." *Middle East and Islamic Studies Collection, Cornell University*. http://www.library.cornell.edu/colldev/mideast/kash.htm (accessed 21 Aug. 2003).
   Includes translation of poem "I Have Decided to Sail."

Kashgari, B. "Seeking Forgiveness." *Poetry Page*. Ed. T. Copple. http://gcuc.ncf.ca/poetry.html#forgive (accessed 21 Aug. 2003).
   Another poem "Trance" can be read at http://gcuc.ncf.ca/poetry.html#trance.

Translations

The Unattainable Lotus: A Bilingual Edition. London: Saqi, 2001.

al-Katib al-Isfahani, 'Imad al-Din Muhammad ibn Muhammad, 1125–1201

Web Sites

Christie, N.G.F. "The Presentation of the Franks in Selected Muslim Sources from the Crusades of the 12th Century." *De Re Militari*. Ed. P. Konieczny. 6 Aug. 2003. Society for Medieval Military History. http://www.deremilitari.org/RESOURCES/ARTICLES/christie.htm (accessed 20 Aug. 2003).
   An unpublished master's thesis, includes a chapter on al-Katib al-Isfahani.

al-Katib al-Isfahani, I. al-D.M. ibn M. "Battle of Hittin, 1187." *The Crusades: Voices and Perspectives*. Ed. G. McDowell. http://www.umich.edu/~iinet/worldreach/assets/docs/crusades/hittinarab.html (accessed 21 Aug. 2003).

Translations

The Life of Saladin. Trans. H. Gibb. Oxford: Clarendon, 1973.

Biography and Criticism

Hillenbrand, C. "'Imad al-Din al-Isfahani." Meisami and Starkey, *Encyclopedia of Arabic Literature*. 392–393.

Rabbat, N. "My Life with Salah al-Din: The Memoirs of 'Imad al-Din al-Katib al-Isfahani." *Edebiyat*, n.s., 7 (1997): 267–287.

Richards, D.S. "'Imad al-Din al-Isfahani: Administrator, Litterateur and Historian." *Crusaders and Muslims in Twelfth-Century Syria*. Ed. M. Shatzmiller. Leiden: Brill, 1993. 133–146.

al-Khal, Yusuf, 1917–1988

Web Sites

"The Wayfarers." Koepke, L. Home Page. http://projects.ups.edu/engl/fall2001/203a/lkoepke/wayfarers.htm (accessed 21 Aug. 2003).

Translations

"After the Fifth of June." Trans. M. Jayyusi and N.S. Nye. Jayyusi, *Modern Arabic Poetry*. 298–300.

Asfour, *When the Words Burn*. 146–152.
   Includes translations of "The Eternal Dialogue" and "The Long Poem."

Boullata, *Modern Arab Poets*. 41–48.
   Includes "The Deserted Well," "The Eternal Dialogue," "Repentance," and "Sin."

"Cain the Immortal." Trans. S. Boulus and S. Hazo. Jayyusi, *Modern Arabic Poetry*. 295–296.

"Death." Fairbairn and al-Gosaibi, *Feathers and the Horizon*. 88.

Khouri and Algar, *Anthology of Modern Arabic Poetry*. 53–59.
   Includes translations of "Birth of the Poet," "Old Age," and "The Voyage."

"Quartet for the Last Days." Trans. A. Haydar and M. Beard. *Literary Review* 37 (1994): 506–507.

"'The Roots' by Yusuf al-Khal." Trans. S.M. Toorawa. *Journal of Arabic Literature* 19 (1988): 179–182.

al-Udhari, *Modern Poetry of the Arab World.* 51–58.
     Includes translations of "Enough, She Said," "The Harvest," "The Last Supper," "Let the Roots Speak," "The Long Poem," and "Prayers in a Temple."

Biography and Criticism

Abu-Deeb, K. "al-Khal, Yusuf." Meisami and Starkey, *Encyclopedia of Arabic Literature.* 429–430.

Allen, *Modern Arabic Literature.* 180–183.

De Moor, C.M. "al-Khal, Yusuf." Serafin, *Encyclopedia of World Literature in the 20th Century.* Vol. 2. 626–627.

Khalifah, Sahar, 1941–

Web Sites

Khalifah, S. "My Life, Myself, and the World." *Aljadid* 39 (2002). http://www.aljadid.com/features/0839khalifeh.html (accessed 21 Aug. 2003).

———. "Renowned Palestinian Writer Sahar Khalifeh: Men Are Not Used to Taking a Brave Look at Things That Might Hurt Their Soul." Interviewed by S. Abu Sharar and G. Joha. *Unionsverlag.* http://www.unionsverlag.com/info/link.asp?link_id=1109 (accessed 21 Aug. 2003).

Kutschera, C. "Palestine: The Aftermath of the (First) Intifada." *Chris Kutschera 30 Ans de Reportage.* Ed. C. Kutschera. http://www.chris-kutschera.com/%0A/Sahar%20Khalifa.htm (accessed 31 Aug. 2003).
     On her novel *Bab al-Sahah.*

"Palestinian Novelists, Sahar Khalifeh." *Khalil Sakakini Cultural Centre.* http://www.sakakini.org/novelists/sahar.htm (accessed 21 Aug. 2003).
     Biography, bibliography, translation of excerpt from *The Inheritance.*

"Sahar Khalifa." *Arab World Books.* http://www.arabworldbooks.com/authors/sahar_khalifa.html (accessed 21 Aug. 2003).

Uthman, N.K. "Occupied Writing: An Introduction to Sahar Khalifeh." *Postcolonial Studies.* Ed. D. Bahri. 3 Feb. 2003. Emory University. http://www.emory.edu/ENGLISH/Bahri/Khalifeh.html (accessed 21 Aug. 2003).

Translations

"From 'Memoirs of an Unrealistic Woman.'" Trans. M. Cooke. *Blood into Ink: South Asian and Middle Eastern Women Write War.* Ed. M. Cooke and R. Rustomji-Kerns. Boulder: Westview, 1994. 101–104.

"From 'Memoirs of an Unrealistic Woman.'" Trans. S. Jabsheh and C. Tingley. Jayyusi, *Anthology of Modern Palestinian Literature.* 589–596.

Wild Thorns. Trans. T. Le Gassick and E. Fernea. London: Al Saqi, 1985.

Biography and Criticism

Bamia, A.A. "Feminism in Revolution: The Case of Sahar Khalifa." *Tradition, Modernity, and Postmodernity in Arabic Literature: Essays in Honor of Professor Issa J. Boullata*. Ed. K. Abdel-Malek and W. Hallaq. Brill: Leiden, 2000. 173–185.

Harlow, B. "Partitions and Precedents." *Intersections: Gender, Nation, and Community in Arab Women's Novels*. Ed. L.S. Majaj, P.W. Sunderman, and T. Saliba. Syracuse: Syracuse UP, 2002. 113–131.

Palestinian Writers. Dir. M. Bellinelli. Prod. RTSI-Televisione svizzera. Videocassette. Filmakers Library, 2001.

Peled, M. "Sahar Khalifah's "Abbad al-Shams': A Feminist Challenge." *Writer, Culture, Text: Studies in Modern Arabic Literature*. Ed. A. Elad. Fredericton, N.B.: York, 1993. 37–46.

Suleiman, Y. "Khalifa, Sahar." Meisami and Starkey, *Encyclopedia of Arabic Literature*. 431–432.

al-Khalili, 'Ali, 1943–

Web Sites

"From 'Ask Me About Distance.'" *Hanthala Palestine*. http://hanthala.virtualave.net/poetry.html (accessed 21 Aug. 2003).

"Palestinian Poets, Ali El Khalili." *Khalil Sakakini Cultural Centre*. http://www.sakakini.org/poets/ali-index.htm (accessed 21 Aug. 2003). Includes translation of "Dialectics of the Homeland."

Translations

Jayyusi, *Anthology of Modern Palestinian Literature*. 192–197.
    Includes translations of "Dialectics of the Homeland" and "From 'What Is Your Purpose, Murderous Beauty?'" by H.M. Ashrawi and translations of "Departure" and "This Country" by S.K. Jayyusi.

al-Khansa', d. ca. 645

Web Sites

Al Mustafa, F.A. "Al Khansa: Manifesting the Spirit of Islam." *Al Shindagh*. Jan.–Feb. 1999. http://www.alshindagah.com/january99/womeninislam.htm (accessed 21 Aug. 2003).

"Khansa/al-Khansa/Tumadir bint 'Amr." *Other Women's Voices*. Ed. D. Disse. 6 May 2003. http://home.infionline.net/~ddisse/khansa.html (accessed 21 Aug. 2003).
    Includes biography, translations of several poems, links to more translations, and references to print sources.

Translations

"al-Khansa'." Arberry, *Arabic Poetry*. 38.

The HarperCollins World Reader. Antiquity to the Early Modern World. Ed. M.A. Caws and C. Prendergast. New York: HarperCollins College Publishers, 1994. 944.
    Includes translations of "It Is as If Sakhr" and "Oh, Would That My Mother" by J. Bellamy.

"Khansa." Trans. A. al-Udhari. *Classical Poems by Arab Women.* London: Saqi Books, 1999. 58–60.

"Khansa of Sulaim." Tuetey, *Classical Arabic Poetry.* 119–120.

Biography and Criticism

Gelder, G.J.H. van. "al-Khansa'." Meisami and Starkey, *Encyclopedia of Arabic Literature.* 435.

Kilany, H. "Al-Khansa'." Pendergast and Pendergast, *Reference Guide to World Literature.* 28–29.

al-Kharrat, Idwar, 1926–

Web Sites

Ghazoul, F.J. "The Phenomenal Kharrat." Rev. of *Idwar al-Kharrat: Mughamir Hatta al-Nihayah. Al-Ahram Weekly On-Line* 13–19 July 2000. http://weekly.ahram.org.eg/2000/490/books1.htm (accessed 21 Aug. 2003).

Woffenden, R. "Word Perfect." *Cairo Times* 9–15 Jan. 2003. http://www.cairotimes.com/content/archiv06/al-kharrat0643.html (accessed 21 Aug. 2003).

Autobiography and Interviews

"The Relative and the Absolute in Avant-Garde Narration." Interviewed by S. Hafez. Trans. M. Awadalla. Ghazoul and Harlow, *The View from Within.* 228–245.

"Without the Possibility of Experimenting with Form, I Think Modern Writing Has No Meaning." Interviewed by M. Obank. *Banipal* 6 (1999): 31–33.

Translations

"Birds' Footsteps in the Sand." Johnson-Davies, *Arabic Short Stories.* 116–127.

"By the Water's Edge." Trans. N. Farag. Rev. J. Wahba. Manzalaoui, *Arabic Short Stories.* 219–226.

"The Charge." Johnson-Davies, *Under the Naked Sky.* 108–119.

City of Saffron. Trans. F. Liardet. London: Quartet, 1989.

Girls of Alexandria. Trans. F. Liardet. London: Quartet Books, 1993.

"'An Open Wound' by Idwar Al-Kharrat: Translation and Commentary." Trans. C. Cobham. *Journal of Arabic Literature* 15 (1984): 121–134.

Rama and the Dragon. Trans. F. Ghazoul and J. Verlenden. Cairo: American U in Cairo P, 2002.

"Within the Walls." Johnson-Davies, *Egyptian Short Stories.* 15–29.

Biography and Criticism

Allen, *Modern Arabic Literature.* 183–187.

Cobham, C. "al-Kharrat, Edwar." Serafin, *Encyclopedia of World Literature in the 20th Century.* Vol. 2. 628–629.

"al-Kharrat, Edwar." *Contemporary Authors* 136 (1992): 5.

Stagh, M. *The Limits of Freedom of Speech: Prose Literature and Prose Writers in Egypt under Nasser and Sadat.* Stockholm: Almqvist and Wiksell, 1993. 171–183.

Starkey, P. "al-Kharrat, Idwar." Meisami and Starkey, *Encyclopedia of Arabic Literature*. 437–438.

Starr, D.A. "al-Kharrat, Idwar (Edwar al-Kharrat)" Gikandi, *Encyclopedia of African Literature*. 266.

Khazindar, Walid, 1950–

Web Sites

"Palestinian Poets, Walid Khazindar." *Khalil Sakakini Cultural Centre*. http://www.sakakini.org/poets/walid-index.htm (accessed 21 Aug. 2003).
     Includes translations of "Distant Light," "Half the Night," "Houses," "Night Is a Flash," and "Some Other Ember."

Translations

Jayyusi, *Anthology of Modern Palestinian Literature*. 198–203.
     Includes a translation of "Belonging" by L. Jayyusi and J. Reed; translations of "Absence," "At Least," "Brambles," "Houses," "That Day," and "You Will Arrive: Bewildered" by L. Jayyusi and W.S. Merwin; and a translation of "The Storm" by A. Shammas and N.S. Nye.

al-Khuli, Lutfi, 1928–1999

Web Sites

"Lutfi El-Kholi." *Al-Ahram Weekly On-Line* 11–17 Feb. 1999. http://weekly.ahram.org.eg/1999/416/kholi.htm (accessed 21 Aug. 2003).
     Includes remembrances by I. Nafie, M. Sid-Ahmed, and A.-M. Said.

"Lutfi El-Kholi." *Egypt*. http://www.us.sis.gov.eg/egyptianfigures/html/Kholi.htm (accessed 21 Aug. 2003).

Nkrumah, G. "Lutfi El-Kholi: The Warrior Dove." *Al-Ahram Weekly On-Line* 2–8 July 1998. http://weekly.ahram.org.eg/1998/384/pe1.htm (accessed 21 Aug. 2003).

Translations

"The Man Who Saw the Sole of His Left Foot in a Cracked Mirror." Johnson-Davies, *Egyptian Short Stories*. 43–50.

Biography and Criticism

Badawi, M.M. *Modern Arabic Drama in Egypt*. Cambridge: Cambridge UP, 1987. 149–150.

Ginat, R. *Egypt's Incomplete Revolution: Lutfi al-Khuli and Nasser's Socialism in the 1960s*. London: Cass, 1997.

al-Khuri, Ilyas, 1948–

Web Sites

Alcalay, A. "1001 Palestinian Nights." Rev. of *Bab al-Shams* (Hebrew and French translations). *The Village Voice* 18 Mar. 2002. http://www.villagevoice.com/issues/0212/alcalay.php (accessed 22 Aug. 2003).

al-Khuri, I. "Politics and Culture in Lebanon." Interviewed by M.B. Young. *The Lebanese Center for Policy Studies*. http://www.lcps-lebanon.org/pub/breview/br5/khourybr5.html (accessed 22 Aug. 2003).

———. "The Autumn of Literature: The Dictator as Novelist." *Aljadid* 33 (2000). http://www.aljadid.com/features/0633khoury.html (accessed 22 Aug. 2003).

On the novel *Zubaybah wa-al-Malik* (*Zubaybah and the King*), purportedly written by S. Hussein.

Autobiography and Interviews

"Elias Khoury: The Necessity to Forget—and Remember." Interviewed by S. Mejcher. *Banipal* 12 (2001): 8–14.

Translated excerpts from Mejcher's *Geschichten uber Geschichte: Erinnerung im Romanwerk von Elias Khoury* (Wiesbaden: Reichert, 2001).

Translations

Gates of the City. Trans. P. Haydar. Minneapolis: U of Minnesota P, 1993.

The Journey of Little Gandhi. Trans. P. Haydar. Minneapolis: U of Minnesota P, 1994.

The Kingdom of Strangers. Trans. P. Haydar. Fayetteville: U of Arkansas P, 1996.

Little Mountain. Trans. M. Tabet. Minneapolis: U of Minnesota P, 1989.

Biography and Criticism

Amyuni, M.T. "Khuri, Ilyas [Elias Khoury]" Meisami and Starkey, *Encyclopedia of Arabic Literature*. 447.

———. "The Arab Artist's Role in Society: Three Case Studies: Naguib Mahfouz, Tayeb Salih, and Elias Khoury." *Arabic and Middle Eastern Literatures* 2 (1999): 203–222.

Ghandour, S. "History, Religion, and the Construction of Subjectivitiy in Elias Khoury's 'Rihlat Ghandi al-Saghir.'" *Tradition, Modernity, and Postmodernity in Arabic Literature: Essays in Honor of Professor Issa J. Boullata*. Ed. K. Abdel-Malek and W. Hallaq. Brill: Leiden, 2000. 186–202.

al-Khuwarizmi, Muhammad ibn Musa, fl. 813–846

Web Sites

Gin, C. "Muhammad Bin Musa Al-Khwarizmi." *SJSU Virtual Museum: The History of Mathematics, Science, and Technology: A Culturally Affirming View*. Ed. R.H. Barba. Aug. 1997. San Jose State University. http://www.sjsu.edu/depts/Museum/alkhwa.html (accessed 22 Aug. 2003).

"Al-Khawarizmi." *MuslimHeritage.com*. http://www.muslimheritage.com/day_life/ (accessed 22 Aug. 2003).

"Mohammad bin Musa al-Khawarizmi." *The Window: Philosophy on the Internet*. Ed. C. Marvin and F. Sikernitsky. http://caribou.cc.trincoll.edu/depts_phil/philo/phils/muslim/khawariz.html (accessed 22 Aug. 2003).

O'Connor, J.J. and E.F. Robertson. "Abu Ja'far Muhammad ibn Musa Al-Khwarizmi." *The MacTutor History of Mathematics Archive*. http://www-gap.dcs.st-and.ac.uk/~history/Mathematicians/Al-Khwarizmi.html (accessed 22 Aug. 2003).

Translations

The Algebra of Mohammed ben Musa. Ed. and Trans. F. Rosen. Hildesheim; New York: G. Olms, 1986.

Biography and Criticism

Conrad, L.I. "al-Khwarazmi, Abu Ja'far Muhammad ibn Musa." Meisami and Starkey, *Encyclopedia of Arabic Literature.* 450–451.

Toomer, G.J. "al-Khwarizmi, Abu Ja'far Muhammad ibn Musa." Gillispie, *Dictionary of Scientific Biography.* Vol. 7. 358–365.

al-Kindi, d. ca. 873

Web Sites

"Al-Kindi." *Center for Islam and Science.* http://www.cis-ca.org/voices/k/al-kindi.htm (accessed 22 Aug. 2003).

"Al-Kindi: Encyclopaedic Scholar of the Baghdad 'House of Wisdom.'" *MuslimHeritage.com.* http://www.muslimheritage.com/day_life/ (accessed 22 Aug. 2003).

Kennedy-Day, K. "al-Kindi, Abu Yusuf Ya'qub ibn Ishaq." *Islamic Philosophy Online.* http://www.muslimphilosophy.com/ip/kin.htm (22 Aug. 2003).

"Kindi (al-)" *Malaspina Great Books.* http://www.malaspina.com/site/person_716.asp (accessed 22 Aug. 2003).

O'Connor, J.J., and E.F. Robertson. "Abu Yusuf Yaqub ibn Ishaq al-Sabbah Al-Kindi." *The MacTutor History of Mathematics Archive.* http://www-gap.dcs.st-and.ac.uk/~history/Mathematicians/Al-Kindi.html (accessed 14 Aug. 2003).

"Yaqub ibn Ishaq al-Kindi." *The Window: Philosophy on the Internet.* Ed. C. Marvin and F. Sikernitsky. http://caribou.cc.trincoll.edu/depts_phil/philo/phils/muslim/kindi.html (accessed 22 Aug. 2003).

Translations

al-Kindi's Metaphysics. Trans. A.L. Ivry. Albany: State U of New York P, 1974.

The Medical Formulary, or Aqrabadhin. Trans. M. Levey. Madison: U of Wisconsin P, 1966.

Scientific Weather Forecasting in the Middle Ages. Trans. G. Bos and C. Burnett. London: Kegan Paul; New York: Distributed by Columbia UP, 2000.

Biography and Criticism

Butterworth, C.E. "al-Kindi." McGreal, *Great Thinkers of the Eastern World.* 439–442.

Endress, G. "al-Kindi, Abu Yusuf." Meisami and Starkey, *Encyclopedia of Arabic Literature.* 451–452.

Jolivet, J. and R. Rashed. "al-Kindi, Abu Yusuf Ya'qub ibn Ishaq al-Sabbah." Gillispie, *Dictionary of Scientific Biography.* Vol. 15. 261–267.

Klein-Franke, F. "al-Kindi." Nasr and Leaman, *History of Islamic Philosophy.* 165–177.

Martin, M.A. "Abu Yusuf Ya'qub al-Kindi." Atiyeh, *The Genius of Arab Civilization*. 98–99.

Zimmerman, F.W. "Al-Kindi." *Religion, Learning and Science in the 'Abbasid Period*. Ed. M.J.L. Young, J.D. Latham, and R.B. Serjeant. Cambridge History of Arabic Literature. Cambridge: Cambridge UP, 1990. 364–369.

Layla al-Akhyaliyah, d. ca. 700

Web Sites

"Laila Akhyaliyya/Layla al-Akhyaliyyah." *Other Women's Voices*. Ed. D. Disse. 6 May 2003. http://home.infionline.net/~ddisse/laila.html (22 Aug. 2003).
  Biographical details, links to translations of two poems, and print sources with excerpts of her poems in translation.

Translations

"Laila al-Akhyaliyya." Trans. A. al-Udhari. *Classical Poems by Arab Women*. London: Saqi Books, 1999. 80–82.

Biography and Criticism

al-Sajdi, D. "Trespassing the Male Domain: The Qasidah of Layla al-Akhyaliyyah." *Journal of Arabic Literature* 31 (2000): 121–146.

Seidensticker, T. "Layla al-Akhyaliyya." Meisami and Starkey, *Encyclopedia of Arabic Literature*. 463.

Leo, Africanus, ca. 1492–ca. 1550

Web Sites

De Rouvray, C. *Leo Africanus: A 16th Century Exploration of Morocco*. 18 May 2003. http://www.leoafricanus.com/ (accessed 22 Aug. 2003).
  Comprehensive site about the man and his travels, including photos of sites that Leo visited, maps showing his routes, notes, and links to other sites. Cristel de Rouvray spent ten months in Morocco on a Fulbright grant in 2000–2001, researching Leo.

Leo, A. "Leo Africanus: Description of Timbuktu." *Resources for the Study of World Civilizations*. Ed. P. Brians. Washington State University. http://www.wsu.edu:8080/~wldciv/world_civ_reader/world_civ_reader_2/leo_africanus.html (accessed 22 Aug. 2003).

Masonen, P. "Leo Africanus: The Man with Many Names." Masonen, P. Home Page. http://www.uta.fi/~hipema/leo.htm (accessed 22 Aug. 2003).

Translations

A Geographical Historie of Africa Written in Arabic and Italian by John Leo. Trans. J. Pory. Ed. L. Jones. Pittsburgh: Jones' Research and Pub. Co., 1994.

Biography and Criticism

Glick, T.F. "Leo the African." Gillispie, *Dictionary of Scientific Biography*. Vol. 8. 190.

Irwin, R. "Leo Africanus." Meisami and Starkey, *Encyclopedia of Arabic Literature.*
    466–467.

al-Maghut, Muhammad, 1934–

Web Sites

Magda's Night Gallery. Ed. Magda. Dec. 2002. http://www.geocities.com/SoHo/
    Cafe/1324/maghut.htm (accessed 22 Aug. 2003).
    Includes translations of "From the Doorstep to Heaven" and "Shade and Noon
Sun."

"Mohammad al-Maghut." *Masthead* 7 (2003). http://au.geocities.com/masthead_2/
    issue7/maghut.html (accessed 22 Aug. 2003).
    Translations of "The Hill" and "Stars and Rains."

"Muhammad al-Maghut, 'The Orphan.'" *PovertyNet.* Ed. G. Prennushi. 31 July 2003.
    Poverty Reduction Group, World Bank. http://www.worldbank.org/poverty/
    povlit/povlit2p5.htm (accessed 22 Aug. 2003).

Translations

Asfour, *When the Words Burn.* 108–116.
    Includes translations of "An Arab Traveller in Space," "The Dead Man," "Ice
and Fire," "The Orphan," "The Postman's Fear," and "When the Words Burn."

The Fan of Swords. Trans. M. Jayyusi and N.S. Nye. Ed. S.K. Jayyusi. Washington,
    D.C.: Three Continents, 1991.

"The Hunchback Sparrow." Trans. M. Manzalaoui. Rev. A. Parkin and H. Heliel.
    Arabic Writing Today: Drama. Ed. M. Manzalaoui. Cairo: American Research
    Center in Egypt, 1977. 555–639.

Joy Is Not My Profession. Trans. J. Asfour and A. Burch. Montreal: Signal Editions,
    1994.

al-Udhari, *Modern Poetry of the Arab World.* 85–89.
    Includes translations of "An Arab Traveller in a Space Station," "The Noonday
Sun and the Shade," "The Orphan," "The Postman's Fear," "Siege," "Tourist," and
"Winter."

Biography and Criticism

Abu-Deeb, K. "al-Maghut, Muhammad." Meisami and Starkey, *Encyclopedia of
    Arabic Literature.* 488–489.

Allen, *Modern Arabic Literature.* 189–192.

Asfour, J. "Adonis and Muhammad al-Maghut: Two Voices in a Burning Land."
    Journal of Arabic Literature 20 (1989): 20–30.

———. "al-Maghut, Muhammad." Serafin, *Encyclopedia of World Literature in the
    20th Century.* Vol. 3. 155–156.

Loloi, P. "Maghut, Muhammad al-." *Contemporary World Writers.* Ed. T. Chevalier.
    2nd ed. Detroit: St. James, 1993. 336–337.

Mahfuz, Najib, 1912–

Web Sites

Hafez, S. "Representing the Nation." *Al-Ahram Weekly On-Line* 13–19 Sept. 2001.
   http://weekly.ahram.org.eg/2001/551/bo1.htm (accessed 22 Aug. 2003).
   The introduction to the Everyman's Library 2001 edition of *The Cairo Trilogy.*
Places Mahfuz within the context of Arabic literature.

Mondal, A. "Naguib Mahfouz and His Women: 'The Cairo Trilogy.'" *SOAS Literary
   Review* 1 (1999). http://www.soas.ac.uk/soaslit/issue1/MONDAL.PDF
   (accessed 22 Aug. 2003).

"Naguib Mahfouz." *AUC Libraries.* 4 Aug. 2003. American University in Cairo.
   http://lib.aucegypt.edu/screens/mahfouz.html (accessed 22 Aug. 2003).
   Includes links to other sites, but mainly a long list of books and articles by and
about Mahfuz.

"Naguib Mahfouz." *Books and Writers.* http://www.kirjasto.sci.fi/mahfouz.htm
   (accessed 22 Aug. 2003).

"Naguib Mahfouz, Biased to Grassroots (People & Facts)" *Egypt.* http://
   www.sis.gov.eg/eginfnew/culture/html/cul0110.htm (accessed 22 Aug. 2003).

"The Nobel Prize in Literature 1988." *Nobel e-Museum.* Exec. Ed. A.W. Levinovitz.
   21 Aug. 2003. Nobel Foundation. http://www.nobel.se/literature/laureates/
   1988/mahfouz-bio.html (accessed 22 Aug. 2003).
   Includes biography, translation of his Nobel lecture, links to other sites.

Puente, S.G. "Naguib Mahfouz's 'Sanna Helwa.'" *Middle East Times* 7 Dec. 1997.
   http://www.metimes.com/issue49/commu/02mahfouz.htm (accessed 22 Aug.
   2003).

Said, E. "Cruelty of Memory." *Al-Ahram Weekly On-Line*, 13–19 Dec. 2001. http://
   weekly.ahram.org.eg/2001/564/2sc1.htm (accessed 22 Aug. 2003).
   Mahfuz's views of Egyptian history, written by a well-known literary and cultural critic.

   This is one of several articles, interviews, and translations published in a special
section of *Al-Ahram Weekly* on the occasion of Mahfuz's 90th birthday. See the complete list at http://weekly.ahram.org.eg/2001/564/special.htm.

Woffenden, R. "Scribe of the Alley." *Cairo Times* 6–12 Dec. 2000. http://
   www.cairotimes.com/content/archiv05/mahfouz.html (accessed 22 Aug. 2003).

"Writers Reviewed: Naguib Mahfouz." *Socialist Review* 206 (1997). http://
   pubs.socialistreviewindex.org.uk/sr206/writers.htm (accessed 22 Aug. 2003).
   A socialist interpretation of his life and work.

Autobiography and Interviews

Echoes of an Autobiography. Trans. D. Johnson-Davies. New York: Doubleday, 1997.
Naguib Mahfouz at Sidi Gaber: Reflections of a Nobel Laureate, 1994–2001.
   Interviewed by M. Salamawy. Cairo: American U in Cairo P, 2001.

Translations

Adrift on the Nile. Trans. F. Liardet. New York: Doubleday, 1993.

Akhenaten, Dweller in Truth. Trans. T. Abu-Hassabo. New York: Anchor Books, 2000.

Arabian Nights and Days. Trans. D. Johnson-Davies. New York: Doubleday, 1995.

Autumn Quail. Trans. R. Allen. Rev. J. Rodenbeck. Cairo: American U in Cairo P, 1985.

The Beggar. Trans. K.W. Henry and N.K.N. al-Warraki. Cairo: American U in Cairo P, 1986.

The Beginning and the End. Trans. R.H. Awad. Ed. M.R. Smith. Cairo: American U in Cairo P, 1985.

The Cairo Trilogy. Trans. W.M. Hutchins, et al. New York: Everyman's Library, 2001. Includes *Palace Walk, Palace of Desire* and *Sugar Street*.

Children of Gebelawi. Trans. P. Stewart. London: Heinemann, 1981.

Children of the Alley. Trans. P. Theroux. New York: Doubleday, 1996.

The Day the Leader Was Killed. Trans. M. Mashem. New York: Anchor Books, 2000.

Fountain and Tomb. Trans. S. Sobhy, E. Fattouh, and J. Kenneson. Washington, D.C.: Three Continents, 1988.

God's World. Trans. A. Abadir and R. Allen. Minneapolis: Bibliotheca Islamica, 1973.

The Harafish. Trans. C. Cobham. New York: Doubleday, 1994.

The Journey of Ibn Fattouma. Trans. D. Johnson-Davies. New York: Doubleday, 1992.

Midaq Alley. Trans. T. Le Gassick. Washington, D.C.: Three Continents, 1977.

Miramar. Trans. F. Moussa-Mahmoud. 2nd U.S. ed., augmented. Washington, D.C.: Three Continents, 1989.

Mirrors. Trans. R. Allen. Cairo: American U in Cairo P, 1999.

Respected Sir; Wedding Song; The Search. Trans. R. El-Enany, O.E. Kenny, and M. Islam. New York: Anchor Books, 2001.

The Thief and the Dogs. Trans. T. Le Gassick and M.M. Badawi. Rev. J. Rodenbeck. Cairo: American U in Cairo P, 1984.

The Time and the Place and Other Stories. Trans. D. Johnson-Davies. New York: Doubleday, 1991.

Biography and Criticism

Abu-Haider, J. "'Awlad Haratina' by Najib Mahfuz: An Event in the Arab World." *Journal of Arabic Literature* 16 (1985): 119–131.

Allen, R. "Autobiography and Memory: Mahfuz's 'Asda al-Sira al-Dhatiyya.'" Ostle, Moor, and Wild, *Writing the Self*. 207–216.

———. "Mahfouz, Naguib (Abdel Aziz Al-Sabilgi)." Serafin, *Encyclopedia of World Literature in the 20th Century*. Vol. 3. 157–158.

———. "Mahfuz, Najib." Meisami and Starkey, *Encyclopedia of Arabic Literature*. 490–492.

————. "Mahfuz, Najib (Naguib Mahfouz)" Gikandi, *Encyclopedia of African Literature*. 306–309.

————. *Modern Arabic Literature*. 192-204.

————. "Najib Mahfuz, 1911–." *African Writers*. Ed. C.B. Cox. New York: Charles Scribner's Sons, 1997. 451–465.

————. "Najib Mahfuz: Nobel Laureate in Literature, 1988." *World Literature Today* 63.1 (1989): 5–9.

————. "The 1988 Nobel Prize in Literature, Najib Mahfuz." *Dictionary of Literary Biography Yearbook* 1988: 3–12.

————. "'Thartharah fawq al-Nil', Najib Mahfuz." *The Arabic Novel: An Historical and Critical Introduction*. 2nd ed. Syracuse: Syracuse UP, 1995. 140–147.

Amyuni, M.T. "The Arab Artist's Role in Society: Three Case Studies: Naguib Mahfouz, Tayeb Salih, and Elias Khoury." *Arabic and Middle Eastern Literatures* 2 (1999): 203–222.

Beard, M. and A. Haydar, eds. *Naguib Mahfouz: from Regional Fame to Global Recognition*. Syracuse: Syracuse UP, 1993.

Carlisle, B.K. "Mahfouz, Naguib (Abdel Aziz Al-Sabilgi)" *Contemporary Authors* 128 (1990): 262–264.

Coppola, C. "Mahfuz, Nagib (Abdel Aziz al-Sailgi)." *Reference Guide to Short Fiction*. Ed. N. Watson. Detroit: St. James, 1994. 333–335.

DeYoung, T. "'Midaqq Alley' by Najib Mahfuz." *African Literature and Its Times*. Ed. J. Moss and L. Valestuk. World Literature and Its Times 2. Detroit: Gale, 2000. 259–268.

El-Enany, R. "The Dichotomy of Islam and Modernity in the Fiction of Naguib Mahfouz." *The Postcolonial Crescent: Islam's Impact on Contemporary Literature*. Ed. J.C. Hawley. New York: Lang, 1998. 71–83.

————, ed. *Naguib Mahfouz: the Pursuit of Meaning*. London: Routledge, 1993.

Elkhadem, S. "Najib Mahfuz's Political Novels." *On Egyptian Fiction: Five Essays*. Fredericton, N.B.: York, 2001.17–21.

Gordon, H. *Naguib Mahfouz's Egypt: Existential Themes in His Writings*. New York: Greenwood, 1990.

Hutchins, W.M. "Mahfouz, Naguib (Abdel Aziz al-Sabilgi)." Pendergast and Pendergast, *Reference Guide to World Literature*. 636–638.

————. "Mahfuz, Nagib (Abdel Aziz al-Sabilgi)." *Contemporary World Writers*. Ed. T. Chevalier. 2nd ed. Detroit: St. James, 1993. 337–339.

Kirkpatrick, H. *The Modern Egyptian Novel: A Study in Social Criticism*. Oxford: Middle East Centre, St. Antony's College; London: Ithaca, 1974. 71–88, 94–113.

Le Gassick, T., ed. *Critical Perspectives on Naguib Mahfouz*. Washington, DC: Three Continents, 1991.

"Mahfouz, Naguib (Abdel Aziz Al-Sabilgi)." *Contemporary Authors New Revision Series* 55 (1997): 261–266; 101 (2002): 271–277.

Mehrez, S. *Egyptian Writers between History and Fiction: Essays on Naguib Mahfouz, Sonallah Ibrahim, and Gamal al-Ghitani*. Cairo: American U in Cairo P, 1994. 17–38, 78–95.

Mikhail, M.N. *Studies in the Short Fiction of Mahfouz and Idris*. New York: New York UP, 1992.

Milson, M. *Najib Mahfuz: The Novelist-Philosopher of Cairo*. New York: St. Martin's, 1998.

Moosa, M. *The Early Novels of Naguib Mahfouz: Images of Modern Egypt*. Gainesville: U of Florida P, 1994.

Naguib Mahfouz: From Regional Fame to Global Recognition. Eds. M. Beard and A. Haydar. Syracuse: Syracuse UP, 1993.

"Najib Mahfuz." *Contemporary Literary Criticism* 52 (1989): 291–305; 55 (1989): 170–189; 153 (2002): 229–375.

Peled, M. *Religion, My Own: The Literary Works of Najib Mahfuz*. New Brunswick: Transaction, 1983.

Sakkut, H. *The Egyptian Novel and Its Main Trends: From 1913 to 1952*. Cairo: American U in Cairo P, 1971. 72–76, 114–142.

———. "Naguib Mahfouz and the Sufi Way." Trans. N. Radwan. Ghazoul and Harlow, *The View from Within*. 90–98.

Somekh, S. *The Changing Rhythm: A Study of Najib Mahfuz's Novels*. Leiden: Brill, 1973.

Stagh, M. *The Limits of Freedom of Speech: Prose Literature and Prose Writers in Egypt under Nasser and Sadat*. Stockholm: Almqvist and Wiksell, 1993. 157–170.

Mahmud, Zaki Najib, 1905–1993

Web Sites

"Zaki Naguib Mahmoud." *Egypt*. http://www.sis.gov.eg/calendar/html/c1261022.htm (accessed 23 Aug. 2003).

A shorter, slightly different biography can be read at http://www.us.sis.gov.eg/egyptianfigures/html/Mahmoud.htm.

Biography and Criticism

Staif, A.-N. "Mahmud, Zaki Najib." Meisami and Starkey, *Encyclopedia of Arabic Literature*. 493–494.

al-Majdhub, Muhammad al-Mahdi, 1919–1982

Web Sites

El Tayyeb, H.A. "Al-Majdub." *Sudan Site*. 31 Jan. 1998. http://www.geocities.com/Athens/Oracle/1296/al_majdub.htm (accessed 23 Aug. 2003).

Includes "The Birth" in English and Arabic.

Translations

Jayyusi, *Modern Arabic Poetry*. 319–328.

Includes a translation of "Birth" by S.K. Jayyusi and C. Doria and a translation of "The Rain" by M. Sorenson.

Biography and Criticism

Berkley, C. "al-Majdhub, [Muhammad] al-Mahdi." Meisami and Starkey, *Encyclopedia of Arabic Literature*. 496.

al-Mala'ikah, Nazik, 1923–

Web Sites

Callaghan, M, et al. *Nazik al-Mala'ika.* http://www.humboldt.edu/~me2/engl240/
    student_projects/Al-Mala_ika/frontpage.html (accessed 23 Aug. 2003).
    Designed as a student project for an English class at Humboldt State University.
Includes biography, bibliography, and translations of "Love Song for Words," "I Am,"
"Jamila," "Washing Off Disgrace," "Cholera," with commentary.

"Nazik al-Mala'ika." *Books and Writers.* http://www.kirjasto.sci.fi/malaika.htm
    (accessed 23 Aug. 2003).

"Nazik al-Malaika and the Search for the Self Poetry." *Arabicnews.com* 16 Apr. 1998.
    http://www.arabicnews.com/ansub/Daily/Day/980416/1998041604.html
    (accessed 23 Aug. 2003).

Nazik al-Malaika: A Tribute Page. http://www.koolpages.com/almalaika/images/
    nazikpage.html (accessed 23 Aug. 2003).
    Includes links to a portion of an autobiographical essay, an essay on women,
and translations of several poems and short stories. The same site hosts a more extensive page in Arabic at http://www.koolpages.com/almalaika/nazikapage.html.

Translations

Asfour, *When the Words Burn.* 78–80.
    Includes translations of "Let Us Dream Together" and "When I Killed My
Love."

Handal, *The Poetry of Arab Women.* 176–182.
    Includes a translation of "Cholera" by H. Haddawy, with N. Handal, and a
translation of "Five Hymns to Pain" by H. Haddawy.

Jayyusi, *Modern Arabic Poetry.* 329–338.
    Includes translations of "Lilies for the Prophet," "Love Song for Words," "Song
for the Moon," and "The Visitor Who Never Came" by M. Sorenson and C. Middleton.

"New Year." Al-Udhari, *Modern Poetry of the Arab World.* 35.

"Who Am I?" Khouri and Algar, *Anthology of Modern Arabic Poetry.* 79–81.

Women of the Fertile Crescent: An Anthology of Modern Poetry by Arab Women. Ed.
    and trans. K. Boullata. Washington, D.C.: Three Continents, 1978. 13–22.
    Includes translations of "I Am," "Insignificant Woman," "Jamila," "My
Silence," and "Washing Off Disgrace."

Biography and Criticism

Allen, *Modern Arabic Literature.* 204–208.

Husni, R. "al-Mala'ika, Nazik Sadiq." Meisami and Starkey, *Encyclopedia of Arabic
    Literature.* 498–500.

Jayyusi, S.K. "al-Mala'ika, Nazik." Serafin, *Encyclopedia of World Literature in the
    20th Century.* Vol. 3. 166–167.

Mamduh, 'Aliyah, 1944–

Web Sites

Mamduh, 'A. "A Secret Language Has Formed Inside the Arabic Language."
   Interviewed by M. Chollet. *Autodafe: The Censored Library.* July 2003.
   International Parliament of Writers. http://www.autodafe.org/correspondence/
   cor_art_02.htm (accessed 23 Aug. 2003).
   Her essay on trying to assimilate while living in different cities can be read at
http://www.autodafe.org/autodafe/autodafe_02/art_15.htm.

Autobiography

"Creatures of Arab Fear." *In the House of Silence: Autobiographical Essays by Arab
   Women Writers.* Ed. F. Faqir. Trans. S. Eber and F. Faqir. Reading: Garnet,
   1998. 63–72.

Translations

Mothballs. Trans. P. Theroux. Reading, UK: Garnet, 1996.

"Presence of the Absent Man." Johnson-Davies, *Under the Naked Sky.* 223–233.

al-Manfaluti, Mustafa, 1876?–1924

Web Sites

"Moustafa Lotfi el Manfalouti and Social Reform." *Egypt.* http://www.sis.gov.eg/
   calendar/html/cl120797.htm (accessed 23 Aug. 2003).

Rakha, Y. "Of Things Discovered in the Deep." *Al-Ahram Weekly On-Line* 30 Dec.
   1999–5 Jan. 2000. http://weekly.ahram.org.eg/1999/462/writers.htm (accessed
   23 Aug. 2003).

Biography and Criticism

de Moor, E.C.M. "al-Manfaluti, Mustafa Lutfi." Meisami and Starkey, *Encyclopedia
   of Arabic Literature.* 506.

Elkhadem, S. *History of the Egyptian Novel: Its Rise and Early Beginnings.*
   Fredericton, N.B.: York, 1985. 21–22.

al-Maqrizi, Ahmad ibn 'Ali, 1364–1442

Web Sites

al-Maqrizi, A. ibn 'A. "Account of the Crusade of St. Louis." *Internet Medieval
   Sourcebook.* http://www.fordham.edu/halsall/source/makrisi.html (accessed 23
   Aug. 2003).

Translations

Al-Maqrizi's Book of Contention and Strife. Trans. C.E. Bosworth. Manchester: U of
   Manchester, 1980.

Mamluk Economics. Trans. A. Allouche. Salt Lake City: U of UT, 1994.

Biography and Criticism

Richards, D.S. "al-Maqrizi." Meisami and Starkey, *Encyclopedia of Arabic
   Literature.* 509.

Mardam, Khalil, 1895?–1959

Web Sites

"National Anthem: Syria." *National Anthems*. Ed. M. Fromm. http://
www.thenationalanthems.com/country/syria.htm (accessed 23 Aug. 2003).
The lyrics are adapted from a poem by Mardam.

Translations

"The Wooing." Trans. A.J. Arberry. *Modern Arabic Poetry*. Cambridge: Cambridge
UP, 1967. 14–15.

Biography and Criticism

Nourallah, R. "Mardam Bek, Khalil." Meisami and Starkey, *Encyclopedia of Arabic
Literature*. 509–510.

al-Mas'udi, d. 956?

Web Sites

"Abul Hasan Ali Al-Mas'udi." *The Window: Philosophy on the Internet*. Ed. C.
Marvin and F. Sikernitsky. http://caribou.cc.trincoll.edu/depts_phil/philo/phils/
muslim/masudi.html (accessed 23 Aug. 2003).

al-Mas'udi. "The Book of Golden Meadows." *Internet Medieval Sourcebook*. http://
www.fordham.edu/halsall/source/masoudi.html (accessed 23 Aug. 2003).
Long excerpts on the early Abbasid caliphs.

Translations

The Meadows of Gold: The Abbasids. Trans. and Ed. P. Lunde and C. Stone. London:
Kegan Paul; New York: Distributed by Routledge, Chapman, and Hall, 1989.

Biography and Criticism

Ahmad, S. "al-Mas'udi, Abu 'l-Hasan 'Ali ibn al-Husayn ibn 'Ali." Gillispie,
Dictionary of Scientific Biography. Vol. 9. 171–172.

al-Azmeh, A. "al-Mas'udi." Meisami and Starkey, *Encyclopedia of Arabic Literature*.
514–515.

Khalidi, T. *Islamic Historiography: The Histories of Mas'udi*. Albany: State U of
New York P, 1975.

Shboul, A.M.H. *Al-Masudi and His World: A Muslim Humanist and His Interest in
Non-Muslims*. London: Ithaca, 1979.

Matar, Muhammad Afifi, 1935–

Web Sites

"Muhammad Afifi Mattar." *Jehat.com*. http://www.jehat.com/en/
default.asp?action=article&ID=88 (accessed 19 Apr. 2004).
Includes translation of "Recital."

Translations

Quartet of Joy. Trans. F. Ghazoul and J. Verlenden. Fayetteville: U of Arkansas P,
1997.

"A Visitation." Trans. S. Slyomovics. *Journal of Arabic Literature* 20 (1989): 69–70.

Biography and Criticism

Al Masri, K. "Matar, Muhammad 'Afifi." Gikandi, *Encyclopedia of African Literature*. 319.

Ghazoul, F.J. "The Greek Component in the Poetry and Poetics of Muhammad 'Afifi Matar." *Journal of Arabic Literature* 25 (1994): 135–151.

Snir, R. "Matar, Muhammad 'Afifi." Meisami and Starkey, *Encyclopedia of Arabic Literature*. 515–516.

al-Mawardi, 'Ali ibn Muhammad, 974?–1058

Web Sites

"Abu al-Hasan al-Mawardi." *The Window: Philosophy on the Internet*. Ed. C. Marvin and F. Sikernitsky. http://caribou.cc.trincoll.edu/depts_phil/philo/phils/muslim/mawardi.html (accessed 23 Aug. 2003).

Translations

The Laws of Islamic Governance. Trans. A. Yate. London: Ta-Ha, 1996.

The Ordinances of Government. Trans. W.H. Wahbi. Reading, UK: Center for Muslim Contribution to Civilization: Garnet, 1996.

Biography and Criticism

Mikhail, H. *Politics and Revelation: Mawardi and After*. Edinburgh: Edinburgh UP, 1995.

Weiss, B. "al-Mawardi, 'Ali ibn Muhammad." Meisami and Starkey, *Encyclopedia of Arabic Literature*. 519.

al-Mazini, Ibrahim 'Abd al-Qadir, 1889–1949

Web Sites

"Ibrahim Abdel Qader Al Mazini." *Egypt*. http://www.sis.gov.eg/calendar/html/cl060897.htm (accessed 23 Aug. 2003).

Translations

Al-Mazini's Egypt. Trans. W. Hutchins. Washington, D.C.: Three Continents, 1983.

"The Wilted Rose." Trans. F. Bitar. *Treasury of Arabic Love Poems, Quotations and Proverbs*. Ed. F. Bitar. New York: Hippocrene, 1996. 55.

Biography and Criticism

Allen, *Modern Arabic Literature*. 214–219.

Allen, R. "al-Mazini, Ibrahim 'Abd al-Qadir." Meisami and Starkey, *Encyclopedia of Arabic Literature*. 521–522.

Badawi, M.M. "Al-Mazini the Novelist." *Journal of Arabic Literature* 4 (1973): 112–145.

Elkhadem, S. *History of the Egyptian Novel: Its Rise and Early Beginnings*. Fredericton, N.B.: York, 1985. 39–44.

Kirkpatrick, H. *The Modern Egyptian Novel: A Study in Social Criticism.* Oxford: Middle East Centre, St. Antony's College; London: Ithaca, 1974. 26–30.

Sakkut, H. *The Egyptian Novel and Its Main Trends: From 1913 to 1952.* Cairo: American U in Cairo P, 1971. 22–27.

Mikha'il, Dunya, 1965–

Web Sites

"Dunya Mikhail." *Masthead* 7 (2003). http://au.geocities.com/masthead_2/issue7/mikhail.html (accessed 23 Aug. 2003).
　　Translations of "The Cup," "Pronouns," and "The War Works Hard."

"Dunya Mikhail." *Readings by Iraqi Poets.* 12 Mar. 2002. Faulconer Gallery, Grinnell College. http://web.grinnell.edu/faulconergallery/iraq/poetry/Mikhail/ (accessed 23 Aug. 2003).
　　Includes translations of "Christmas," "Pomegranate," "Statements," "The Prisoner," and "The War Works Hard," with audio and video of her reading.

Ghazoul, F.J. "Confronting Loss." Rev. of *Diary of a Wave Outside the Sea. Al-Ahram Weekly On-Line* 11–17 Nov. 1999. http://weekly.ahram.org.eg/1999/455/bk5_455.htm (accessed 23 Aug. 2003).

"Iraqi Poems." *Guardian* 1 Mar. 2001. http://books.guardian.co.uk/Print/0,3858,4614907,00.html (accessed 23 Aug. 2003).
　　Translations of "America," "The Jewel," and "The Prisoner."

Translations

Handal, *The Poetry of Arab Women.* 208–213.
　　Includes translations of "The Chaldean Ruins" and "The Dawn Fairy" by S. Kawar and a translation of "Rain" by S. Kawar, with N. Handal.

Minah, Hanna, 1924–

Web Sites

Hassan, F.S. "Experience as Essence: A Review of Al Wallaah by Syrian Novelist Hanna Minah." *Aljadid* 5 (1996). http://almashriq.hiof.no/general/000/070/079/al-jadid/aljadid-wallaah.html (accessed 23 Aug. 2003).

Translations

Fragments of Memory: A Story of a Syrian Family. Trans. O. Kenny and L. Kenny. Austin: Center for Middle Eastern Studies, U of Texas at Austin, 1993.

Sun on a Cloudy Day. Trans. and Ed. B. Frangieh and C. Brown. Pueblo, Colo.: Passeggiata, 1997.

Biography and Criticism

Allen, *Modern Arabic Literature.* 219–224.

Allen, R. "Mina, Hanna." Meisami and Starkey, *Encyclopedia of Arabic Literature.* 526.

Ghandour, S. "Mina, Hanna." Serafin, *Encyclopedia of World Literature in the 20th Century.* Vol. 3. 270.

al-'Id, Y. "The Autobiographical Novel and the Dual Function: A Study of Hanna Mina's 'Trilogy.'" Trans. D. Manisty. Ostle, Moor, and Wild, *Writing the Self.* 157–177.

Mirsal, Iman, 1966–

Web Sites

"Iman Mersal." *Arab World Books.* http://www.arabworldbooks.com/authors/ iman_mersal.htm (accessed 23 Aug. 2003).

"Iman Mersal." *Masthead* 7 (2003). http://au.geocities.com/masthead_2/issue7/ mersal.html (accessed 23 Aug. 2003).
  Includes translations of "Dividers," "ECG," "House of Mirrors," "In Neutrality," "Many Times," "News of Your Death," "Not Likely," "Portrait," "Resemblance," "Simply Sleeping," "Screams," "That Is Good," "Visits," and "You Have Lost Wisdom."

Translations

"Iman Mersal: Egypt's Postmodern Poet." *Tradition, Modernity, and Postmodernity in Arabic Literature: Essays in Honour of Professor Issa J. Boullata.* Ed. K. Abdel-Malek and W. Hallaq. Leiden: Brill, 2000. 411–414.
  Includes a translation of "Crossing the Threshold" by K. Abdel-Malek.

Ojaide, T., and T.M. Sallah, eds. *The New African Poetry: An Anthology.* Boulder: Rienner, 1999. 53–54.
  Includes translations of "Abortion," "Confessions," and "I Usually Look around Me" by C. Burt.

"Solitude Exercises." Trans. K. Mattawa with I. Mirsal. Handal, *The Poetry of Arab Women.* 204–207.

Mosteghanemi, Ahlem, 1953–

Web Sites

"Ahlam Mustaghanmi." *Arab World Books.* http://www.arabworldbooks.com/authors/ ahlam_mustaghanmi.html (accessed 23 Aug. 2003).

Ghazoul, F.J. "Memory and Desire." Rev. of *Memory in the Flesh. Al-Ahram Weekly On-Line* 24–30 Dec. 1998. http://weekly.ahram.org.eg/1998/409/cu2.htm (accessed 23 Aug. 2003).

Mosteghanemi, A. "To Colleagues of the Pen." *Al-Ahram Weekly On-Line* 24–30 Dec. 1998. http://weekly.ahram.org.eg/1998/409/cu1.htm (accessed 23 Aug. 2003).
  Her speech on accepting the Naguib Mahfouz Medal for Literature in 1998.

Autobiography

"Writing against Time and History." *In the House of Silence: Autobiographical Essays by Arab Women Writers.* Ed. F. Faqir. Trans. S. Eber and F. Faqir. Reading: Garnet, 1998. 79–90.

Translations

Memory in the Flesh. Trans. B.A. Sreih. Cairo: American U in Cairo P, 2000.

Biographies and Criticism

Bamia, A.A. "Mustaghanmi, Ahlam." Serafin, *Encyclopedia of World Literature in the 20th Century*. Vol. 3. 332.

McLarney, E. "Unlocking the Female in Ahlam Mustaghanami." *Journal of Arabic Literature* 33 (2002): 24–44.

Sheble, R. "Mustaghanmi, Ahlam." Gikandi, *Encyclopedia of African Literature*. 349–350.

Muhammad 'Abduh, 1849–1905

Web Sites

Harder, E. "Muhammad 'Abduh." *Center for Islam and Science*. http://www.cisca.org/voices/a/abduh.htm (accessed 23 Aug. 2003).

"Imam Muhammad Abdou, the Innovator of the Nation's Thought." *Egypt*. http://www.sis.gov.eg/calendar/html/cl110798.htm (accessed 23 Aug. 2003).

"Introduction to Muhammad Abduh." Khater, A. Home Page. http://social.chass.ncsu.edu/khater/personal/muhammad_abduh_unity_of_theology.htm (accessed 23 Aug. 2003). Includes translation of two chapters from *The Theology of Unity*.

Robinson, N. "'Abduh, Muhammad." *Islamic Philosophy Online*. http://www.muslimphilosophy.com/ip/rep/H049.htm (accessed 28 Aug. 2003).

Translations

The Theology of Unity. Trans. I. Masa'ad and K. Cragg. London: Allen and Unwin, 1966.

Biography and Criticism

Adams, C.C. *Islam and Modernism in Egypt: A Study of the Modern Reform Movement Inaugurated by Muhammad Abduh*. New York: Russell and Russell, 1968.

Ahmed, J.M. *The Intellectual Origins of Egyptian Nationalism*. London: Oxford UP, 1960.

Cragg, K. "'Abduh, Muhammad." *Oxford Encyclopedia of the Modern Islamic World*. Ed. J.L. Esposito. New York: Oxford UP, 1995. Vol. 1. 11–12.

Haddad, Y. "Muhammad Abduh: Pioneer of Islamic Reform." *Pioneers of Islamic Revival*. Ed. A. Rahnema. London: Zed, 1994. 30–63.

Kedourie, E. *Afghani and 'Abduh: An Essay on Religious Unbelief and Political Activism in Modern Islam*. New York: Humanities, 1966.

Kerr, M.H. *Islamic Reform: The Political and Legal Theories of Muhammad Abduh and Rashid Rida*. Berkeley: U of California P, 1966.

Zebiri, K. "'Abduh, Muhammad." Meisami and Starkey, *Encyclopedia of Arabic Literature*. 20–21.

Muhammad Farid, 1868–1919

Web Sites

"The Birth of Muhammad Farid." *Egypt*. http://www.sis.gov.eg/calendar/html/cl200197.htm (accessed 23 Aug. 2003).

Autobiography

The Memoirs and Diaries of Muhammad Farid, an Egyptian Nationalist Leader (1868–1919). Trans. A. Goldschmidt, Jr. San Francisco: Mellen U Research P, 1992.

Biography and Criticism

Crabbs, J. "Farid, Muhammad." Meisami and Starkey, *Encyclopedia of Arabic Literature.* 221.

Gershoni, I. Rev. of *Memoirs and Diaries of Muhammad Farid, an Egyptian Nationalist Leader (1868–1919).* Trans. A. Goldschmidt, Jr. *Asian and African Studies* 27 (1993): 313–341.

Muhammad Rashid Rida, 1865–1935

Web Sites

Ghazali, A.S. *Islam in the Post-Cold War Era.* http://www.ghazali.net/book2/chapter6/Page_2/body_page_2.html (accessed 23 Aug. 2003).
Chapter 6, page 2, has a section on Muhammad Rashid Rida.

"Muhammad Rashid Rida." *Center for Islam and Science.* http://cis-ca.org/voices/r/rida.htm (accessed 23 Aug. 2003).

M.R. Rida. "Socialism, Bolsehvism and Religion." *The Free Arab Voice.* Ed. I. Alloush. http://www.freearabvoice.org/reference/bolshevismAndReligion.htm (accessed 23 Aug. 2003).

Biography and Criticism

Busool, A.N. "Rashid Rida's Struggle to Establish a Modern Islamic State." *American Journal of Islamic Studies* 1 (1984): 83–99.

———. "Shaykh Muhammad Rashid Rida's Relations with Jamal al-Da'in al-Afghani and Muhammad 'Abduh." *Muslim World* 66 (1976): 272–286.

Kerr, M.H. *Islamic Reform: The Political and Legal Theories of Muhammad Abduh and Rashid Rida.* Berkeley: U of California P, 1966.

Shahin, E.E. "Muhammad Rashid Rida's Perspectives on the West as Reflected in al-Manar." *Muslim World* 79 (1989): 113–132.

———. "Rashid Rida, Muhammad." *Oxford Encyclopedia of the Modern Islamic World.* Ed. J.L. Esposito. New York: Oxford UP, 1995. Vol. 3. 410–412.

Sirriyeh, E. "Rashid Rida's Autobiography of the Syrian Years, 1865–1897." *Arabic and Middle Eastern Literatures* 3 (2000): 179–194.

Sluglett, P. "Rida, (Muhammad) Rashid." Meisami and Starkey, *Encyclopedia of Arabic Literature.* 662.

Tauber, E. "Rashid Rida as Pan-Arabist before World War I." *Muslim World* 79 (1989): 102–112.

———. "Rashid Rida's Political Attitutdes during World War I." *Muslim World* 85 (1995): 107–121.

Muhammad, Zakariya, 1951–

Web Sites

Mohammed, Z. "Lives in Ruins." *Guardian* 22 Apr. 2002. http://
    www.guardian.co.uk/g2/story/0,3604,688283,00.html (accessed 23 Aug. 2003).
    His eyewitness report on conditions in Ramallah during the Israeli occupation
in March 2002.

"Palestinian Poets, Zakaria Mohammed." *Khalil Sakakini Cultural Centre*. http://
    www.sakakini.org/poets/zakaria-index.htm (accessed 23 Aug. 2003).
    Includes translations of "Emigration," "Night," "The Reapers," "The Rose and
the Bull," "Sun Stroke," and "A Tavern."

"Zakariyya Muhammad." *Autodafe: The Censored Library*. July 2003. International
    Parliament of Writers. http://www.autodafe.org/bookshop/palestine/
    khaznadar.htm#2 (accessed 23 Aug. 2003).
    Includes translations of "Ant," "Caravan," "The Dead," and "The Island."

Translations

Jayyusi, *Anthology of Modern Palestinian Literature*. 224–229.
    Includes translations of "Apology." "The Cafe Mistress," "Emigration," "Every-
thing," "My Things," "A Tavern," and "A Woman" by L. Jayyusi and J. Reed.

Munif, 'Abd al-Rahman, 1933–

Web Sites

"Abdelrahman Munif." *al-Bab.com*. Ed. B. Whitaker. http://www.al-bab.com/arab/
    literature/munif.htm (accessed 23 Aug. 2003).
    With links to several articles about Munif.

"Abdelrahman Munif." *Books and Writers*. http://www.kirjasto.sci.fi/munif.htm
    (accessed 23 Aug. 2003).

Nixon, R. "The Hidden Lives of Oil." *Middle East and Islamic Studies Collection,
    Cornell University*. http://www.library.cornell.edu/colldev/mideast/hidoil.htm
    (accessed 23 Aug. 2003).
    Essay on what Munif's *Cities of Salt* can teach students about the human conse-
quences of oil exploration and drilling.

Autobiography and Interviews

"Clashing with Society at Gut Level." *Banipal* 3 (1998): 8–14.

Story of a City: A Childhood in Amman. Trans. S. Kawar. London: Quartet, 1996.

Translations

Cities of Salt. Trans. P. Theroux. London: Cape, 1988.

Endings. Trans. R. Allen. London; New York: Quartet, 1988.

The Trench. Trans. P. Theroux. New York: Pantheon Books, 1991.

Variations on Night and Day. Trans. P. Theroux. New York: Pantheon Books, 1993.

Biography and Criticism

Allen, *Modern Arabic Literature*. 224–228.

Allen, R. "'Al-Nihayat', 'Abd al-Rahman Munif." *The Arabic Novel: An Historical and Critical Introduction*. 2nd ed. Syracuse: Syracuse UP, 1995. 222–230.

———. "Munif, Abdelrahman." Serafin, *Encyclopedia of World Literature in the 20th Century*. Vol. 3. 321–322.

Badawi, M.M. "Two Novelists from Iraq: Jabra and Munif." *Journal of Arabic Literature* 23 (1992): 140–154.

Brennan, C. "Munif, Abdelrahman." *Contemporary Authors* 144 (1994): 316–318.

Hafez, S. "Munif, 'Abd al-Rahman." *Contemporary World Writers*. Ed. T. Chevalier. 2nd ed. Detroit: St. James, 1993. 367–369.

Hamarneh, W. "Munif, 'Abd al-Rahman." Meisami and Starkey, *Encyclopedia of Arabic Literature*. 550–551.

al-Muqaddasi, Muhammad ibn Ahmad, b. ca. 946

Web Sites

"Al-Muqaddasi: An Encyclopaedic Scholar." *MuslimHeritage.com*. http://www.muslimheritage.com/day_life/ (accessed 23 Aug. 2003).

Translations

The Best Divisions for Knowledge of the Regions. Trans. B.A. Collins. Rev. M.H. al-Tai. Reading, UK: Center for Muslim Contribution to Civilisation: Garnet, 1994.

Biography and Criticism

Ahmad, S.M. "al-Maqdisi, Shams al-Din Abu 'Abd Allah Muhammad ibn Ahmad ibn Abi Bakr al-Banna' al-Shami al-Maqdisi al-Bashshari." Gillispie, *Dictionary of Scientific Biography*. Vol. 9. 88–89.

Richter-Bernburg, L. "al-Muqaddasi." Meisami and Starkey, *Encyclopedia of Arabic Literature*. 551.

Musa, Nabawiyah, 1886–1951

Web Sites

"Nabawiya Moussa, Pioneer of Women Education in Egypt." *Egypt Magazine* 28 (2002). http://www.sis.gov.eg/public/magazine/iss028e/html/mag04.htm (accessed 23 Aug. 2003).

"Nabawya Moussa, Pioneer of Women's Education in Egypt." *Egypt*. http://www.sis.gov.eg/calendar/html/cl300498.htm (accessed 23 Aug. 2003).

Translations

Badran and Cooke, *Opening the Gates*. 257–269.

　　　Includes translations of "The Difference between Men and Women and Their Capacities for Work" and "The Effect of Books and Novels on Morals" by A. Badran and M. Badran.

Biography and Criticism

Booth, M. "Musa, Nabawiyya." Meisami and Starkey, *Encyclopedia of Arabic Literature*. 554.

Musa, Salamah, 1887–1958

Web Sites

"Salama Moussa, Prominent Man of Letters and Thinker." *Egypt.* http:// www.sis.gov.eg/calendar/html/cl040897.htm (accessed 23 Aug. 2003).

Autobiography

The Education of Salama Musa. Trans. L.O. Schuman. Leiden: Brill, 1961.

Biography and Criticism

Egger, V. *A Fabian in Egypt: Salamah Musa and the Rise of the Professional Classes in Egypt, 1909–1939.* Lanham: UP of America, 1986.

Mikhail, M. "Musa, Salama." Meisami and Starkey, *Encyclopedia of Arabic Literature*. 554–555.

al-Mutanabbi, Abu al-Tayyib Ahmad ibn al-Husayn, 915 or 916–965

Web Sites

"Mutanabi, Abul Tayyeb al-." *Damascus Online.* http://www.damascus-online.com/ se/bio/mutanabi.htm (accessed 23 Aug. 2003).

"Princeton Online Arabic Poetry." *Princeton Online Poetry Project.* 27 Jan. 2003. Princeton University. http://www.princeton.edu/~arabic/poetry/ (accessed 23 Aug. 2003).

   Short introduction, Arabic text and audio recitation of "To Sayf al-Dawla."

Translations

"al-Mutanabbi." Arberry, *Arabic Poetry*. 84–90.

"Mutanabbi of Madhhij." Tuetey, *Classical Arabic Poetry*. 264–268.

Poems of al-Mutanabbi. Trans. A.J. Arberry. London: Cambridge UP, 1967.

Biography and Criticism

Hamori, A. "Al-Mutanabbi." *'Abbasid Belles-Lettres.* Ed. J. Ashtiany, et al. Cambridge History of Arabic Literature. Cambridge: Cambridge UP, 1990. 300–314.

———. *The Composition of Mutanabbi's Panegyrics to Sayf al-Dawla.* Leiden: Brill, 1992.

Meisami, J.S. "al-Mutanabbi." Meisami and Starkey, *Encyclopedia of Arabic Literature*. 558–560.

Sharlet, J. "Al-Mutanabbi, Ahmad ibn al-Husayn Abu al-Tayyib al-Ju'fi al-Kindi." Pendergast and Pendergast, *Reference Guide to World Literature*. 29–30.

Zwettler, M. "Abu at-Tayyib Ahmad bin al-Husayn al-Mutanabbi." Atiyeh, *The Genius of Arab Civilization*. 80–82.

Nabarawi, Sayza, 1897–1985

Web Sites

"Siza Nabarawi, a Prominent Leader of Feminist Movement." *Egypt.* http://
www.sis.gov.eg/calendar/html/cl240298.htm (accessed 23 Aug. 2003).

Translations

"Double Standard." Trans. C. Petrey. Badran and Cooke, *Opening the Gates.*
279–281.

Biography and Criticism

Booth, M. "Nabarawi, Sayza." Meisami and Starkey, *Encyclopedia of Arabic
Literature.* 569.

al-Nafzawi, 'Umar ibn Muhammad, fl. 1410–1434

Web Sites

al-Nafzawi, 'U. ibn M. "The Perfumed Garden of the Shaykh Nefwazi." *Internet
Sacred Text Archive.* Ed. J.B. Hare. 22 Aug. 2003. http://www.sacred-texts.com/
sex/garden/index.htm (accessed 23 Aug. 2003).
Translation by Sir Richard Burton.

Translations

The Perfumed Garden of Sensual Delight. Trans. J. Colville. London: Kegan Paul,
1999.

The Perfumed Garden of the Cheikh Nefzaoui: A Manual of Arabian Erotology. Trans.
R.F. Burton. New York: New American Library, 1999.

Biography and Criticism

Kennedy, D., and B.E. Casari. "Burnt Offerings: Isabel Burton and 'The Scented
Garden' Manuscript." *Journal of Victorian Culture* 2 (1997): 229–244.

Rowson, E.K. "al-Nafzawi." Meisami and Starkey, *Encyclopedia of Arabic
Literature.* 572–573.

Naji, Ibrahim, 1898–1953

Web Sites

"Anniversary of Ibrahim Nagi." *Egypt.* http://www.sis.gov.eg/calendar/html/
cl250397.htm (accessed 23 Aug. 2003).

Magda's Night Gallery. Ed. Magda. Dec. 2002. http://www.geocities.com/SoHo/
Cafe/1324/naji.htm (accessed 23 Aug. 2003).
Includes four works by Ibrahim Naji: "The Burning Flute," "The Dream of
Infatuation," "Farewell," and "Oblivion."

Translations

"Burning Letters." Fairbairn and al-Gosaibi, *Feathers and the Horizon.* 116.

"The Return." Trans. A.J. Arberry. *Modern Arabic Poetry.* Cambridge: Cambridge
UP, 1967. 49.

Biography and Criticism

Allen, *Modern Arabic Literature.* 234–237.

Ostle, R.C. "Naji, Ibrahim." Meisami and Starkey, *Encyclopedia of Arabic Literature*. 576–577.

———. "Romantic Poetry and the Tradition: The Case of Ibrahim Nagi." *Arabicus Felix: Luminosus Britannicus: Essays in Honour of A.F.L. Beeston on His Eightieth Birthday*. Ed. A. Jones. Reading: Ithaca, 1991. 202–212.

Naqqash, Samir

Web Sites

Forget Baghdad: A Film by Samir. http://www.forgetbaghdad.com/index.php?topic=naqqashandlang=e (accessed 23 Aug. 2003).
   Web site for a film about four Iraqi-Jewish communists, including Naqqash.

Naqqash, S. Home Page. http://www.geocities.com/ruti_v/index.htm (accessed 23 Aug. 2003).
   Includes a biography, list of publications with short summaries, and bibliography of articles about him (largely in Arabic and Hebrew).

Autobiography and Interviews

"Signs in the Great Disorder: An Interviewed by Samir Naqqash." Interviewed by A. Alcalay. *Literary Review* 37 (1994): 195–205.

Biography and Criticism

Keys to the Garden: New Israeli Writing. Ed. A. Alcalay. San Francisco: City Lights, 1996. 100–111.
   Includes an interview and translations of "Prophesies of a Madman in a Cursed City" and excerpt from *The Angels' Genitalia*.

Nasif, Malak Hifni, 1886–1918

Web Sites

"Bahethat al Badia (The Scholar of the Desert), Malak Hefni Nassef." *Egypt*. http://www.sis.gov.eg/women/figures/html/malak.htm (accessed 23 Aug. 2003).

Nassef, M. "I Remember My Sister . . ." *Al-Ahram Weekly On-Line* 9–15 Mar. 2000. http://weekly.ahram.org.eg/2000/472/feat2.htm (accessed 23 Aug. 2003).

Translations

Badran and Cooke, *Opening the Gates*. 134–136, 227–238.
   Includes translations of "Bad Deeds of Men: Injustice" and "A Lecture in the Club of the Umma Party" by M. Badran and A. Badran.

Nasir, Amjad, 1955–

Web Sites

"Amjad Nasser." *Masthead* 7 (2003). http://au.geocities.com/masthead_2/issue7/nasser.html (accessed 23 Aug. 2003).
   Includes translations of "Old Radio," "Once Upon An Evening In a Café," and "Seven Bridges."

Nasser, A. "An Attempt at a Poem for New York." *Vert* 8 (2003). http://www.litvert.com/anasser.html (accessed 23 Aug. 2003).

Autobiography and Interviews

"The Arrival of a Stranger." Interviewed by M. Obank. *Banipal* 3 (1998): 63–67.

Translations

"The Arrival of the Strangers." Trans. S. Kawar. *Modern Poetry in Translation* 13 (1998): 133–134.

"Eleven Stars for Asia." Trans. Z. Khan. *Journal of Arabic Literature* 22 (1991): 146–147.

Nasir, Kamal, 1925–1973

Web Sites

"Kamal Nasir." *Barghouti.com*. http://www.barghouti.com/poets/kamal/ (accessed 23 Aug. 2003).
  Includes text and translation of "The Story."

Translations

"The Leaders of My Country." Asfour, *When the Words Burn*. 215.

"Letter to Fadwa." Trans. S. Elmusa and N.S. Nye. Jayyusi, *Anthology of Modern Palestinian Literature*. 236–237.

"Mona Lisa." Elmessiri, *The Palestinian Wedding*. 35–37.

Biography and Criticism

Nourallah, M.R. "Nasir, Kamal." Meisami and Starkey, *Encyclopedia of Arabic Literature*. 581.

Nasr Allah, Ibrahim, 1954–

Web Sites

Awadat, I. "Jordanian Poet Refuses Allegations of Blasphemy." *The Star* 17 Jan. 2001. http://www.arabia.com/jordan/life/article/english/0,5127,9299,00.html (accessed 23 Aug. 2003).

"Ibrahim Nasrallah." *Masthead* 7 (2003). http://au.geocities.com/masthead_2/issue7/nasrallah.html (accessed 23 Aug. 2003).
  Translations of "Bewildered," "Childhood," "Confession," "Days," "Freedom," "Homeland," and "Poets."

Translations

Jayyusi, *Anthology of Modern Palestinian Literature*. 238–243.
  Includes translations of "Flight," "The Hand," "Passageway," "Song," "Thread," and "A Woman" by L. Jayyusi and J. Reed.

Prairies of Fever. Trans. M. Jayyusi and J. Reed. New York: Interlink, 1993.

"Windows." Fairbairn and al-Gosaibi, *Feathers and the Horizon*. 118.

Nasr Allah, Imili, 1931–

Web Sites

Nasrallah, E. *The Lebanese Novelist Emily Nasrallah*. http://web.cyberia.net.lb/pnsralah/ (accessed 23 Aug. 2003).
  Includes biography, list of works, awards and prizes, and dissertations written about her.

Translations

"Explosion." Trans. T. Khalil-Khouri. *Literary Review* 37 (1994): 420–425.

Flight against Time. Trans. I.J. Boullata. Austin: Center for Middle Eastern Studies, U of Texas at Austin, 1997.

"The Lost Mill." Trans. I.J. Boullata. *Journal of Arabic Literature* 20 (1989): 31–35.

"Our Daily Bread." Trans. T. Khalil-Khouri. *Blood into Ink: South Asian and Middle Eastern Women Write War.* Ed. M. Cooke and R. Rustomji-Kerns. Boulder: Westview, 1994. 67–72.

"September Birds." Trans. M. Yacoubian and M. Cooke. Badran and Cooke, *Opening the Gates.* 144–154.

"Those Memories: From the Novel." Trans. M. Khazali. *Women and the Family in the Middle East: New Voices of Change.* Ed. E.W. Fernea. Austin: U of Texas P, 1985. 183–190.

Biography and Criticism

Cooke, M. "Nasr Allah, Imili (Emily)" Meisami and Starkey, *Encyclopedia of Arabic Literature.* 582.

al-Nawwab, Muzaffar, 1934–

Web Sites

al-Nawwab, M. "Muzaffar Al-Nawwab Remembers a Distant Childhood." Interviewed by S. Antoon. *Al-Ahram Weekly On-Line* 17–23 Apr. 2003. http://weekly.ahram.org.eg/2003/634/bsc7.htm (accessed 23 Aug. 2003).

"Poetry." *Iraq4u.com.* http://www.iraq4u.com/Poetry_search.asp (accessed 23 Aug. 2003).
   Listen to the author read his own poems (choose 3 or 4).

Biography and Criticism

Bardenstein, C. "Stirring Words: Traditions and Subversions in the Poetry of Muzaffar al-Nawwab." *Arab Studies Quarterly* 19.4 (1997): 37–63.

Hamad, W. "Muthaffar al-Nawwab: Portrait of a Poet, Activist, Painter, and, Above All, Humanist." *Arab Review* 3.1 (1994): 22–26.

Nu'aymah, Mikha'il, 1889–1989

Web Sites

"Mikhail Naimy." *Baskinta Online.* 18 Aug. 2003. http://www.baskinta.com/html/mikhael_nouymeh/mikhael.htm (accessed 23 Aug. 2003).
   Photos of the statue in his hometown in Lebanon.

Translations and English Texts

The Book of Mirdad, a Lighthouse and a Haven. Baltimore: Penguin, 1962.

Jayyusi, *Modern Arabic Poetry.* 93–94.
   Includes translations of "Seek Out Another Heart" and "To a Worm" by S. Boulos and T.G. Ezzy.

Khouri and Algar, *Anthology of Modern Arabic Poetry.* 27–35.
    Includes translations of "Autumn Leaves," "My Brother," "Peace of Mind," and "The Struggle."

Modern Arabic Poetry. Cambridge: Cambridge UP, 1967. 64–67.
    Includes translations of "Comrade!," "Now," and "The Tranquil Heart" by A.J. Arberry.

A New Year: Stories, Autobiography, and Poems. Trans. J.R. Perry. Leiden: Brill, 1974.

Biography and Criticism

Allen, *Modern Arabic Literature.* 237–244.

Boullata, I.J. "Mikhail Naimy: Poet of Meditative Vision." *Journal of Arabic Literature* 24 (1993): 173–184.

"Naimy, M." *Contemporary Authors* 124 (1988): 322.

Naimy, N. *The Lebanese Prophets of New York.* Beirut: American U of Beirut, 1985. 57–86.

Nijland, C. *Mikha'il Nu'aymah, Promoter of the Arabic Literary Revival.* Leiden: Nederlands Historisch-Archaeologisch Instituut te Istanbul, 1975.

———. "Nu'ayma, Mikha'il." Meisami and Starkey, *Encyclopedia of Arabic Literature.* 588–589.

———. "Nu'ayma, Mikha'il." Serafin, *Encyclopedia of World Literature in the 20th Century.* Vol. 3. 407–408.

Qabbani, Nizar, 1923–1998

Web Sites

Darwish, A. "Nizzar Qabbani: The Poet Who Challenged Arab Taboos." *MERIA News*, June 1998. http://www.biu.ac.il/SOC/besa/meria/news/1998/98news10.html#a1 (accessed 24 Aug. 2003).

Jehl, D. "Nizar Qabbani, Sensual Arab Poet, Dies at 75." *Middle East and Islamic Studies Collection, Cornell University.* http://www.library.cornell.edu/colldev/mideast/obit-qab.htm (accessed 24 Aug. 2003).

Magda's Night Gallery. Ed. Magda. Dec. 2002. http://www.geocities.com/SoHo/Cafe/1324/qabbani.htm (accessed 24 Aug. 2003).
    Includes the following works by Nizar Qabbani: "A Brief Love Letter," "Dialogue," "I Conquer the World with Words," "Jerusalem," "A Lesson in Drawing," "Love Compared," "On Entering the Sea," "When I Love," and "When I Love You."

Nizar Qabbani. http://www.nizar.net/english.htm (accessed 24 Aug. 2003).
    Biography and chronology of the poet's life, photos, bibliography of works, and translations of 21 poems.

"Nizar Qabbani." *Arab World Books.* http://www.arabworldbooks.com/authors/nizar_qabbani.html (accessed 24 Aug. 2003).

"Nizar Quabbani." *Books and Writers.* http://www.kirjasto.sci.fi/quabba.htm (accessed 24 Aug. 2003).

Qabbani, N. "Poetry Recital by Nizar Qabbani." *Digital Documentation Center.*
American University of Beirut. http://almashriq.hiof.no/ddc/projects/public/
qabbani/ (accessed 24 Aug. 2003).
Listen and watch the poet read his own work.

Woffenden, R., and M. Metwalli. "They Have Announced the Death of Nizar
Qabbani." *Cairo Times* 28 May 1998. http://www.cairotimes.com/content/
culture/qabbani.html (accessed 24 Aug. 2003).

Translations

Arabian Love Poems. Ed. and trans. B.K. Frangieh and C.R. Brown. Washington,
D.C.: Three Continents, 1993.

Asfour, *When the Words Burn*. 93–103.
Includes translations of "Bread, Hashish, and One Moon," "The Dictionary for
Lovers," "The Latest Book of Poems," "Love Compared," "Marginal Notes on the
Book of Defeat," "The Nipple," and "Unemployed."

Bennani, B., ed. and trans. *Bread, Hashish, and Moon*. Greensboro: Unicorn Press,
Inc., 1982. 5–14.
Includes translations of "Ancestral Remains," "Bread, Hashish and Moon,"
"Black Pearls," "Drawing with Words," "The Knight and the Rose," and "Schahriar's
Tears."

Bitar, F., ed. *Treasury of Arabic Love Poems, Quotations and Proverbs*. New York:
Hippocrene, 1996. 79–85.
Includes translations of "A Brief Love Letter," "Dialogue," and "To A Saint" by
M. Khouri and H. Algar.

Jayyusi, *Modern Arabic Poetry*. 371–379.
Includes translations of "The Child Scribbles," "Cup and Rose," "Equation,"
"Foolishness," "Fragments from Notes on the Book of Defeat," "From The Actors,"
"I Conquer the World with Words," "Introduction to Painting with Words," "Lan-
guage," "Poems," "Testament," and "Two African Breasts" by D. Der Hovanessian
and L. Jayyusi (first trans.).

Khouri and Algar, *Anthology of Modern Arabic Poetry*. 161–195.
Includes translations of "A Brief Love Letter," "Bread, Hashish and Moonlight,"
"Pregnant," "To A Saint," "What Value Has the People Whose Tongue Is Tied?," and
"The Whore."

Literary Review 37 (1994): 498–505.
Includes a translation of "Beirut! O Queen of the World" by M.T. Amyuni and
translations of "I Wear You," "The Orange," "When You Find a Man," "With a Newspaper," and "You Are So Beautiful That" by B. Frangieh.

On Entering the Sea: the Erotic and Other Poetry of Nizar Qabbani. Trans. L. Jayyusi
and S. Elmusa. New York: Interlink, 1995.

"Poems." Trans. L. Jayyusi and W.S. Merwin. Jayyusi, *Modern Arabic Poetry*.
368–371.

Republic of Love: Selected Poems in English and Arabic. Trans. N. al-Kalali. Ed. L.
Kavchak. London: Kegan Paul, 2003.

al-Udhari, *Modern Poetry of the Arab World*. 97–104.
>Includes "Footnotes to the Book of the Setback," "I am the Train of Sadness," "Morphine," and "The Ruler and the Sparrow."

Biography and Criticism

Allen, *Modern Arabic Literature*. 244–249.

Boullata, I.J. "Qabbani, Nizar." Meisami and Starkey, *Encyclopedia of Arabic Literature*. 625–626.

———. "Qabbani, Nizar." Serafin, *Encyclopedia of World Literature in the 20th Century*. Vol. 3. 617.

Buturovich, A. "'Only Women and Writing Can Save Us from Death': Erotic Empowering in the Poetry of Nizar Qabbani (d. 1998)." *Tradition, Modernity, and Postmodernity in Arabic Literature: Essays in Honor of Professor Issa J. Boullata*. Ed. K. Abdel-Malek and W. Hallaq. Brill: Leiden, 2000. 141–157.

Loloi, P. "Qabbani, Nizar." *Contemporary World Writers*. Ed. T. Chevalier. 2nd ed. Detroit, Mich.: St. James, 1993. 420–421.

Wild, S. "Nizar Qabbani's Autobiography: Images of Sexuality, Death and Poetry." *Love and Sexuality in Modern Arabic Literature*. Ed. R. Allen, H. Kilpatrick, and E. de Moor. London: Saqi, 1995. 200–209.

Qasim Amin, 1863–1908

Web Sites

Qasim Amin. "Qasim Amin." *History of the Middle East Database*. Ed. T. Thornton. 13 Aug. 2003. http://www.nmhschool.org/tthornton/mehistorydatabase/qasim_amin.htm (accessed 24 Aug. 2003).
>Short extract from *The New Woman*.

"Qassem Ameen." *Egypt*. http://www.us.sis.gov.eg/egyptianfigures/html/kassem.htm (accessed 24 Aug. 2003).
>A summary of his book *The New Woman* can be read at http://www.sis.gov.eg/eginfnew/html/briview.html.

Translations

The Liberation of Women; and, The New Woman: Two Documents in the History of Egyptian Feminism. Trans. S.S. Peterson. Cairo: American U in Cairo P, 2000.

"Nanny Karima and the Hammam." Trans. M. Wahba. Rev. R. Ewart. Manzalaoui, *Arabic Short Stories*. 108–116.

Biography and Criticism

Zebiri, K. "Amin, Qasim." Meisami and Starkey, *Encyclopedia of Arabic Literature*. 86–87.

al-Qasim, Samih, 1939–

Web Sites

al-Qasim, S. "Report of a Bankrupt." *Salam Review*. http://leb.net/bcome/culture/poem5.html (accessed 24 Aug. 2003).

"Palestinian Poets, Samih el Qasim." *Khalil Sakakini Cultural Centre*. http://www.sakakini.org/poets/samih-index.htm (accessed 24 Aug. 2003).
Includes translations of "Ashes" and "Bats."

Translations

Asfour, *When the Words Burn*. 201–207.
Includes translations of "Come, Together We Shall Draw a Rainbow," "Descent," "The Eucharist of Failure," "I Love You as Death Wishes," "So," and "A Speech in the Unemployment Market."

Elmessiri, *The Palestinian Wedding*. 33+.
Includes "The Eternal Fire," "A Homeland," "Joseph," "Kafr Qasim," "Letter from a Prison Camp," "The Man Who Visited Death," "The Thunderbird," "To Najib Mahfuz," and "The Unruly Horse."

Jayyusi, *Anthology of Modern Palestinian Literature*. 254–261.
Includes "Ashes," "Bats," "The Clock," "Drunk," "I Do Not Blame You," "Love Poems," and "You Pretend to Die" by S. Elmusa and N.S. Nye.

———, *Modern Arabic Poetry*. 380–385.
Includes a translation of "From: After the Apocalypse" by S. Elmusa and N.S. Nye and a translation of "Girl from Rafah" by S. Elmusa and C. Doria.

"Resignation from the Death Insurance Company." Boullata, *Modern Arab Poets*. 117–118.

Victims of a Map. London: Al Saqi, 1984. 50–85.
Includes translations by A. al-Udhari of "Abandoning," "Bats," "The Boring Orbit," "The Clock on the Wall," "Confession at Midday," "Conversation Between an Ear of Corn and a Jerusalem Rose Thorn," "End of a Discussion with a Jailer," "Eternity," "How I Became an Article," "Slit Lips," "Sons of War," "The Story of a City," "The Story of the Unknown Man," "Travel Tickets," and "The Will of a Man Dying in Exile."

Biography and Criticism

Allen, *Modern Arabic Literature*. 253–256.

Caspi, M.M., and J.D. Weltsch. *From Slumber to Awakening: Culture and Identity of Arab Israeli Literati*. Lanham, Md.: UP of America, 1998. 51–54.

Suleiman, Y. "al-Qasim, Samih." Meisami and Starkey, *Encyclopedia of Arabic Literature*. 634.

Taha, I. *The Palestinian Novel: A Communication Study*. London: RoutledgeCurzon, 2002. 87–104.

al-Qasimi, Maysun Saqr

Web Sites

"About Maisoon in English." *Arab World Books*. http://www.arabworldbooks.com/authors/maisoon_saqr.htm#english (accessed 24 Aug. 2003).

"Maisoon Saqr al-Kasimi." *World's Women On-Line!* Ed. M. Magenta. http://wwol.is.asu.edu/al-kasimi.html (accessed 24 Aug. 2003).

Al-Qasimi is an artist as well as a writer. This page exhibits one of her works of art.

Translations

"Cycle." Trans. D. Der Hovanessian and L. Jayyusi (first trans.). *The Literature of Modern Arabia: An Anthology.* Ed. S.K. Jayyusi. London: Kegan Paul International, 1988. 168–170.

Handal, *The Poetry of Arab Women.* 249–251.

Includes a translation of "The Morning of Every Sin" by S. Hadidi and translations of "The Cusp of Desire" and "A Dream Recalling a Temptation" by S. Hadidi and N. Handal.

al-Qusaybi, Ghazi 'Abd al-Rahman, 1940–

Web Sites

"Ghazi al-Gosaibi." *Jehat.com.* http://www.jehat.com/en/ default.asp?action=article&ID=84 (accessed 21 Apr. 2004).

Includes translations of the poems "Octopus," "When I Am With You," "Silence," "Oh Desert," and an essay, "Arabic Poetry: A Glimpse into the Soul."

al-Qusaybi, G. 'Abd al-R. "Science, Ethics, and Alternative Visions." Interviewed by E. Masood. *Nature.com.* http://www.nature.com/wcs/c07.html (accessed 24 Aug. 2003).

Al-Qusaybi has also been a diplomat, and it is in this capacity that this interview was conducted.

Saudi Arabian Information Resource. http://www.saudinf.com/main/r1.htm (accessed 24 Aug. 2003).

Includes "A Song" and "Your Eyes."

Autobiography and Interviews

"A True Poet Has to Be Classical and Romantic and a Realist." *Banipal* 5 (1999): 16–19.

Translations and English Texts

An Apartment Called Freedom: A Novel. Trans. L. McLoughlin. London: Kegan Paul International; New York: Distributed by Columbia UP, 1996.

Arabian Essays. London: Kegan Paul International, 1982.

The Dilemma of Development. Trans. L. McLoughlin. Reading: Garnet, 1995.

Dusting the Color from Roses: A Bilingual Collection of Arabic Poetry. Trans. A.A. Ruffai. Rev. H. Lawton. London: Echoes, 1995.

From the Orient and the Desert: Poems. London: Kegan Paul International, 1994.

The Gulf Crisis: An Attempt to Understand. London: Kegan Paul International, 1993.

Jayyusi, S.K., ed. *The Literature of Modern Arabia: An Anthology.* London: Kegan Paul International, 1988. 88–96.

Includes translations of "Little Thoughts," "Love and Black Harbours," "Song in a Tropical Night," and "Your Loving" by S. Boulus and J. Heath-Stubbs.

Love Story. Trans. R. Bray. London: Saqi, 2002.

Seven. Trans. B. Hatim and G. Watterson. London: Saqi, 1999.

Qutb, Sayyid, 1903–1966

Web Sites

Bangash, Z. "Remembering Sayyid Qutb, an Islamic Intellectual and Leader of Rare Insight and Integrity." *Muslimedia* 1–15 Sept. 1999. http://www.muslimedia.com/archives/features99/qutb.htm (accessed 24 Aug. 2003).

Irwin, R. "Is This the Man Who Inspired Bin Laden?" *Guardian* 1 Nov. 2001. http://www.guardian.co.uk/g2/story/0,3604,584478,00.html (accessed 24 Aug. 2003).

Thornton, T. "Sayyid Qutb." *History of the Middle East Database*. Ed. T. Thornton. http://www.nmhschool.org/tthornton/sayyid_qutb.htm (accessed 24 Aug. 2003).

  Includes excerpts from his writings on women and a link to the translation of his book *Milestones*, which can be read at http://www.youngmuslims.ca/online_library/books/milestones/.

Translations

Sayyid Qutb and Islamic Activism: A Translation and Critical Analysis of Social Justice in Islam. Trans. W.E. Shepard. Leiden: Brill, 1996.

Biography and Criticism

Abu-Rabi, I.M. *Intellectual Origins of Islamic Resurgence in the Modern Arab World*. Albany: State U of New York P, 1996.

Akhavi, S. "Qutb, Sayyid." *Oxford Encyclopedia of the Modern Islamic World*. Ed. J.L. Esposito. New York: Oxford UP, 1995. Vol. 3. 400–404.

Carre, O. *Mysticism and Politics: A Critical Reading of 'Fi Zilal al-Qur'an' by Sayyid Qutb* (1906–1966). Trans. C. Artigues. Rev. W. Shepard. Leiden: Brill, 2003.

Tripp, C. "Sayyid Qutb: The Political Vision." *Pioneers of Islamic Revival*. Ed. A. Rahnema. London: Zed, 1994. 154–183.

Zebiri, K. "Qutb, Sayyid." Meisami and Starkey, *Encyclopedia of Arabic Literature*. 642.

Rabi'ah al-'Adawiyah, d. 801?

Web Sites

"Princeton Online Arabic Poetry." *Princeton Online Poetry Project*. 27 Jan. 2003. Princeton University. http://www.princeton.edu/~arabic/poetry/ (accessed 23 Aug. 2003).
  Short introduction, Arabic text and audio recitation of "My Cup and My Wine."

"Rabi'a al-'Adawiyya/Rabi'ah." *Other Women's Voices*. Ed. D. Disse. 6 May 2003. http://www.akron.infi.net/~ddisse/rabia.html (accessed 24 Aug. 2003).
  Includes links to translations and articles and poems from print sources.

Translations

Doorkeeper of the Heart: Versions of Rabi'a. Trans. C. Upton. Putney: Threshold, 1988.

"Raabi'a al-Adwiyya." Trans. A. al-Udhari. *Classical Poems by Arab Women*. London: Saqi Books, 1999. 102–104.

Biography and Criticism

El Sakkakini, W. *First Among Sufis: The Life and Thought of Rabia al-Adawiyya, the Woman Saint of Basra.* Trans. N. Safwat. London: Octagon, 1982.

Helms, B.L. "Rabi'ah as Mystic, Muslim and Woman." *Annual Review of Women in World Religions* 3 (1994): 1–87.

Radtke, B. "Rabi'a al-'Adawiyya." Meisami and Starkey, *Encyclopedia of Arabic Literature.* 643.

Sells, M.A. "Rabi'a al-Adawiyya." McGreal, *Great Thinkers of the Eastern World.* 435–438.

Smith, M. *Rabi'a: The Life and Work of Rabi'a and Other Women Mystics in Islam.* Oxford: Oneworld, 1994.

al-Rafi'i, Mustafa Sadiq, d. 1937

Web Sites

"Mustafa Sadeq Al-Rafei." *Egypt.* http://www.us.sis.gov.eg/egyptianfigures/html/Rafei.htm (accessed 24 Aug. 2003).

Translations

"Soliloquy to the Moon." Trans. A. Afsaruddin. *Edebiyat*, n.s., 7 (1996): 105–114.

Biography and Criticism

Eliraz, G. "The Social and Cultural Conception of Mustafa Sadik al-Rafi'i." *African and Asian Studies* 13 (1979): 101–129.

Mikhail, M. "al-Rafi'i, Mustafa Sadiq." Meisami and Starkey, *Encyclopedia of Arabic Literature.* 644.

al-Razi, Abu Bakr Muhammad ibn Zakariya, 865?–925?

Web Sites

"Abu Bakr Mohammad Ibn Zakariya Razi (-al)" *Malaspina Great Books.* http://www.malaspina.com/site/person_981.asp (accessed 24 Aug. 2003).

"Muhammad ibn Zakariya al-Razi: A Life." Aftab, M.A. Home Page. http://umcc.ais.org/~maftab/ip/hmp/XII-TwentyTwo.pdf (accessed 24 Aug. 2003). Chapter on al-Razi from Sharif, M.M., ed. *A History of Muslim Philosophy.* 2 vols. (Wiesbaden: Harrassowitz, 1963–1966).

"al-Razi." *The Window: Philosophy on the Internet.* Ed. C. Marvin and F. Sikernitsky. http://caribou.cc.trincoll.edu/depts_phil/philo/phils/muslim/razi.html (accessed 24 Aug. 2003).

al-Razi, M. ibn Z. "The Spiritual Physick (Healing)." *CIE Council on Islamic Education.* http://www.cie.org/pdffiles/smplls05.pdf (accessed 24 Aug. 2003). Translation of the section "Of Repelling Anger" from *The Spiritual Physick of Rhazes.* Trans. A.J. Arberry (London: Murray, 1950).

"Al-Razi, the Clinician." *Islamic Culture and the Medical Arts.* Ed. E. Savage-Smith. National Library of Medicine. http://www.nlm.nih.gov/exhibition/islamic_medical/islamic_06.html (accessed 24 Aug. 2003).

Tadjbaksh, H. "The Life of Muhammad Ibn Zakariya Razi and the Discovery of Allergic Asthma." *Iranian Journal of Allergy Asthma & Immunology* 1.1 (2000). http://www.netiran.com/Htdocs/Clippings/Social/200131XXSO04.html (accessed 24 Aug. 2003).

Walker, P.E. "al-Razi, Abu Bakr Muhammad ibn Zakariyya'." *Islamic Philosophy Online*. http://www.muslimphilosophy.com/ip/rep/H043.htm (accessed 28 Aug. 2003).

Translations

"Abu Bakr Muhammad Zakariyya' Razi." *An Anthology of Philosophy in Persia*. Ed. S.H. Nasr with M. Aminrazavi. 2 vols. New York: Oxford UP, 1999. Vol. 1. 353–373.

Biography and Criticism

Butterworth, C.E. "Abu Bakr al-Razi." McGreal, *Great Thinkers of the Eastern World*. 443–445.

Endress, G. "al-Razi, Abu Bakr Muhammad ibn Zakariyya." Meisami and Starkey, *Encyclopedia of Arabic Literature*. 648–649.

Goodman, L.E. "Muhammad ibn Zakariyya' al-Razi." Nasr and Leaman, *History of Islamic Philosophy*. 198–215.

Hamarneh, S.K. "Abu Bakr Muhammad bin Zakariya ar-Razi." Atiyeh, *The Genius of Arab Civilization*. 224.

Iskandar, A.Z. "Al-Razi." *Religion, Learning and Science in the 'Abbasid Period*. Ed. M.J.L. Young, J.D. Latham, and R.B. Serjeant. Cambridge History of Arabic Literature. Cambridge: Cambridge UP, 1990. 370–377.

Pines, S. "al-Razi, Abu Bakr Muhammad ibn Zakariyya." Gillispie, *Dictionary of Scientific Biography*. Vol. 11. 323–326.

Stroumsa, S. *Freethinkers of Medieval Islam: Ibn al-Rawandi, Abu Bakr al-Razi and Their Impact on Islamic Thought*. Leiden: Brill, 1999.

al-Razi, Fakhr al-Din Muhammad ibn 'Umar, 1149 or 1150–1210

Web Sites

Cooper, J. "al-Razi, Fakhr al-Din." *Islamic Philosophy Online*. http://www.muslimphilosophy.com/ip/rep/H044.htm (accessed 24 Aug. 2003).

"Fakhr al-Din al-Razi." *Center for Islam and Science*. http://www.cis-ca.org/voices/r/alRazi-Fakhr%20al-Din.htm (accessed 24 Aug. 2003).

al-Razi, F. al-D.M. ibn 'U. "Imam Razi's 'Ilm al-Akhlaq." Aftab, M.A. Home Page. http://umcc.ais.org/~maftab/ip/pdf/bktxt/razi-akhlak.pdf (accessed 24 Aug. 2003).
Translation of his book on ethics.

Biography and Criticism

Netton, I. and J.S. Meisami. "Fakhr al-Din al-Razi, Abu 'Abd Allah Muhammad ibn 'Umar." Meisami and Starkey, *Encyclopedia of Arabic Literature*. 217.

Rif'at, Alifah

Web Sites

"Alifa Rifaat (Egypt)" *African Writers Series*. http://www.africanwriters.com/
Writers/WriterTop.asp?cPK=RifaatAlifa (accessed 24 Aug. 2003).

Poulakis, V. "Study Guide for Alifa Rifaat's 'My World of the Unknown.'" Poulakis,
V. Home Page. http://www.nv.cc.va.us/home/vpoulakis/Rifaat.htm (accessed 24
Aug. 2003).

Introduction and study questions to this short story, for a class on world literature at Northern Virginia Community College.

Translations

"Another Evening at the Club." Johnson-Davies, *Arabic Short Stories*. 68–74.

Badran and Cooke, *Opening the Gates*. 72–83.

Includes translations of "Honour" and "Who Will Be the Man?" by E. Gold-
wasser and M. Cooke.

Distant View of a Minaret and Other Stories. Trans. D. Johnson-Davies. London:
Quartet, 1983.

"My Wedding Night." *An Arabian Mosaic: Short Stories by Arab Women Writers*.
Trans. D. Cohen-Mor. Potomac, Md.: Sheba, 1993. 23–32.

"My World of the Unknown." Trans. D. Johnson-Davies. *The HarperCollins World
Reader: The Modern World*. Ed. M.A. Case and C. Prendergast. New York:
HarperCollins, 1994. 1698–1708.

Biography and Criticism

Sheble, R. "Rifaat, Alifa." Gikandi, *Encyclopedia of African Literature*. 462.

Rifqah, Fu'ad, 1930–

Web Sites

"Fuad Rifqa." *Masthead* 7 (2003). http://au.geocities.com/masthead_2/issue7/
rifqa.html (accessed 21 Apr. 2004).

Includes translations of "At the Edge of the Tower," "A Garden," "Morning
Star," "Oak Tree," "Oil Lamp," "Sadness," "Siesta," "A Spark," "A Thought," "Wedding," and "A Wish."

Translations

Jayyusi, *Modern Arabic Poetry*. 388–390.

Includes translations of "The Fortune Teller," "Mirrors," and "The Threshold"
by S. Boulus and S. Hazo.

Literary Review 37 (1994): 515–518.

Includes translations of "Address Unknown," "Another Picking Season," "In
Tubingen," "Note from a Soldier," and "A Song for the Evening" by N. Nasr.

al-Udhari, *Modern Poetry of the Arab World*. 83–84.

Includes "An Elegy for Holderlin," "Setting Off," and "Straw Mat."

Rihani, Ameen Fares, 1876–1940

Web Sites

Ameen F. Rihani. 17 July 2003. *Ameen Rihani Organization.* http://
www.ameenrihani.org/ (accessed 24 Aug. 2003).
Extensive site includes biography, bibliography, quotations, museum, portraits,
and excerpts from his works in English and Arabic.

Bushrui, S.F. "The Thought and Works of Ameen Rihani." *Al-Hewar Center: The
Center for Arab Culture and Dialogue.* Ed. S. Ghandour. http://
www.alhewar.com/Bushrui_Rihani.html (accessed 24 Aug. 2003).

Kennicott, P. "For Writer Ameen Rihani, a Postscript and an Introduction." *Middle
East and Islamic Studies Collection, Cornell University.* http://
www.library.cornell.edu/colldev/mideast/amrihn.htm (accessed 24 Aug. 2003).

Saldana, S. "Trying to Bridge Two Great Civilizations." *American Middle-Eastern
Association Founded by Lebanese Internet Developers.* http://amalid.com/
the_beauty_of_arab_culture/
Amin_Rihani_Trying_to_bridge_two_great_civilizations.htm (accessed 24
Aug. 2003).

Translations and English Texts

Arabian Peak and Desert: Travels in al-Yaman. Boston: Houghton Mifflin, 1930.

Around the Coasts of Arabia. Boston: Houghton Mifflin, 1930.

The Book of Khalid. New York: Dodd, Mead, 1911.

Hymns of the Valleys. Trans. H.B. Oueijan. Piscataway: Gorgias, 2002.

Ibn Sa'oud of Arabia. London: Kegan Paul, 2002.

"Light." Khouri and Algar, *An Anthology of Modern Arabic Poetry.* 25.

Biography and Criticism

Allen, *Modern Arabic Literature.* 256–259.

Naimy, N. *The Lebanese Prophets of New York.* Beirut: American U of Beirut, 1985.
11–34.

Nijland, C. "al-Rihani, Amin." Meisami and Starkey, *Encyclopedia of Arabic
Literature.* 662–663.

al-Rimawi, Mahmud, 1948–

Web Sites

al-Rimawi, M. "Two Short-Stories." *Autodafe: The Censored Library.* July 2003.
International Parliament of Writers. http://www.autodafe.org/bookshop/
palestine/al-rimawi.htm (accessed 24 Aug. 2003).
Translations of "Curse" and "A Pleasant Get Together."

Translations

"A Longing for the Good Land." Trans. O. Kenny and T.G. Ezzy. Jayyusi, *Anthology
of Modern Palestinian Literature.* 510–515.

Sa'adah, Antun, 1904–1949

Web Sites

"Syrian Social Nationalist Party." *Fertile Crescent Home Page.* Ed. Cadmus. http://
     leb.net/~fchp/antun.htm (accessed 25 Aug. 2003).
     Includes numerous articles about and translations of writings by Sa'adah.

Al-Zawba'ah. Ed. E. Melhem. http://home.iprimus.com.au/fidamelhem/SSNP/
     (accessed 25 Aug. 2003).
     Site devoted to Sa'adah and the Syrian Socialist National Party. Not well orga-
nized, but lots of information and many translations of speeches and articles by
Sa'adah.

Biography and Criticism

Sluglett, P.J. "Sa'ada, Antun." Meisami and Starkey, *Encyclopedia of Arabic
     Literature.* 669.

Al-Sabah, S.M., 1942–

Web Sites

Al-Sabah, S.M. *Magda's Night Gallery.* Ed. Magda. Dec. 2002. http://
     www.geocities.com/SoHo/Cafe/1324/suad.htm (accessed 14 Aug. 2003).
     Includes translations of "Free Harbor," "Mad Woman," "A Wild Cat," and "You
Alone."

"Poetry." Trans. S. Ghanem. *Al Shindagh* 36 (2000). http://www.alshindagah.com/
     sept2000/poetry.htm (accessed 14 Aug. 2003).
     Translation of "Female 2000."

Translations

*Development Planning in an Oil Economy and the Role of Women: The Case of
     Kuwait.* London: Eastlords, 1983.

Jayyusi, S.K., ed. *The Literature of Modern Arabia: An Anthology.* London: Kegan
     Paul International, 1988. 185–188.
     Includes translations of "A Covenant," "Free Harbour," "A New Definition of
the Third World," "Sojourn Forever," "A Thousand Times More Beautiful," and "You
Alone" by S. Jabsheh and J. Heath-Stubbs.

Biography and Criticism

Michalak-Pikulska, B. "Su'ad al-Sabah: in the Beginning was the Female." *Folia
     Orientalia* 34 (1998): 129–140.

Sabri, Isma'il, 1854–1923

Web Sites

"Ismail Sabri Pasha, Prominent Egyptian Poet." *Egypt.* http://www.sis.gov.eg/online/
     html6/o200322m.htm (accessed 25 Aug. 2003).

Translations

"Conversing His Heart." Trans. F. Bitar. *Treasury of Arabic Love Poems, Quotations,
     and Proverbs.* Ed. F. Bitar. New York: Hippocrene, 1996. 43.

Biography and Criticism

Sadgrove, P.C. "Sabri Pasha, Isma'il." Meisami and Starkey, *Encyclopedia of Arabic Literature*. 673.

al-Sa'dawi, Nawal, 1931–

Web Sites

Arab Culture and Civilization. Ed. M. Toler. National Institute for Technology and Liberal Education. http://www.nitle.org/arabworld/main_menu.php (accessed 25 Aug. 2003).
    Use the Search box to find a seven-part video interview of al-Sa'dawi and her husband, Sharif Hatatah, on the status of women in the Arab world and the changes due to globalization.

Belton, B., and C. Dowding. "Nawal el Saadawi, a Creative and Dissident Life." *Infed.org*. Ed. M.K. Smith. 3 Apr. 2003. http://www.infed.org/thinkers/et-saadawi.htm (accessed 25 Aug. 2003).

"Dr. Nawal el-Saadawi." *Contemporary Africa Database*.17 June 2003. Africa Centre. http://www.africaexpert.org/people/data/person2437.html (accessed 25 Aug. 2003).
    Includes profiles and links to articles about and by her, excerpts from some of her books, book reviews, and other material.

"An Introduction to Nawal el Saadawi." *Two Eyes* 1 (2000). http://home.earthlink.net/~twoeyesmagazine/issue1/nesintro.htm (accessed 25 Aug. 2003).
    Includes an interview by Stephanie McMillan.

Malti-Douglas, F. *Men, Women, and God(s): Nawal El Saadawi and Arab Feminist Poetics*. Berkeley: U of California P, 1995. http://ark.cdlib.org/ark:/13030/ft8c6009n4 (accessed 25 Aug. 2003).

McBride, J. "Nawal Saadawi." *Women's Intellectual Contributions to the Study of Mind and Society*. Ed. L.M. Woolf. http://www.webster.edu/~woolflm/saadawi.html (accessed 25 Aug. 2003).

"Nawal Al Sadawi." *Cairo Times* 10 July 1997. http://www.cairotimes.com/content/people/nawal.html (accessed 25 Aug. 2003).

"Nawal El Saadawi." *Books and Writers*. http://www.kirjasto.sci.fi/sadawi.htm (accessed 25 Aug. 2003).

Nawal El Saadawi, Sherif Hetata. 11 June 2003. http://www.nawalsaadawi.net/index.html (accessed 25 Aug. 2003).
    Includes photos, biographies, articles by and about the author and her husband Sharif Hatatah.

Autobiography and Interviews

"Alone with Pen and Paper." *In the House of Silence: Autobiographical Essays by Arab Women Writers*. Ed. F. Faqir. Trans. S. Eber and F. Faqir. Reading: Garnet, 1998. 111–118.

A Daughter of Isis: The Autobiography of Nawal El Saadawi. Trans. S. Hetata. London: Zed; New York: Distributed by St. Martin's P, 1999.

Memoirs from the Women's Prison. Trans. M. Booth. London: Women's P, 1986.

Memoirs of a Woman Doctor. Trans. C. Cobham. London: Saqi, 1988.

My Travels around the World. Trans. S. Eber. London: Methuen, 1991.

"An Overview of My Life." Trans. A. Tuma. *Contemporary Authors Autobiography Series* 11 (1990): 61–72.

"Reflections of a Feminist." Interviewed by F. Malti-Douglas and A. Douglas. Badran and Cooke, *Opening the Gates.* 394–404.

Walking Through Fire: A Life of Nawal El Saadawi. Trans. S. Hetata. London: Zed; New York: Distributed by Palgrave, 2002.

Translations

The Circling Song. Trans. M. Booth. London: Zed, 1989.

Death of an Ex-Minister. Trans. S. Eber. London: Methuen, 1987.

The Fall of the Imam. Trans. S. Hetata. London: Zed, 1988.

God Dies by the Nile. Trans. S. Hetata. London: Zed, 1985.

The Hidden Face of Eve: Women in the Arab World. Trans. and ed. S. Hetata. London: Zed, 1980.

The Innocence of the Devil. Trans. S. Hetata. Berkeley: U of California P, 1994.

Love in the Kingdom of Oil. Trans. B. Hatim and M. Williams. London: Saqi, 2001.

The Nawal El Saadawi Reader. London: Zed; New York: Distributed by St. Martin's P, 1997.

Searching. Trans. S. Eber. London: Zed, 1991.

She Has No Place in Paradise. Trans. S. Eber. London: Methuen, 1987.

Two Women in One. Trans. O. Nusairi and J. Gough. London: Saqi, 1985.

The Well of Life; and The Thread: Two Short Novels. Trans. S. Hetata. London: Lime Tree, 1993.

Woman at Point Zero. Trans. S. Hetata. London: Zed, 1983.

"Women and Sex." Trans. D.L. Bowen. *Everyday Life in the Muslim Middle East.* Ed. D.L. Bowen and E.A. Early. Bloomington: Indiana UP, 1993. 81–83.

"Women's Resistance in the Arab World and in Egypt." *Women in the Middle East: Perceptions, Realities, and Struggles for Liberation.* Ed. H. Afshar. New York: St. Martin's P, 1993. 139–145.

Biography and Criticism

Amireh, A. "Framing Nawal El Saadawi: Arab Feminism in a Transnational World." *Intersections: Gender, Nation, and Community in Arab Women's Novels.* Ed. L.S. Majaj, P.W. Sunderman, and T. Saliba. Syracuse: Syracuse UP, 2002. 33–67.

Booth, M. "al-Sa'dawi, Nawal." Meisami and Starkey, *Encyclopedia of Arabic Literature.* 673–674.

———. "al-Sa'dawi, Nawal." Serafin, *Encyclopedia of World Literature in the 20th Century.* Vol. 4. 5–6.

"El Saadawi, Nawal." *Contemporary Authors New Revision Series* 92 (2001): 124–128.

Evans, N.H. "El Saadawi, Nawal." *Contemporary Authors* 118 (1986): 143–144.

Hafez, S. "Sa'dawi, Nawal al-." *Contemporary World Writers*. Ed. T. Chevalier. 2nd ed. Detroit: St. James, 1993. 450–451.

Manisty, D. "Nawal al-Sa'adawi, 1931–." *African Writers*. Ed. C.B. Cox. New York: Charles Scribner's Sons, 1997. 721–731.

Mikhail, M.N. "el-Saadawi, Nawal." Gikandi, *Encyclopedia of African Literature*. 469–471.

Royer, D. *A Critical Study of the Works of Nawal El Saadawi, Egyptian Writer and Activist*. Lewiston: Mellen, 2001.

Salti, R.M. "Paradise, Heaven and Other Oppressive Spaces: A Critical Examination of the Life and Works of Nawal el-Saadawi." *Journal of Arabic Literature* 25 (1994): 152–174.

Speace, G.J. "El Saadawi, Nawal." *Contemporary Authors New Revision Series* 44 (1994): 123–126.

Tarabishi, G. *Woman against Her Sex: A Critique of Nawal el-Saadawi*. Trans. B. Hatim and E. Orsini. London: Saqi, 1988.

Zuhur, S. "'Woman at Point Zero' by Nawal El Saadawi." *African Literature and Its Times*. Ed. J. Moss and L. Valestuk. World Literature and Its Times 2. Detroit: Gale, 2000. 493–502.

Sadr al-Din Shirazi, Muhammad ibn Ibrahim, d. 1641

Web Sites

Cooper, J. "Mulla Sadra (Sadr al-Din Muhammad al-Shirazi)." *Islamic Philosophy Online*. http://www.muslimphilosophy.com/ip/rep/H027.htm (accessed 25 Aug. 2003).

Kalin, I. "Sadr al-Din Shirazi (Mulla Sadra)." *Center for Islam and Science*. http://www.cis-ca.org/voices/s/sadra.htm (accessed 25 Aug. 2003).

McLean, G.F. *Ways to God: Personal and Social at the Turn of the Millennia: The Iqbal Lecture, Lahore*. Washington, D.C.: Council for Research in Values and Philosophy, 1999. http://www.crvp.org/book/Series01/I-17/contents.htm (accessed 25 Aug. 2003).
Chapter 7 deals with Sadr al-Din Shirazi.

"Sadr Al-Din Mohammad Shirazi." *IranChamber.com*. http://www.iranchamber.com/personalities/msadra/mulla_sadra.php (accessed 25 Aug. 2003).

SIPRIn: Sadra Islamic Philosophy Research Institute. http://www.mullasadra.org (accessed 25 Aug. 2003).
Includes biography, list of works, and articles about him.

Translations

The Metaphysics of Mulla Sadra: Kitab al-Mashahir, The Book of Metaphysical Prehensions. Trans. P. Morewedge. New York: SSIPS, 1992.

Biography and Criticism

Aminrazavi, M. "Mulla Sadra (Sadr al-Din Shirazi)" McGreal, *Great Thinkers of the Eastern World*. 484–488.

Cooper, J. "Mulla Sadra." Meisami and Starkey, *Encyclopedia of Arabic Literature*. 549.

Morris, J.W. *The Wisdom of the Throne: An Introduction to the Philosophy of Mulla Sadra*. Princeton: Princeton UP, 1981.

Nasr, S.H. "Mulla Sadra: His Teachings." Nasr and Leaman, *History of Islamic Philosophy*. 643–662.

Rahman, F. *The Philosophy of Mulla Sadra (Sadr al-Din al-Shirazi)*. Albany: State U of New York P, 1975.

Ziai, H. "Mulla Sadra: His Life and Works." Nasr and Leaman, *History of Islamic Philosophy*. 635–642.

al-Sa'id, Aminah, 1914–1995

Web Sites

"Amina Al Saied, a Pioneer of Journalism." *Egypt*. http://www.sis.gov.eg/calendar/html/cl1308.htm (accessed 25 Aug. 2003).

Translations

"Feast of Unveiling, Feast of the Renaissance." Trans. A. Badran and M. Badran. Badran and Cooke, *Opening the Gates*. 357–365.

Handal, *The Poetry of Arab Women*. 262–266.
    Includes translations of "I Present Myself to the World" and "One Day I Know the Page" by L. McNair.

"Why, Reverence Shaikh?" Trans. N. Radwan. Badran and Cooke, *Opening the Gates*. 357–365.

Biography and Criticism

Mikhail, M. "al-Sa'id, Amina." Meisami and Starkey, *Encyclopedia of Arabic Literature*. 676–677.

Qader, N. "Said, Amina." Gikandi, *Encyclopedia of African Literature*. 477–478.

Salih, al-Tayyib, 1929–

Web Sites

Salih, al-T. "A Handful of Dates." *Exploring Africa: Africa in the Classroom*. African Studies Center, Michigan State University. http://ex.matrix.msu.edu/africa/curriculum/lm11/teachers4africanshortstories.htm (accessed 25 Aug. 2003).

"Tayeb Salih." *Sudan Site*. 31 Jan. 1998. http://www.geocities.com/Athens/Oracle/1296/tayeb_salih.htm (accessed 25 Aug. 2003).

Autobiography and Interviews

"Tayeb Salih: There Is a Much Wider Potential Readership for Arabic Literature Than Publishers Are Prepared to Admit." Interviewed by M. Shaheen. *Banipal* 10–11 (2001): 82–84.

Translations

Bandarshah. Trans. D. Johnson-Davies. London: Kegan Paul; Paris: UNESCO, 1996.

"The Cypriot Man." Johnson-Davies, *Arabic Short Stories*. 75–83.

"A Letter to Aileen." Trans. N.S. Doniach. *Journal of Arabic Literature* 11 (1980): 76–79.

Season of Migration to the North. Trans. D. Johnson-Davies. London: Heinemann, 1969.

The Wedding of Zein and Other Stories. Trans. D. Johnson-Davis. London: Heinemann Educational, 1968.

Biography and Criticism

Abu-Deeb, K. "Salih, al-Tayyib." *Contemporary World Writers*. Ed. T. Chevalier. 2nd ed. Detroit: St. James, 1993. 455–457.

Allen, *Modern Arabic Literature*. 264–270.

Allen, R. "'Mawsim al-Hijrah ila al-Shamal', al-Tayyib Salih." *The Arabic Novel: An Historical and Critical Introduction*. 2nd ed. Syracuse: Syracuse UP, 1995. 159–167.

Amyuni, M.T. "The Arab Artist's Role in Society: Three Case Studies: Naguib Mahfouz, Tayeb Salih, and Elias Khoury." *Arabic and Middle Eastern Literatures* 2 (1999): 203–222.

———. "Salih, al-Tayyib." Meisami and Starkey, *Encyclopedia of Arabic Literature*. 681.

Al-Haggagi, A.S. al-D. "The Mythmaker: Tayeb Salih." Trans. O. Abou-Bakr. Ghazoul and Harlow, *The View from Within*. 99–133.

Hassan, W.S. "Salih, al-Tayyib." Gikandi, *Encyclopedia of African Literature*. 478–479.

Littleton, J. "'Season of Migration to the North' by Tayeb Salih." *African Literature and Its Times*. Ed. J. Moss and L.Valestuk. World Literature and Its Times 2. Detroit: Gale, 2000. 367–375.

Nasr, A.A. "Popular Islam in Al-Tayyib Salih." *Journal of Arabic Literature* 11 (1980): 88–104.

Sadgrove, P. "Al-Tayyib Salih, 1929–." *African Writers*. Ed. C.B. Cox. New York: Charles Scribner's Sons, 1997. 733–744.

Salim, 'Ali, 1936–

Web Sites

"Ali Salem: Egyptian Writer Shunned for His Views on Israel." *Middle East and Islamic Studies Collection, Cornell University*. http://www.library.cornell.edu/colldev/mideast/alsalem.htm (accessed 25 Aug. 2003).

Salim, 'A. "I Want to Start a Kindergarten for Extremism." *MEMRI Special Dispatch* 8 Nov. 2001. http://www.memri.de/uebersetzungen_analysen/laender/aegypten/egypt_salem_08_11_01.pdf (accessed 25 Aug. 2003).

———. "Man of Letters." Interviewed by E. Farnsworth. *NewsHour*. PBS. 27 Nov. 2001. http://www.pbs.org/newshour/bb/terrorism/july-dec01/playwright_11-27.html.
Transcript, video, and audio.

————. "My Drive to Israel." *Middle East Quarterly* 9.1 (2002). http://
   www.meforum.org/article/130 (accessed 25 Aug. 2003).
   Excerpts from his book, with a good introduction.

Woffenden, R., and S. Negus. "Outcast of the Art World." *Cairo Times* 4 Sept. 1997.
   http://www.cairotimes.com/content/culture/salem.html (accessed 25 Aug.
   2003).

Youssef, R. "One in 61 Million." *Middle East Times* 29 June 1997. http://
   www.metimes.com/issue26/commu/1salem.htm (accessed 25 Aug. 2003).

Translations

"The Coffee Bar." Trans. L. Jayyusi and T.G. Ezzy. *Short Arabic Plays: An
   Anthology.* Ed. S.K. Jayyusi. New York: Interlink, 2003. 328–355.

"The Comedy of Oedipus: You're the One Who Killed the Beast." Trans. P. Cachia
   and D. O'Grady. *Modern Arabic Drama: An Anthology.* Ed. S.K. Jayyusi and R.
   Allen. Bloomington: Indiana UP, 1995. 353–386.

A Drive to Israel: An Egyptian Meets His Neighbors. Trans. R.J. Silverman. Tel Aviv:
   Moshe Dayan Center for Middle Eastern and Africa Studies, Tel Aviv U.;
   Syracuse: Distributed by Syracuse UP, 2001.

"The Wheat Well." Trans. D. Johnson-Davies. *Egyptian One-Act Plays.* London:
   Heinemann; Washington, D.C.: Three Continents P, 1981. 69–99.

Biography and Criticism

Badawi, M.M. *Modern Arabic Drama in Egypt.* Cambridge: Cambridge UP, 1987.
   197–205.

Farag-Badawi, N.R. "Ali Salem ('Ali Salim): A Modern Egyptian Dramatist." *Journal
   of Arabic Literature* 12 (1981): 87–100.

Starkey, P. "Salim, 'Ali." Meisami and Starkey, *Encyclopedia of Arabic Literature.*
   681.

al-Samman, Ghadah, 1942–

Web Sites

Jensen, K. "Ghada Samman's 'Beirut '75' Unmasks Gender and Class in Post-
   Colonial Society." Rev. of *Beirut '75. Aljadid* 25 (1999). http://
   www.aljadid.com/reviews/0525jensen.html (accessed 25 Aug. 2003).

al-Samman, G. "Street Walker." *Gender Issues & Literature in the Middle East.* http://
   www.u.arizona.edu/~talattof/women-lit/introduction.htm (accessed 25 Aug.
   2003).

Translations

"Another Scarecrow." *An Arabian Mosaic: Short Stories by Arab Women Writers.*
   Trans. D. Cohen-Mor. Potomac, Md.: Sheba, 1993. 141–154.

Asfour, *When the Words Burn.* 132–134.
   Includes translations of "Imprisonment of a Question Mark" and "Imprisonment of a Rainbow."

Beirut '75: A Novel. Trans. N.N. Roberts. Fayetteville: U of Arkansas P, 1995.

Beirut Nightmares. Trans. N.N. Roberts. London: Quartet, 1997.

Handal, *The Poetry of Arab Women.* 274–276.

Includes a translation of "The Lover of Blue Writing above the Sea!" by S. Ahmed and M. Cooke and a translation of "The Lover of Rain in an Inkwell" by M. Cooke with R. McKane.

"Old Enough to be Your Father." *Modern Syrian Short Stories.* Trans. M.G. Azrak. Rev. M.J.L. Young. Washington, D.C.: Three Continents, 1988. 71–76.

"Our Constitution—We the Liberated Women." Trans. M. Cooke. Badran and Cooke, *Opening the Gates.* 137–143.

The Square Moon: Supernatural Tales. Trans. I.J. Boullata. Fayetteville: U of Arkansas P, 1998.

Biography and Criticism

Allen, *Modern Arabic Literature.* 270–275.

Awwad, H.A. *Arab Causes in the Fiction of Ghadah al-Samman (1961–1975).* Sherbrooke: Naaman, 1983.

Boullata, I.J. "al-Samman, Ghada." Meisami and Starkey, *Encyclopedia of Arabic Literature.* 686–687.

Sannu', Ya'qub ibn Rafa'il, 1839–1912

Web Sites

Sanua, V.D. "Egypt for the Egyptians: The Story of Abu Naddara (James Sanua) 1839–1912, a Jewish Egyptian Patriot." *Welcome to FASSAC.* http://www.sephardicstudies.org/naddara.html (accessed 25 Aug. 2003).

Biography and Criticism

Badawi, M.M. *Early Arabic Drama.* Cambridge: Cambridge UP, 1988. 31–42.

———. "The Father of the Modern Egyptian Theatre: Ya'qub Sannu'." *Journal of Arabic Literature* 16 (1985): 132–145.

Ceccato, R. Dorigo. "Autobiographical Features in the Works of Ya'qub Sanu'." Ostle, Moor, and Wild, *Writing the Self.* 51–60.

Gendzier, I.L. *The Practical Visions of Ya'qub Sanu'.* Cambridge: Distributed for the Center for Middle Eastern Studies of Harvard U by Harvard UP, 1966.

Moreh, S. "New Light on Ya'qub Sanua's Life and Editorial Work Through His Paris Archive." *Writer, Culture, Text: Studies in Modern Arabic Literature.* Ed. A. Elad. Fredericton, N.B.: York, 1993. 101–115.

———. "Ya'qub Sanu': His Religious Identity and Work in the Theater and Journalism, According to the Family Archive." *The Jews of Egypt: A Mediterranean Society in Modern Times.* Ed. S. Shamir. Boulder: Westview, 1987. 111–129.

Sadgrove, P. "Sanu', Ya'qub (James Sanua)" Meisami and Starkey, *Encyclopedia of Arabic Literature.* 688.

al-Sa'udi, Muna, 1945–

Web Sites

Mona Saudi. http://www.geocities.com/mona_saudi/new_page_1.htm (accessed 25 Aug. 2003).
     Primarily devoted to her sculpture, also includes text and translation of the poem "An Ocean of Dreams."

"Mona Saudi." *World's Women On-Line!* Ed. M. Magenta. http://wwol.is.asu.edu/saudi.html (accessed 25 Aug. 2003).

al-Sa'udi, M. "Darkness." *Gender Issues & Literature in the Middle East*. http://www.u.arizona.edu/~talattof/women-lit/introduction.htm (accessed 25 Aug. 2003).

Translations

An Ocean of Dreams. Trans. T.T. Nasir. Pueblo: Passeggiata, 1999.

Women of the Fertile Crescent. Washington, D.C.: Three Continents, 1978. 23–42.
     Includes translations by K. Boullata of "And I Erase the Face," "And Let Her Die," "Blind City," "The City Trembles Beneath the Dawn," "Darkness Is," "How Do I Enter the Silence of Stones," "I Left My Home to Its Walls," "In Her Heart She Planted a Tree," "I Shall Sculpt for You Both Two," "Morning Unleafed," "Out of the Murky Debris," "So Drunk Am I," "Through Galaxies of Stars," "When the Loneliness of the Tomb," and "Why Don't I Write."

al-Sayigh, Mayy, 1940–

Web Sites

"Palestinian Poets, May Sayigh." *Khalil Sakakini Cultural Centre*. http://www.sakakini.org/poets/may-index.htm (accessed 25 Aug. 2003).
     Includes translation of poem "Departure."

Translations

Jayyusi, *Anthology of Modern Palestinian Literature*. 280–283.
     Includes translations of "Departure," "Elegy for Imm 'Ali," and "From 'Beirut under Siege'" by L. Jayyusi and N.S. Nye.

"Lament." Trans. C. Doria with the help of S.K. Jayyusi. Jayyusi, *Modern Arabic Poetry*. 416–419.

"A Love Poem to My Aunt—a Name Pursued." Elmessiri, *The Palestinian Wedding*. 219–221.

Sayigh, Tawfiq, 1924–1971

Web Sites

Tawfiq Sayigh: Public Poet, Private Artist. Ed. T. Dunivant, et al. http://www.humboldt.edu/~me2/engl240/student_projects/Sayigh/ (accessed 25 Aug. 2003).
     Created as a student project for an English class at Humboldt State University, includes translations of poems ("A National Hymn," "al-Qasida K #1," "al-Qasida K #10," "al-Qasida K #24") with commentary, biography, and bibliography.

Translations

"Also and Also." Trans. S. Simawe and E.D. Watson. *Modern Poetry in Translation*
14 (1998–1999): 169–175.

"A Few Questions I Pose to the Unicorn." Trans. Z.A.H. Ali. *Journal of Arabic
Literature* 30 (1999): 33–54.

Boullata, *Modern Arab Poets*. 135–148.
Includes translations of "1," "6," "10," "24," "28," and "A National Hymn."

Jayyusi, *Anthology of Modern Palestinian Literature*. 284–292.
Includes translations of "From 'The Poem K,'" "Poem 28," and "To Enter a
Country" by A. Haydar and J. Reed.

Jayyusi, *Modern Arabic Poetry*. 420–426.
Includes a translation of "Out of the Depths I Cry unto You, O Death!" by A.
Royal and S. Hazo and a translation of "Phantom" by A. Royal and T.G. Ezzy.

Khouri and Algar, *Anthology of Modern Arabic Poetry*. 211–223.
Includes translations of "Alarm," "And Then?," "Poem 22," "Poem 23," and
"The Sermon on the Mount."

"What's Next." Al-Udhari, *Modern Poetry of the Arab World*. 91–92.

Biography and Criticism

Ali, Z.A.H. "The Aesthetics of Dissonance: Echoes of Nietzsche and Yeats in Tawfiq
Sayigh's Poetry." *Journal of Arabic Literature* 30 (1999): 1–32.

Allen, *Modern Arabic Literature*. 275–279.

Boullata, I.J. "The Beleaguered Unicorn: A Study of Tawfiq Sayigh." *Journal of
Arabic Literature* 4 (1973): 69–93.

DeYoung, T. "Sayigh, Tawfiq." Serafin, *Encyclopedia of World Literature in the 20th
Century*. Vol. 4. 44–45.

Starkey, P. "Sayigh, Tawfiq." Meisami and Starkey, *Encyclopedia of Arabic
Literature*. 695–696.

al-Sayyab, Badr Shakir, 1926–1964

Web Sites

"Badr Shakir al-Sayyab." *Jehat.com*. http://www.jehat.com/en/
default.asp?action=article&ID=59 (accessed 21 Apr. 2004).
Includes a short essay by Fadhil Sultani and translations of the poems "Death
and the River," "Rain Song," and "Return to Jaykur."

al-Sayyab, B.S. "In the Arab Maghreb." *Spotlight on the Muslim Middle East: Issues
of Identity*. Ed. H.S. Greenberg and L. Mahony. 1995. American Forum for
Global Education. http://www.globaled.org/muslimmideast/spage4.php
(accessed 25 Aug. 2003).
Scroll down to this translation.

Translations

Asfour, *When the Words Burn*. 138–145.
Includes translations of "[From] The Book of Job [Part I of X]," "Christ after
Crucifixion," "River of Death," and "Song of the Rain."

Bennani, B., ed. and trans. *Bread, Hashish and Moon*. Greensboro: Unicorn, 1982.
17–25.
Includes translations of "City of Sinbad," "Garcia Lorca," and "The Messiah
after the Crucifixion."

Boullata, *Modern Arab Poets*. 3–10.
Includes translations of "A City Without Rain" and "The Song of Rain."

Jayyusi, *Modern Arabic Poetry*. 427–442.
Includes translations of "Death and the River," "In the Arab Maghreb," "Jaikur
and the City," "Rain Song," and "Song in August" by L. Jayyusi and C. Middleton.

Khouri and Algar, *Anthology of Modern Arabic Poetry*. 83–107.
Includes translations of "Before the Gate of God," "Burning," "City of Sinbad,"
"For I Am a Stranger," "An Ode to Revolutionary Iraq," and "The River and Death."

Biography and Criticism

Allen, *Modern Arabic Literature*. 279–288.

Boullata, I.J. "The Poetic Technique of Badr Shakir al-Sayyab." *Journal of Arabic
Literature* 2 (1971): 104–115.

———. "al-Sayyab, Badr Shakir." Meisami and Starkey, *Encyclopedia of Arabic
Literature*. 696–697.

———. "al-Sayyab, Badr Shakir." Serafin, *Encyclopedia of World Literature in the
20th Century*. Vol. 4. 45–46.

DeYoung, T. *Placing the Poet: Badr Shakir al-Sayyab and Postcolonial Iraq*. Albany:
State U of New York P, 1998.

Shaheen, M. *The Modern Arabic Short Story: Shahrazad Returns*. 2nd ed. rev. and
exp. New York: Palgrave Macmillan, 2002. 88–92.

Simawe, S.A. "Modernism and Metaphor in Contemporary Arabic Poetry." *World
Literature Today* 75 (2001): 275–284.

al-Shabbi, Abu al-Qasim, 1909–1934

Web Sites

al-Shabbi, Abu al-Q. "The New Morning." *AboutLaw.com*. http://aboutlaw.com/
languages/poetry-arabic.htm (accessed 25 Aug. 2003).
To see the Arabic text and listen to it being read, go to the previous page.

Translations

"Abu al-Qasim ash-Shabbi (Tunisian Poet 1909–34)" *Literature East & West* 31
(1977): 318–321.
Includes translations of "My Heart Said to God" and "The Songs of Sorrows"
by S. Masliyah.

Modern Arabic Poetry. Cambridge: Cambridge UP, 1967. 52–54.
Includes translations of "I Weep for Love" and "To the Tyrant" by A.J. Arberry.

"In the Shadow of the Valley of Death." Khouri and Algar, *Anthology of Modern
Arabic Poetry*. 137.

Jayyusi, *Modern Arabic Poetry*. 97–99.

Includes translations of "Life's Will" and "Quatrains from 'Song of Ecstasy'" by S. Boulos and C. Middleton.

Biography and Criticism

Abdel-Jaouad, H. "al-Shabbi, Abu al-Qasim." Serafin, *Encyclopedia of World Literature in the 20th Century.* Vol. 4. 82.

Allen, *Modern Arabic Literature.* 289–293.

Khouri, M. "al-Shabbi as a Romantic." *Arabic Literature in North Africa: Critical Essays and Annotated Bibliography.* Cambridge, MA: Dar Mahjar, 1982. 3–17.

Ostle, R. "Abu al-Qasim al-Shabbi, 1909–1934." *African Writers.* Ed. C.B. Cox. New York: Charles Scribner's Sons, 1997. 791–797.

———. "Abu'l-Qasim al-Sabbi (1909–1934) between Tradition and Modernity." *Oriente Moderno,* n.s., 16 (1997): 143–150.

———. "al-Shabbi, Abu al-Qasim." Meisami and Starkey, *Encyclopedia of Arabic Literature.* 700.

Shafiq, Durriyah, 1908–1975

Web Sites

"Dorreya Shafik." *Egypt.* http://www.sis.gov.eg/women/figures/html/dorreya.htm (accessed 25 Aug. 2003).

Translations

"Islam and the Constitutional Rights of Woman." Trans. A. Badran and M. Badran. Badran and Cooke, *Opening the Gates.* 352–356.

Biography and Criticism

Nelson, C. *Doria Shafik, Egyptian Feminist: A Woman Apart.* Gainesville: U of Florida P, 1996.

———. "Dora Shafik's French Writing: Hybridity in a Feminist Key." *Alif* 20 (2000): 109–139.

———. "Feminist Expression as Self-Identity and Cultural Critique: The Discourse of Doria Shafik." *The Postcolonial Crescent: Islam's Impact on Contemporary Literature.* Ed. J.C. Hawley. New York: Lang, 1998. 95–120.

Sha'rawi, Huda, 1879–1947

Web Sites

"Anniversary of Hoda Sha'rawi, Pioneer of Feminist Movement." *Egypt.* http://www.sis.gov.eg/calendar/html/cl121297.htm (accessed 25 Aug. 2003).

Bois, D. "Huda Shaarawi." *Distinguished Women of Past and Present.* Ed. D. Bois. http://www.distinguishedwomen.com/biographies/shaarawi.html (accessed 25 Aug. 2003).

"Huda Shaarawi." *Sunshine for Women.* http://www.pinn.net/~sunshine/whm2001/huda2.html (accessed 25 Aug. 2003).

Short selections from her autobiography, *Harem Years,* can be read at http://www.pinn.net/~sunshine/book-sum/huda.html.

Sha'rawi, H. "Pan-Arab Feminism: An Eternal Message." *Civil Society: Democratization in the Arab World* 80 (1998). http://www.ibnkhaldun.org/newsletter/1998/aug/opinion1.html (accessed 25 Aug. 2003).

Spatz, M. "Huda Shaarawi." *Postcolonial Studies*. Ed. D. Bahri. 3 Feb. 2003. Emory University. http://www.emory.edu/ENGLISH/Bahri/Shaarawi.html (accessed 25 Aug. 2003).

Autobiography

Harem Years: The Memoirs of an Egyptian Feminist, 1879–1924. Trans. and ed. M. Badran. New York: Feminist at the City U of New York, 1987.

Translations

"Pan-Arab Feminism." Trans. A. Badran and M. Badran. Badran and Cooke, *Opening the Gates*. 337–340.

Biography and Criticism

Ahmed, L. "Between Two Worlds: The Formation of a Turn-of-the-Century Egyptian Feminist." *Life/Lines: Theorizing Women's Autobiography*. Ed. B. Brodzki and C. Schenck. Ithaca: Cornell UP, 1988. 154–174.

Booth, M. "Sha'rawi, Huda (born Nur al-Huda Sultan)." Meisami and Starkey, *Encyclopedia of Arabic Literature*. 704–705.

Kahf, M. "Huda Sha'rawi's Mudhakkirati: The Memoirs of the First Lady of Arab Modernity." *Arab Studies Quarterly* 20 (1998): 53–82.

al-Sharqawi, 'Abd al-Rahman, 1920–1987

Web Sites

"Abdel-Rahman Al-Sharqawi, an Innovative Poet, Critic, Novelist and Intellectual." *Egypt*. http://www.sis.gov.eg/calendar/html/cl091197.htm (accessed 21 Apr. 2004).

Arab Culture and Civilization. Ed. M. Toler. National Institute for Technology and Liberal Education. http://www.nitle.org/arabworld/main_menu.php (accessed 25 Aug. 2003).

Use the Search box to find the video clip from Yusuf Shahin's film adaptation of the novel *al-Ard*, with English subtitles.

Translations

Egyptian Earth. Trans. D. Stewart. London: Saqi, 1990.

"The Scorpion Hunter." Trans. D. Bishai. Rev. R. Ewart. Manzalaoui, *Arabic Short Stories*. 180–192.

Biography and Criticism

Allen, *Modern Arabic Literature*. 293–298.

Badawi, M.M. *Modern Arabic Drama in Egypt*. Cambridge: Cambridge UP, 1987. 217–220.

Jad, A.B. "'Abd ar-Rahman ash-Sharqawi's 'al-Ard.'" *Journal of Arabic Literature* 7 (1976): 88–100.

Kirkpatrick, H. *The Modern Egyptian Novel: A Study in Social Criticism*. Oxford: Middle East Centre, St. Antony's College; London: Ithaca, 1974. 126–140.

"Sharkawi, A(bdel)-R(ahman)." *Contemporary Authors* 125 (1989): 416.

Starkey, P. "al-Sharqawi, 'Abd al-Rahman." Meisami and Starkey, *Encyclopedia of Arabic Literature*. 707.

al-Sharuni, Yusuf, 1924–

Web Sites

"Youssef El-Sharouni." *Arab World Books*. http://www.arabworldbooks.com/authors/youssef_elsharouni.html (accessed 25 Aug. 2003).

Translations

Blood Feud. Trans. D. Johnson-Davies. London: Heinemann, 1984.

"The Crowd." Trans. N. Farag. Rev. P. Ward-Green. Manzalaoui, *Arabic Short Stories*. 328–342.

"The Crush of Life." Johnson-Davies, *Egyptian Short Stories*. 103–117.

"Glimpses from the Life of Maugoud Abdul Maugoud and Two Postscripts." Johnson-Davies, *Arabic Short Stories*. 46–67.

"The Man and the Farm." *Modern Arabic Short Stories*. Trans. D. Johnson-Davies. London: Oxford UP, 1967. 56–66.

Biography and Criticism

Allen, *Modern Arabic Literature*. 298–301.

Mikhail, M. "al-Sharuni, Yusuf." Meisami and Starkey, *Encyclopedia of Arabic Literature*. 708.

"Al Sharouni, Youssef." *Contemporary Authors* 131 (1991): 12–13.

Shawqi, Ahmad, 1868–1932

Web Sites

"Ahmed Shawki Museum." *Tour Egypt*. http://www.touregypt.net/shawkimuseum.htm (accessed 25 Aug. 2003).

Guide to the museum in his old home, together with a biography and photographs.

"Birthday of Ahmed Shawki, the Prince of Poets." *Egypt*. http://www.us.sis.gov.eg/calendar/html/cl161096.htm (accessed 25 Aug. 2003).

A review of the English translation of his *Quais & Laila (Majnun Layla)* can be read at http://www.sis.gov.eg/public/magazine/iss019e/html/art07txt.htm.

Al-Lawati, A. "Ahmed Shawqi." Al-Lawati, A. Home Page. http://www.personal.psu.edu/users/a/h/aha112/hmwk3.html (accessed 25 Aug. 2003).

Al Roussan, R. "'Prince of Poets' Remembered." *The Star* 2–8 Nov. 2000. http://star.arabia.com/article/0,5596,16_96,00.html (accessed 25 Aug. 2003).

Shawqi, A. "Knowledge and Teaching and the Teacher's Task." *Spotlight on the Muslim Middle East: Issues of Identity*. Ed. H.S. Greenberg and L. Mahony. 1995. American Forum for Global Education. http://www.globaled.org/muslimmideast/spage4.php (accessed 25 Aug. 2003).

Scroll down on the Web site to read this poem.

Translations

Jayyusi, *Modern Arabic Poetry*. 100–103.
> Includes translations of "An Andalusian Exile," "Bois de Boulogne," and "Thoughts on Schoolchildren" by M.M. Badawi and J. Heath-Stubbs.

"Shauqi." Arberry, *Arabic Poetry*. 154–161.

"They Deceived Her." Trans. F. Bitar. *Treasury of Arabic Love Poems, Quotations, and Proverbs*. Ed. F. Bitar. New York: Hippocrene, 1996. 45.

Biography and Criticism

Badawi, M.M. *Modern Arabic Drama in Egypt*. Cambridge: Cambridge UP, 1987. 207–215.

Elkhadem, S. *History of the Egyptian Novel: Its Rise and Early Beginnings*. Fredericton, N.B.: York, 1985. 20–21.

Kadhim, H.N. "The Poetics of Postcolonialism: Two Qasidahs by Ahmad Shawqi." *Journal of Arabic Literature* 28 (1997): 179–218.

Mahmoud, A.A. "Ahmad Shauqi's 'al-Sitt Huda' as a Satirical Comedy of Manners." *Journal of Arabic Literature* 19 (1988): 183–191.

Ostle, R.C. "Shawqi, Ahmad." Meisami and Starkey, *Encyclopedia of Arabic Literature*. 709.

al-Shaykh, Hanan, 1945–

Web Sites

Beydoun, L. "Hanan Al Shaykh (Writer)" *Lebwa: Lebanese Women's Awakening*. http://www.lebwa.org/life/shaykh.php (accessed 25 Aug. 2003).

Chalala, E. "Hanan Al-Shaykh on Life, Dreams and Pain of Afghan Women." *Aljadid* 37 (2001). http://www.aljadid.com/essays/0737chalala.html (accessed 25 Aug. 2003).

Ghazaleh, P. "Hanan Al-Shaykh: From the Rooftops." *Al-Ahram Weekly On-Line* 11–17 Nov. 1999. http://weekly.ahram.org.eg/1999/455/profile.htm (accessed 25 Aug. 2003).

"Hanan al-Shaykh." *Books and Writers*. http://www.kirjasto.sci.fi/shaykh.htm (accessed 25 Aug. 2003).

Milani, A. "A Warm, Sad Blues Riff on Life in Beirut." Rev. of *Beirut Blues*. *San Francisco Chronicle* 13 Aug. 1995. http://www.sfgate.com/cgi-bin/article.cgi?file=/chronicle/archive/1995/08/13/RV26382.DTL (accessed 25 Aug. 2003).

al-Shaykh, H. "My Mother, the Muslim." *Newsweek Web Exclusive* 8 Jan. 2003. http://www.msnbc.com/news/684177.asp?0dm=C12NOandcp1=1 (accessed 25 Aug. 2003).

Woffenden, R. "Four in a Foreign Land." Rev. of *Only in London. Cairo Times* 3–9 Jan. 2002. http://www.cairotimes.com/content/archiv05/alshaykh.html (accessed 25 Aug. 2003).

Translations

Beirut Blues: A Novel. Trans. C. Cobham. New York: Anchor, 1995.

"A Girl Called Apple." Trans. M. Cooke. Badran and Cooke, *Opening the Gates*.
    155–159.

I Sweep the Sun off Rooftops. Trans. C. Cobham. New York: Doubleday, 1998.

Literary Review 37 (1994): 433–443.
    Includes a translation of "The Scratching of Angels' Pens" by C. Cobham and a
translation of "The Women's Swimming Pool" by D. Johnson-Davies.

"The Man Shouldn't Know of This." Johnson-Davies, *Under the Naked Sky*.
    166–168.

Only in London. Trans. C. Cobham. New York: Pantheon, 2001.

"The Persian Rug." *An Arabian Mosaic: Short Stories by Arab Women Writers*. Trans.
    D. Cohen-Mor. Potomac, Md.: Sheba, 1993. 49–55.

The Story of Zahra. Trans. P. Ford. New York: Anchor, 1994.

Women of Sand and Myrrh. Trans. C. Cobham. London: Quartet, 1989.

Biography and Criticism

Allen, R. "'Hikayat Zahrah', Hanan al-Shaykh." *The Arabic Novel: An Historical and
    Critical Introduction*. 2nd ed. Syracuse: Syracuse UP, 1995. 231–244.

Cooke, M. "al-Shaykh, Hanan." Meisami and Starkey, *Encyclopedia of Arabic
    Literature*. 710–711.

———. "al-Shaykh, Hanan." Serafin, *Encyclopedia of World Literature in the 20th
    Century*. Vol. 4. 91.

Ghandour, S. "Hanan al-Sahykh's 'Hikayat Zahra': A Counter-Narrative and a
    Counter-History." *Intersections: Gender, Nation, and Community in Arab
    Women's Novels*. Ed. L.S. Majaj, P.W. Sunderman, and T. Saliba. Syracuse:
    Syracuse UP, 2002. 231–249.

"al-Shaykh, Hanan." *Contemporary Authors* 135 (1992): 12–13.

"al-Shaykh, Hanan." *Contemporary Authors New Revision Series* 111 (2003): 1–3.

al-Shidyaq, Ahmad Faris, 1804?–1887

Web Sites

"Arabic Printed Books." *The British Library*. http://www.bl.uk/collections/
    arabpb.html (accessed 25 Aug .2003).
    The image of the book at the bottom of the page shows an Arabic font designed
by al-Shidyaq.

Roper, G. "Ahmad Faris al-Shidyaq and the Libraries of Europe and the Ottoman
    Empire." *Libraries & Culture* 33.3 (1998). http://www.gslis.utexas.edu/~landc/
    fulltext/LandC_33_3_Roper.pdf (accessed 25 Aug. 2003).

Translations

"al-Shidyaq." Arberry, *Arabic Poetry*. 136–148.

Biography and Criticism

Roper, G. "Faris Al-Shidyaq and the Transition from Scribal to Print Culture in the
    Middle East." *The Book in the Islamic World : The Written Word and
    Communication in the Middle East*. Ed. G.N. Atiyeh. Albany: State U of New
    York P, 1995. 209–231.

Sadgrove, P.C. "al-Shidyaq, (Ahmad) Faris." Meisami and Starkey, *Encyclopedia of Arabic Literature*. 712–713.

Starkey, P. "Fact and Fiction in 'al-Saq 'ala al-Saq.'" Ostle, Moor, and Wild, *Writing the Self*. 30–38.

Shumayyil, Shibli, d. 1917

Web Sites

Shumayyil, S. "Social Killing." *The Free Arab Voice*. Ed. I. Alloush. http://www.freearabvoice.org/reference/socialKilling.htm (accessed 25 Aug. 2003).

Biography and Criticism

Anawati, G.C. "Shibli Shumayyil: Medical Philosopher and Scientist." *The Islamic World from Classical to Modern Times: Essays in Honor of Bernard Lewis*. Ed. C.E. Bosworth, et al. Princeton: Darwin, 1989. 637–650.

Fakhry, M. "The Materialism of Shibli Shumayyil." *Quest for Understanding: Arabic and Islamic Studies in Memory of Malcolm H. Kerr*. Eds. S. Seikaly, R. Baalbaki, and P. Dodd. Beirut: American U of Beirut, 1991. 59–70.

Sadgrove, P.C. "Shumayyil, Shibli." Meisami and Starkey, *Encyclopedia of Arabic Literature*. 716.

Shuqayr, Mahmud, 1941–

Web Sites

Shuqayr, M. "Three Short-Stories." *Autodafe: The Censored Library*. July 2003. International Parliament of Writers. http://www.autodafe.org/bookshop/palestine/choukeir.htm (accessed 25 Aug. 2003).
Includes translations of "Another Cafe," "Fragments," and "Wool."

Autobiography and Interviews

"My Journey in Writing." Trans. L. Winslow. *Banipal* 7 (2000): 10.

Translations

Modern Poetry in Translation. 14 (1998–1999): 178–180.
Includes translations of "Childbirth," "Heart," "Loneliness," "Love," "No One," "Punishment," and "Statue" by L. Winrow.

"The Orphans' Cow." *The Modern Arabic Short Story: Shahrazad Returns*. Trans. M. Shaheen. 2nd ed. rev. and exp. New York: Palgrave Macmillan, 2002. 221–226.

"Ten Short Stories." Trans. L. Winslow. *Banipal* 7 (2000): 11–12.

Biography and Criticism

Shaheen, M. *The Modern Arabic Short Story: Shahrazad Returns*. 2nd ed. rev. and exp. New York: Palgrave Macmillan, 2002. 121–123.

al-Siba'i, Yusuf, 1917–1978

Web Sites

"Yousef Al-Seba'ie." *Egypt*. http://www.us.sis.gov.eg/egyptianfigures/html/Yousef.htm (accessed 25 Aug. 2003).

Translations

"The Country Boy." Johnson-Davies, *Egyptian Short Stories*. 88–92.

"The Master-Milkman." Trans. N. Farag. Rev. D. Kirkhan and R. Ewart. Manzalaoui, *Arabic Short Stories*. 147–155.

Biography and Criticism

Abdel-Malek, Z.N. "The Influence of Diglossia on the Novels of Yuusif al-Sibaa'i." *Journal of Arabic Literature* 3 (1972): 132–141.

Sakkut, H. *The Egyptian Novel and Its Main Trends: From 1913 to 1952*. Cairo: American U in Cairo P, 1971. 37–40.

Starkey, P. "al-Siba'i, Yusuf." Meisami and Starkey, *Encyclopedia of Arabic Literature*. 717–718.

Sirat Bani Hilal

Web Sites

Rakha, Y. "Upstaging the Master." *Al-Ahram Weekly On-Line* 21–27 Nov. 2002. http://weekly.ahram.org.eg/2002/613/cu1.htm (accessed 25 Aug. 2003). Review of a live performance of the epic.

Criticism

Canova, G. "Banu Hilal, Romance of." Meisami and Starkey, *Encyclopedia of Arabic Literature*. 133.

Connelly, B. *Arab Folk Epic and Identity*. Berkeley: U of California P, 1986.

Norris, H.T. "The Rediscovery of the Ancient Sagas of the Banu Hilal." *Bulletin of the School of Oriental and African Studies* 51 (1988): 462–481.

Reynolds, D.F. *Heroic Poets, Poetic Heroes: The Ethnography of Performance in an Arabic Oral Epic Tradition*. Ithaca: Cornell UP, 1995.

Slyomovics, S. *The Merchant of Art: An Egyptian Hilali Oral Epic Poet in Performance*. Berkeley: U of California P, 1987.

Sirat Sayf ibn Dhi Yazan

Web Sites

Schemm, P. "Kings, Heroes, Sorcerers and Djinn." Rev. of *The Adventures of Sayf Ben Dhi Yazan*. Trans. L. Jayyusi. *Middle East Times* 22 Oct. 1999. http://www.metimes.com/issue99-43/cultent/kings__heroes.htm (accessed 25 Aug. 2003).

Translations

The Adventures of Sayf ben Dhi Yazan: An Arab Folk Epic. Trans. L. Jayyusi. Bloomington: Indiana UP, 1996.

Criticism

Canova, G. "Sayf ibn Dhi Yazan, Romance of." Meisami and Starkey, *Encyclopedia of Arabic Literature*. 695.

al-Suhrawardi, Yahya ibn Habash, 1152 or 1153–1191

Web Sites

Cooper, J. "al-Suhrawardi, Shihab al-Din Yahya." *Islamic Philosophy Online.* http://www.muslimphilosophy.com/ip/rep/H031.htm (accessed 25 Aug. 2003).

"Suhrawardi." *Islamic Esotericism.* Ed. M.A. Kazlev. 27 Sept. 1999. http://www.kheper.net/topics/Islamic_esotericism/Ishraqism/Suhrawardi.htm (accessed 25 Aug. 2003).

"Suhrawardi." *Theosophy Library Online.* http://theosophy.org/tlodocs/teachers/Suhrawardi.htm (accessed 25 Aug. 2003).

Translations

The Book of Radiance. Ed. and trans. H. Ziai. Costa Mesa: Mazda, 1998.

The Mystical and Visionary Treatises of Shihabuddin Yahya Suhrawardi. Trans. W.M. Thackston, Jr. London: Octagon, 1982.

The Philosophical Allegories and Mystical Treatises. Trans. and ed. W.M. Thackston, Jr. Costa Mesa: Mazda, 1999.

The Philosophy of Illumination. Trans. and ed. J. Walbridge and H. Ziai. Provo: Brigham Young UP, 1999.

Biography and Criticism

Aminrazavi, M. "Suhrawardi." McGreal, *Great Thinkers of the Eastern World.* 469–474.

Nasr, S.H. *Three Muslim Sages: Avicenna, Suhrawardi, Ibn Arabi.* Cambridge: Harvard UP, 1964.

Netton, I. and J.S. Meisami. "al-Suhrawardi, Yahya ibn Habash." Meisami and Starkey, *Encyclopedia of Arabic Literature.* 742–743.

Razavi, M.A. *Suhrawardi and the School of Illumination.* Richmond, UK: Curzon, 1997.

Walbridge, J. *The Leaven of the Ancients: Suhrawardi and the Heritage of the Greeks.* Albany: State U of New York P, 2000.

————. *The Wisdom of the Mystic East: Suhrawardi and Platonic Orientalism.* Albany: State U of New York P, 2001.

Ziai, H. "Shihab al-Din Suhrawardi: Founder of the Illuminationist School." Nasr and Leaman, *History of Islamic Philosophy.* 434–464.

Surur, Najib, 1932–1978

Web Sites

Naguib Surur. 17 Nov. 1998. http://www.wadada.net/surur/index.html (accessed 25 Aug. 2003).

Mostly in Arabic, but contains translation of the poem "Drink Delirium" as well as a critique of Surur as a poet. The Arabic text and an audio file of his most controversial poem ("Kuss Ummiyat") can be found at http://www.wadada.net/surur/ummiyyat/index.html, together with links to information on his son's arrest and conviction for publishing the poem on the Web.

"Naguib Surur." *Books and Writers.* http://www.kirjasto.sci.fi/surur.htm (accessed 25 Aug. 2003).

Translations

"Sindbad the Porter." *The Modern Arabic Short Story: Shahrazad Returns.* Trans. M. Shaheen. 2nd ed. rev. and exp. New York: Palgrave Macmillan, 2002. 171–177.

Biography and Criticism

Allen, *Modern Arabic Literature.* 306–309.

Cachia, P. "Folk Themes in the Works of Najib Surur." *Arabic and Middle Eastern Literatures* 3 (2000): 195–204.

Sadgrove, P.C. "Surur, Najib Muhammad." Meisami and Starkey, *Encyclopedia of Arabic Literature.* 745.

Shaheen, M. *The Modern Arabic Short Story: Shahrazad Returns.* 2nd ed. rev. and exp. New York: Palgrave Macmillan, 2002. 70–76.

al-Suyuti, 1445–1505

Web Sites

"Jalau'd-Din as-Suyuti." *Islamic Paths.* http://www.islamic-paths.org/Home/English/ History/Personalities/Content/Suyuti.htm (accessed 25 Aug. 2003).

Translations

As-Suyuti's Medicine of the Prophet. London: Ta-Ha, 1994.

"Four Perfumes of Arabia: A Translation of al-Suyuti's 'al-Maqama al-Miskiyya.'" Trans. G.J. van Gelder. *Parfums d'Orient.* Ed. R. Gyselen. Res Orientales 11. Bures-sur-Yvette: Groupe pour l'Etude de la Civilisation du Moyen-Orient, 1998. 203–212.

History of the Caliphs. Trans. H.S. Jarrett. Amsterdam: Oriental, 1970.

Biography and Criticism

Irwin, R. "al-Suyuti." Meisami and Starkey, *Encyclopedia of Arabic Literature.* 746.

Sartain, E.M. *Jalal al-Din al-Suyuti.* 2 vols. Cambridge: Cambridge UP, 1975.

al-Tabari, 838?–923

Web Sites

"Abu Ja'far Muhammad b. Jarir b. Yazid al-Tabari." *Center for Islam and Science.* http://www.cis-ca.org/voices/t/tabari.htm (accessed 25 Aug. 2003).

Ahmad, J. "Tabari." *Renaissance: a Monthly Islamic Journal* 5.5 (1995). http:// www.renaissance.com.pk/myletfor95.html (accessed 25 Aug. 2003).

Translations

The Commentary on the Qur'an. Trans. J. Cooper. Ed. W.F. Madelung and A. Jones. Oxford: Oxford UP, 1987.

The History of al-Tabari. 39 vols. Albany: SU New York P, 1985–1999.

Each volume has its own title and translator. For a complete list, see the publisher's Web site, http://www.sunypress.edu/index.asp?site=True.

Biography and Criticism

Conrad, L.I. "Notes on al-Tabari's History." *Journal of the Royal Asiatic Society* 3 (1993): 191–206.

Daniel, E.L. "al-Tabari, Muhammad ibn Jarir." Meisami and Starkey, *Encyclopedia of Arabic Literature*. 750–751.

al-Tabari, 'Ali ibn Sahl Rabban, 9th century

Web Sites

"Ali ibn Rabban Tabari (-al)" *Malaspina Great Books*. http://www.malaspina.com/site/person_1095.asp (accessed 25 Aug. 2003).

Translations

The Book of Religion and Empire. Trans. A. Mingana. Manchester: Longmans, 1922.

Biography and Criticism

Hamarneh, S. "Contributions of 'Ali al-Tabari to Ninth-Century Arabic Culture." *Folia Orientalia* 12 (1970): 91–101.

Taha, 'Ali Mahmud, 1903 or 1904–1949

Web Sites

Magda's Night Gallery. Ed. Magda. Dec. 2002. http://www.geocities.com/SoHo/Cafe/1324/taha.htm (accessed 25 Aug. 2003).

Includes three poems by 'Ali Mahmud Taha: "The Blind Musician," "Egyptian Serenade," and "A Rustic Song."

Translations

Modern Poetry in Translation 14 (1998–1999): 44–49.

Includes translations of "Ambergris," "Fooling the Killers," "The Kid Goats of Jamil," and "Never Mind" by P. Cole, Y. Hejazi, and G. Levin.

Biography and Criticism

Allen, *Modern Arabic Literature*. 309–313.

Ostle, R.C. "Taha, 'Ali Mahmud." Meisami and Starkey, *Encyclopedia of Arabic Literature*. 752.

al-Tahawi, Miral, 1968–

Web Sites

Elmessiri, N. "Out of the Tent and into the Harem Quarters." Rev. of *The Tent*. *Al-Ahram Weekly On-Line* 6–12 Aug. 1998. http://weekly.ahram.org.eg/1998/389/cu2.htm (accessed 25 Aug. 2003).

"Miral el-Tahawi." *Arab World Books*. http://www.arabworldbooks.com/authors/miral_eltahawi.htm (accessed 25 Aug. 2003).

"Unveiling the Lives of Egypt's Bedouin Women." *Washington Post* 17 June 2002. http://www.arabworldbooks.com/news18.html (accessed 25 Aug. 2003).

Woffenden, R. "Coming of Age." Rev. of *Blue Aubergine*. *Cairo Times* 24–30 Oct. 2002. http://www.cairotimes.com/content/archiv06/book0633.html (accessed 25 Aug. 2003).

Translations

Blue Aubergine. Trans. A. Calderbank. Cairo: American U in Cairo P, 2002.

The Tent: A Novel. Trans. A. Calderbank. Cairo: American U in Cairo P, 1998.

Tahir, Baha', 1935–

Web Sites

"Bahaa Taher." *Arab World Books*. http://www.arabworldbooks.com/authors/
   bahaa_taher.htm (accessed 25 Aug. 2003).

Tahir, B. *Aunt Safiyya and the Monastery: A Novel*. Berkeley: U of California P, 1996.
   http://ark.cdlib.org/ark:/13030/ft3b69n847 (accessed 25 Aug. 2003).

Translations

"Advice from a Sensible Young Man." Johnson-Davies, *Arabic Short Stories*.
   40–45.

"Last Night I Dreamt of You." *Egyptian Tales and Short Stories of the 1970s and
   1980s*. Ed. W.M. Hutchins. Cairo: American U in Cairo P, 1987. 3–24.

Love in Exile. Trans. F.A. Wahab. Cairo: American U in Cairo P, 2001.

"Suddenly it Rained." Johnson-Davies, *Egyptian Short Stories*. 40–42.

Biography and Criticism

Allen, R. "Tahir, Baha'." Meisami and Starkey, *Encyclopedia of Arabic Literature*.
   752.

Al Masri, K. "Tahir, Baha'." Gikandi, *Encyclopedia of African Literature*.
   530–531.

al-Tahtawi, Rifa'ah Rafi', 1801–1873

Web Sites

"Al-Tahtawi's Impact on Egyptian Thought Assessed." *Egypt*. http://www.sis.gov.eg/
   online/html7/o280422b.htm (accessed 25 Aug. 2003).

Gran, P. "Tahtawi in Paris." *Al-Ahram Weekly On-Line* 10–16 Jan. 2002. http://
   weekly.ahram.org.eg/2002/568/cu1.htm (accessed 25 Aug. 2003).

"Refa'ah Rafie' Al Tahtawi." *Egypt*. http://www.sis.gov.eg/egyptinf/culture/html/
   tahtawi.htm (accessed 25 Aug. 2003).

al-Tahtawi, R.R. "Kitab Takhlis al-Ibriz ila Talkhis Paris." Khater, A. Home Page. 22
   Jan. 2001. http://social.chass.ncsu.edu/khater/personal/Tahtawi.htm (accessed
   25 Aug. 2003).
   Translation of excerpts from his book on Paris.

Biography and Criticism

Crabbs, J. "al-Tahtawi, Rifa'a Rafi'." Meisami and Starkey, *Encyclopedia of Arabic
   Literature*. 753–754.

Elkhadem, S. *History of the Egyptian Novel: Its Rise and Early Beginnings*.
   Fredericton, N.B.: York, 1985. 6–8.

Heyworth-Dunne, J. "Rifa'ah Badawi Rafi' al-Tahtawi: The Egyptian Revivalist."
   Bulletin of the School of Oriental and African Studies 9 (1937–1939): 961–967;
   10 (1940–1942): 399–415.

al-Takarli, Fu'ad, 1927–

Web Sites

Mower, E. "There's No Substitute for Life." Rev. of *The Long Way Back*. *Kikah.com: Middle East Literature & Arts*. http://www.kikah.com/ indexenglish.asp?code=kkbooks (accessed 25 Aug. 2003).

Translations

"The Cloud." Johnson-Davies, *Under the Naked Sky*. 65–70.

"The Dying Lamp." *Modern Arabic Short Stories*. Trans. D. Johnson-Davies. London: Oxford UP, 1967. 51–55.

The Long Way Back. Trans. C. Cobham. Cairo: American U in Cairo P, 2001.

Biography and Criticism

Allen, *Modern Arabic Literature*. 323–326.

Walther, W. "Distant Echoes of Love in the Narrative Work of Fu'ad al-Tikirli." *Love and Sexuality in Modern Arabic Literature*. Ed. R. Allen, H. Kilpatrick, and E. de Moor. London: Saqi, 1995. 131–139.

———. "Studies in Human Psyche and Human Behavior under Political and Social Pressure: The Recent Literary Works of Fu'ad al-Takarli." *Arab Studies Quarterly* 19.4 (1997): 21–36.

———. "al-Takarli, Fu'ad." Meisami and Starkey, *Encyclopedia of Arabic Literature*. 755.

al-Tanukhi, al-Muhassin ibn 'Ali, 940?–994

Web Sites

HH362/History of the Middle East. Baghdad: Center of Medieval Middle Eastern Civilization. http://www.usna.edu/Users/history/tucker/hh362/Baghdad.htm (accessed 26 Aug. 2003).

   The second selection is from his book of anecdotes. Reading for a history course at U.S. Naval Academy.

al-Tanukhi, al-M. ibn 'A. "Ruminations and Reminiscences." *Internet Medieval Sourcebook*. http://www.nipissingu.ca/department/history/muhlberger/2805/ tabltk.htm (accessed 25 Aug. 2003).

Translations

The Table-Talk of a Mesopotamian Judge. Trans. D.S. Margoliouth. London: Royal Asiatic Soc., 1922.

Biography and Criticism

Seidensticker, T. "al-Tanukhi." Meisami and Starkey, *Encyclopedia of Arabic Literature*. 757–758.

Tarafah ibn al-'Abd, 6th century

Web Sites

"The Mu'allaqa of Ibn Tarafa." Joris, Pierre. *Homad Page*. http://www.albany.edu/ ~joris/Tarafa.html (accessed 25 Aug. 2003).

"The Ode of Tarafah." *Middle East and Islamic Studies Collection, Cornell University.* http://www.library.cornell.edu/colldev/mideast/taraf.htm (accessed 25 Aug. 2003).

Translations

"The Mu'allaqa of Tarafa." Trans. M. Sells. *Journal of Arabic Literature* 17 (1986): 21–33.

Biography and Criticism

Arberry, A.J. *The Seven Odes.* London: George Allen and Unwin; New York: The Macmillan Company, 1957. 67–89.

Bauer, T. "Tarafa ibn al-'Abd." Meisami and Starkey, *Encyclopedia of Arabic Literature.* 759.

Taymur, Mahmud, 1894–1973

Web Sites

"Mahmoud Taymour, a Pioneer of Modern Arabic Novel." *Egypt.* http://www.sis.gov.eg/eginfnew/culture/html/cul0101.htm (accessed 25 Aug. 2003).

A slightly different version of his biography can be read at http://www.sis.gov.eg/calendar/html/cl060697.htm.

Translations

"The Court Rules." Trans. M. Shaheen. Rev. A. Parkin and M. Manzalaoui. *Arabic Writing Today: Drama.* Ed. M. Manzalaoui. Cairo: American Research Center in Egypt, 1977. 53–63.

"The Enemy." Trans. A. McDermott. Rev. L. Knight and D. Kirkham. Manzalaoui, *Arabic Short Stories.* 47–53.

"'Little Pharaoh,' a Short Story by Mahmud Taimur." Trans. G.M.N. Wickens. *Journal of Arabic Literature* 10 (1979): 109–116.

"Longing." Trans. R. Kimber. *Journal of Arabic Literature* 17 (1986): 97–104.

"Summer Journey." *Modern Arabic Short Stories.* Trans. D. Johnson-Davies. London: Oxford UP, 1967. 169–175.

Biography and Criticism

Allen, *Modern Arabic Literature.* 317–323.

Badawi, M.M. *Early Arabic Drama.* Cambridge: Cambridge UP, 1988. 101–120.

———. *Modern Arabic Drama in Egypt.* Cambridge: Cambridge UP, 1987. 88–111.

Elkhadem, S. *History of the Egyptian Novel: Its Rise and Early Beginnings.* Fredericton, N.B.: York, 1985. 36–39.

Moor, E.C.M. de. "Taymur, Mahmud." Meisami and Starkey, *Encyclopedia of Arabic Literature.* 761–762.

Peled, M. "Taymur, Mahmud." Serafin, *Encyclopedia of World Literature in the 20th Century.* Vol. 4. 302–303.

Sakkut, H. *The Egyptian Novel and Its Main Trends: From 1913 to 1952.* Cairo: American U in Cairo P, 1971. 28–30, 104–107.

al-Taymuriyah, 'A'ishah, 1840 or 1841–1902 or 1903

Web Sites

Elbendary, A. "Reintroducing Aisha." *Al-Ahram Weekly On-Line* 16–22 May 2002. http://weekly.ahram.org.eg/2002/586/cu4.htm (accessed 25 Aug. 2003).

Translations

Badran and Cooke, *Opening the Gates*. 125–133.
    Includes translations of "Family Reform Comes Only Through the Education of Girls" and "Introduction to the Results of Circumstances in Words and Deeds" by M. Booth.

Biography and Criticism

Booth, M. "al-Taymuriyya, 'A'isha 'Ismat." Meisami and Starkey, *Encyclopedia of Arabic Literature*. 763.

Hatem, M. "'A'isha Taymur's Tears and the Critique of the Modernist and the Feminist Discourses on Nineteenth-Century Egypt." *Remaking Women: Feminism and Modernity in the Middle East*. Ed. L. Abu-Lughod. Princeton: Princeton UP, 1998. 73–87.

Thabit ibn Qurrah al-Harrani, d. 901

Web Sites

"Arab Translators." *Loq-Man Translations*. http://www.loqmantranslations.com/ArabicFacts/ArabTranslators.html (accessed 26 Aug. 2003).

O'Connor, J.J., and E.F. Robertson. "Al-Sabi Thabit ibn Qurra al-Harrani." *The MacTutor History of Mathematics Archive*. http://www-gap.dcs.st-and.ac.uk/~history/Mathematicians/Thabit.html (accessed 26 Aug. 2003).

"Thabit ibn Qurrah al-Harrani." *Malaspina Great Books*. http://www.malaspina.com/site/person_968.asp (accessed 26 Aug. 2003).

"Thabit ibn Qurrah (Thebit)" *The Enlightenment*. Ed. A. Naqvi. http://www.thenlightenment.com/history/ms6.html (accessed 26 Aug. 2003).

Biography and Criticism

Conrad, L.I. "Thabit ibn Qurra." Meisami and Starkey, *Encyclopedia of Arabic Literature*. 765.

Goodman, L.E. "The Translation of Greek Materials into Arabic." *Religion, Learning, and Science in the 'Abbasid Period*. Ed. M.J.L. Young, J.D. Latham, and R.B. Serjeant. Cambridge History of Arabic Literature. Cambridge: Cambridge UP, 1990. 477–497. See especially 485–486.

Rosenfeld, B.A., and A.T. Grigorian. "Thabit ibn Qurra, al-Sabi' al-Harrani." Gillispie, *Dictionary of Scientific Biography*. Vol. 13. 288–295.

Sabra, A.I. "Abu al-Hasan Thabit bin Qurrah as-Sabi' al-Harrani." Atiyeh, *The Genius of Arab Civilization*. 198–199.

Tuqan, Fadwa, 1917–

Web Sites

Gender Issues & Literature in the Middle East. http://www.u.arizona.edu/~talattof/
    women-lit/introduction.htm (accessed 26 Aug. 2003)
    Includes "Gone Are Those We Love" and "Labor Pains."

Magda's Night Gallery. Ed. Magda. Dec. 2002. http://www.geocities.com/SoHo/
    Cafe/1324/tuqan.htm (accessed 26 Aug. 2003).
    Includes five poems: "Enough for Me," "In the Ocean," "I Won't Sell His
Love," "No Separation," and "The Rock."

"Palestinian Poets, Fadwa Tuqan." *Khalil Sakakini Cultural Centre.* http://
    www.sakakini.org/poets/fadwa-index.htm (accessed 26 Aug. 2003).
    Includes translations of two poems, "Enough for Me" and "The Deluge and the
Tree."

Tuqan, F. "I Found It." *The Women's Center News* 9.2 (2001). http://
    www.louisville.edu/provost/womenctr/news/wcnews92tuqan.html (accessed 26
    Aug. 2003).

———. "Martyrs of the Intifada." Al-Sayeh, K. Home Page. 13 June 1999. http://
    www.hally.net/personal/khaled/palestine/intifada/intifada.htm (accessed 26
    Aug. 2003).

———. "The Vision of Henry." *The Shi'a Homepage.* http://www.shia.org/
    tuqan.html (accessed 26 Aug. 2003).

———. "Waiting at the Allenby Bridge." *Crossing Borders* 11 (2001). http://
    www.crossingborder.org/newspaper/no11/pdf/PP.08-.pdf (accessed 26 Aug. 2003).

Autobiography

A Mountainous Journey: An Autobiography. Trans. O. Kenny. Poetry trans. N.S. Nye.
    St. Paul, MN: Graywolf, 1990.

Translations

Elmessiri, *The Palestinian Wedding.* 67+.
    Includes translations of "Eytan in the Steel Trap," "My Sad City," and "The
Seagull and the Negation of Negation."

Fernea, E.W., ed. *Women and the Family in the Middle East: New Voices of Change.*
    Austin: U of Texas P, 1985. 163–168.
    Includes translations of "Between Ebb and Flow," "Etan in the Steel Netting,"
"A Painful Longing," and "A Small Song to Despair" by T. Mitchell.

Handal, *The Poetry of Arab Women.* 306–308.
    Includes translations of "Elegy of a Knight" and "A Prayer to the New Year" by
S. Kawar.

"In Front of the Closed Door." Boullata, *Modern Arab Poets.* 119–123.

Jayyusi, *Anthology of Modern Palestinian Literature.* 310–316.
    Includes "The Deluge and the Tree," "Enough for Me," The Sibyl's Prophecy,"
and "Song of Becoming" by N.S. Nye and S.K. Jayyusi.

————, *Modern Arabic Poetry*. 455–462.
   Includes "Face Lost in the Wilderness," "I Found It," "In the Aging City," and "In the Flux" by P.A. Byrne with the help of the S.K. Jayyusi and N.S. Nye.

"Song of Becoming." Trans. N.S. Nye and S.K. Jayyusi. *Blood into Ink: South Asian and Middle Eastern Women Write War.* Ed. M. Cooke and R. Rustomji-Kerns. Boulder: Westview, 1994. 236–237.

Women of the Fertile Crescent. Washington, D.C.: Three Continents, 1978. 145–156.
   Includes translations of "Gone Are Those We Love," "Hamza," "Labor Pains," "My Freedom," "To Etan," and "To Her Sister and Comrade in the Resistance" by K. Boullata.

Biography and Criticism

Algazy, J. "Fadwa Touqan, Poetess of Nablus." *Mediterraneans/Mediterraneennes* 6 (1994): 54–58.

Allen, *Modern Arabic Literature*. 326–329.

Boullata, I.J. "Tuqan, Fadwa." Meisami and Starkey, *Encyclopedia of Arabic Literature*. 785–786.

DeYoung, T. "Love, Death, and the Ghost of al-Khansa': The Modern Female Poetic Voice in Fadwa Tuqan's Elegies for Her Brother Ibrahim." *Tradition, Modernity, and Postmodernity in Arabic Literature: Essays in Honor of Professor Issa J. Boullata*. Ed. K. Abdel-Malek and W. Hallaq. Brill: Leiden, 2000. 45–47.

Tuqan, Ibrahim 'Abd al-Fattah, 1905–1941

Web Sites

"Ibrahim Tukan." *Barghouti.com*. http://www.barghouti.com/poets/tukan/ (accessed 26 Aug. 2003).
   Includes text and translation of "My Homeland."

Translations

Jayyusi, *Anthology of Modern Palestinian Literature*. 317–319.
   Includes a translation of "Commando" by L. Jayyusi and J. Heath-Stubbs and translations of "From 'Brokers,'" "From 'Dead Hearts,'" "From 'In Beirut,'" and "From 'Lest We Lose'" by S. Jabsheh and N.S. Nye.

————, *Modern Arabic Poetry*. 106–108.
   Includes a translation of "The Martyr" by L. Jayyusi and J. Heath-Stubbs and a translation of "Perplexity" by C. Tingley, with the help of S.K. Jayyusi and J. Heath-Stubbs.

Biography and Criticism

Boullata, I.J. "Ibrahim Tuqan's Poem 'Red Tuesday'." *Tradition and Modernity in Arabic Literature*. Ed. I.J. Boullata and T. DeYoung. Fayetteville: U of Arkansas P, 1997. 87–100.

Starkey, P. "Tuqan, Ibrahim." Meisami and Starkey, *Encyclopedia of Arabic Literature*. 786.

al-Tusi, Nasir al-Din Muhammad ibn Muhammad, 1201–1274

Web Sites

Alakbarov, F. "A 13th-Century Darwin?: Tusi's Views on Evolution." *Azerbaijan International* 9.2 (2001). http://www.azer.com/aiweb/categories/magazine/ 92_folder/92_articles/92_tusi.html (accessed 26 Aug. 2003).

Badakhchani, S.J. "Nasir al-Din Tusi." *The Internet Encyclopedia of Philosophy*. Ed. J. Fieser. http://www.utm.edu/research/iep/t/tusi.htm (accessed 13 Aug. 2003).

Cooper, J. "al-Tusi, Khwajah Nasir." *Islamic Philosophy Online*. http:// www.muslimphilosophy.com/ip/rep/H036.htm (accessed 26 Aug. 2003).

O'Connor, J.J., and E.F. Robertson. "Nasir al-Din al-Tusi." *The MacTutor History of Mathematics Archive*. http://www-gap.dcs.st-and.ac.uk/~history/ Mathematicians/Al-Tusi_Nasir.html (accessed 14 Aug. 2003).

Autobiography

Contemplation and Action: The Spiritual Autobiography of a Muslim Scholar. Ed. and trans. S.J. Badakhchani. London: Tauris, 1998.

Translations

"Nasir al-Din Tusi." *An Anthology of Philosophy in Persia*. Ed. S.H. Nasr with M. Aminrazavi. 2 vols. New York: Oxford UP, 1999. Vol. 2. 342–378.

Nasir al-Din al-Tusi's Memoir on Astronomy. Trans. F.J. Ragep. New York: Springer-Verlag, 1993.

Biography and Criticism

Dabashi, H. "Khwajah Nasir al-Din al-Tusi: The Philosopher/Vizier and the Intellectual Climate of His Times." Nasr and Leaman, *History of Islamic Philosophy*. 527–584.

Nasr, S.H. "al-Tusi, Muhammad ibn Muhammad ibn al-Hasan." Gillispie, *Dictionary of Scientific Biography*. Vol. 13. 508–514.

Netton, I.R., and J.S. Meisami. "Nasir al-Din al-Tusi." Meisami and Starkey, *Encyclopedia of Arabic Literature*. 581–582.

'Umar ibn Abi Rabi'ah, 643 or 644–711 or 712

Web Sites

"Arab Love Poetry." *The Humanities Handbook*. Ed. W. Evans. Augusta State University. http://www.aug.edu/langlitcom/humanitiesHBK/handbook_htm/ arab_love_poetry.htm (accessed 26 Aug. 2003).

Scroll down to read the English translation of "Zeyneb at the Ka'bah" and "The Unveiled Maid." This site was converted from the 7th edition of a printed handbook for use by students in a humanities course.

Translations

Bitar, F., ed. *Treasury of Arabic Love Poems, Quotations, and Proverbs*. New York: Hippocrene, 1996. 23–29.

Includes translations of "From the Diwan of 'Umar ibn Abi Rabi'a," "The Suffering Heart," "To 'Aisha," and "To the Beauty" by A. Wormhoudt.

"'Umar ibn Abi Rabi'a." Arberry, *Arabic Poetry*. 40–42.

Biography and Criticism

Jacobi, R. "'Umar ibn Abi Rabi'a." Meisami and Starkey, *Encyclopedia of Arabic Literature*. 791–792.

Usamah ibn Munqidh, 1095–1188

Web Sites

Usamah ibn Munqidh. "'Autobiography,' excerpts on the Franks." *Internet Medieval Sourcebook*. http://www.fordham.edu/halsall/source/usamah2.html (accessed 26 Aug. 2003).

Autobiography

An Arab-Syrian Gentlemen and Warrior in the Period of the Crusades: Memoirs of Usamah ibn-Munqidh. Trans. P.K. Hitti. New York: Columbia UP, 1929.

Biography and Criticism

Irwin, R. "Usama ibn Munqidh." Meisami and Starkey, *Encyclopedia of Arabic Literature*. 796–797.

———. "Usamah ibn Munqidh: An Arab-Syrian Gentleman at the Time of the Crusades Reconsidered." *The Crusades and Their Sources: Essays Presented to Bernard Hamilton*. Ed. J. France and W.G. Zajac. Aldershot: Ashgate, 1998. 71–87.

al-'Uthman, Layla

Web Sites

"Freedom of Expression in Kuwait Remains under Threat." *Amnesty International*. http://web.amnesty.org/library/Index/engMDE170012000?OpenDocumentandof=COUNTRIES%5CKUWAIT?OpenDocumentandof=COUNTRIES%5CKUWAIT (accessed 26 Aug. 2003).

"Laila Othman." *Writer's Guild*. http://www.goa-world.net/writers-guild/lothman.htm (accessed 26 Aug. 2003).

al-'Uthman, Layla. "An Author Responds: The 'Crime' of Disturbing Calm Waters with a Pen." *Aljadid* 29 (1999). http://www.aljadid.com/features/0529othman.html (accessed 26 Aug. 2003).

Translations

"The Picture." *An Arabian Mosaic: Short Stories by Arab Women Writers*. Trans. D. Cohen-Mor. Potomac, Md.: Sheba, 1993. 77–84.

"Pulling Up Roots." Trans. L.M. Kenny and N.S. Nye. *The Literature of Modern Arabia: An Anthology*. Ed. S.K. Jayyusi. London: Kegan Paul International, 1988. 483–488.

Biography and Criticism

Michalak-Pikulska, B. "Life and Work of Layla al-'Uthman, the Contemporary Kuwaiti Woman Writer." *Folia Orientalia* 30 (1994): 101–112.

Mikhail, M. "al-'Uthman, Layla." Meisami and Starkey, *Encyclopedia of Arabic Literature*. 798–799.

Rahmer, A. "The Development of Women's Political Consciousness in the Short
 Stories of the Kuwaiti Author Layla al-'Uthman." *Love and Sexuality in
 Modern Arabic Literature*. Ed. R. Allen, H. Kilpatrick and E. de Moor. London:
 Saqi, 1995. 175–183.

Waddah al-Yaman, 'Abd al-Rahman ibn Isma'il, d. ca. 708

Web Sites

Al-Udhari, A. "Waddah al-Yaman: National Poet." *The British-Yemeni Society*. http://
 www.al-bab.com/bys/articles/waddah96.htm (accessed 26 Aug. 2003).

Waddah al-Yaman, 'Abd al-R. ibn I. "Poetry from the Years of Conquest." *Mosaic:
 Perspectives on Western Civilization*. http://college.hmco.com/history/west/
 mosaic/chapter4/source228.html (accessed 26 Aug. 2003).

Biography and Criticism

Seidensticker, T. "Waddah al-Yaman." Meisami and Starkey, *Encyclopedia of Arabic
 Literature*. 801.

Walladah bint al-Mustakfi, d. 1091 or 1092

Web Sites

"Notable Women." *Women in World History Curriculum*. Ed. L. Reese. http://
 www.womeninworldhistory.com/notables.html (accessed 26 Aug. 2003).

Translations

"Four Poems to Ibn Zaydun." *Andalusian Poems*. Trans. C. Middleton and L. Garza-
 Falcon. Boston: Godine, 1993. 16.

"Wallada bint al-Mustakfi." Trans. A. al-Udhari. *Classical Poems by Arab Women*.
 London: Saqi Books, 1999. 184–194.

Biography and Criticism

Alvarez, L. "Wallada bint al-Mustakfi." Meisami and Starkey, *Encyclopedia of Arabic
 Literature*. 803–804.

Nichols, J.M. "Wallada, the Andalusian Lyric, and the Question of Influence."
 Literature East & West 21 (1977): 286–291.

Wannus, Sa'd Allah, 1941–1997

Web Sites

Arab Culture and Civilization. Ed. M. Toler. National Institute for Technology and
 Liberal Education. http://www.nitle.org/arabworld/main_menu.php (accessed
 26 Aug. 2003).
  Use the Search box to find the English translation of the play "The King is the
King."

Selaiha, N. "A Hair-Razing Adventure." *Al-Ahram Weekly On-Line* 9–15 Mar. 2000.
 http://weekly.ahram.org.eg/2000/472/cu3.htm (accessed 26 Aug. 2003).
  Review of a new staging of "The Head of Memluk Geber." Another review by
Selaiha, of "Drunken Days," can be read at http://weekly.ahram.org.eg/1999/418/
cu2.htm.

Translations

Jayyusi, S.K., ed. *Short Arabic Plays: An Anthology.* New York: Interlink, 2003.
    412–451.
    Includes a translation of "The Glass Cafe" by F. Azzam and A. Brownjohn and
a translation of "The King's Elephant" by G. Maleh and C. Tingley.

"The King is the King." Trans. Ghassan Maleh and Thomas G. Ezzy. *Modern Arabic
    Drama: an Anthology.* Ed. Salma Khadra Jayyusi and Roger Allen.
    Bloomington: Indiana UP, 1995. 77–120.

"Theater and the Thirst for Dialogue." *Middle East Report* 203 (1997): 14–15.

"A Translation of 'Sahrah ma'a Abi Khalil al-Qabbani' by Sa'dallah Wannus." Trans.
    S.M. Toorawa. *Arabic and Middle Eastern Literatures* 3 (2000):
    19–49.

Biography and Criticism

Allen, *Modern Arabic Literature.* 336–340.

Allen, R. "Arabic Drama in Theory and Practice: The Writings of Sa'dallah Wannus."
    Journal of Arabic Literature 15 (1984): 94–113.

———. "Wannus, Sa'd Allah." Meisami and Starkey, *Encyclopedia of Arabic
    Literature.* 804.

———. "Wannus, Sa'dallah." Serafin, *Encyclopedia of World Literature in the 20th
    Century.* Vol. 4. 458–459.

Ruocco, M. "Islamic Modernism in a Recent Play by Sa'd Allah Wannus." *Law,
    Christianity, and Modernism in Islamic Society.* Ed. U. Vermeulen and J.M.F.
    van Reeth. Orientalia Lovaniensia Analecta 86. Leuven: Peeters, 1998.
    279–289.

Wattar, al-Tahir, 1936–

Web Sites

Wattar, al-T. *Tahar Ouettar.* 23 June 2003. http://wattar.cv.dz/ (accessed 26 Aug.
    2003).
    The author's Web site is largely in Arabic and French, but choose "Romans"
from the right-hand column, and you can read the English translations of *The Earth-
quake* and *Saint Tahir Returns to His Holy Shrine.* A review of the first by Gaber
Asfour can be accessed at http://wattar.cv.dz/lire/chahadat/ZILZAL/
JABR%20ASFOR.htm.

Translations

"The Gangway to the Elevator." Trans. H. Abdel-Jaouad. *Literary Review* 41 (1998):
    275–280.

Biographies and Criticism

Allen, *Modern Arabic Literature.* 340–342.

Bamia, A. "Wattar, al-Tahir." Serafin, *Encyclopedia of World Literature in the 20th
    Century.* Vol. 4. 465.

Bois, M. "Wattar, al-Tahir." Meisami and Starkey, *Encyclopedia of Arabic Literature.*
    808.

al-Sa'afin, I. "Modern Arabic Novel and Tradition: al-Tahir Wattar as a Case Study." *Oriente Moderno,* n.s. 16 (1997): 195–201.

Salhi, Z.S. "Wattar, al-Tahir." Gikandi, *Encyclopedia of African Literature*. 561.

Siddiq, M. "The Contemporary Arabic Novel in Perspective." *World Literature Today* 60 (1986): 206–211.

Yakhlif, Yahya, 1944–

Web Sites

Galford, H. Rev. of *A Lake beyond the Wind. Washington Report on Middle East Affairs* 20.1 (2001). http://www.washington-report.org/backissues/010201/0101103.html (accessed 26 Aug. 2003).

"Palestinian Novelists, Yahyia Yakhluf." *Khalil Sakakini Cultural Centre*. http://www.sakakini.org/novelists/yahyia.html (accessed 26 Aug. 2003).

Yakhlif, Y. "Chapter One: Samakh, the South Shore, 1948." *PARC: Palestinian American Research Center*. http://www.parcenter.org/resources/literature_region/lit_region.html (accessed 26 Aug. 2003).
Translation of the first chapter of *A Lake beyond the Wind*.

Translations

A Lake Beyond the Wind. Trans. M. Jayyusi and C. Tingley. New York: Interlink, 1999.

"That Rose of a Woman." Trans. S. Jabsheh and N.S. Nye. Jayyusi, *Anthology of Modern Palestinian Literature*. 577–586.

Yaqut ibn 'Abd Allah al-Hamawi, 1179?–1229

Web Sites

HH362/History of the Middle East. Baghdad: Center of Medieval Middle Eastern Civilization. http://www.usna.edu/Users/history/tucker/hh362/Baghdad.htm (accessed 26 Aug. 2003).
Translation of the description of Baghdad, from his geographical dictionary. Reading for a history course at U.S. Naval Academy.

Yaqut ibn 'Abd Allah al-Hamawi. "Baghdad under the Abbasids." *Internet Medieval Sourcebook*. http://www.fordham.edu/halsall/source/1000baghdad.html (accessed 26 Aug. 2003).

Translations

The Introductory Chapters of Yaqut's Mu'jam al-Buldan. Trans. and ann. W. Jwaideh. Leiden: Brill, 1959.

Biography and Criticism

Ahmad, S.M. "Yaqut al-Hamawi al-Rumi, Shihab al-Din Abu 'Abdallah Yaqut ibn 'Abd Allah." Gillispie, *Dictionary of Scientific Biography*. Vol. 14. 546–548.

Ostafin, B. "Yaqut: Geographer, Compiler or Adib? According to the Preface to His Dictionary." *Folia Orientalia* 30 (1994): 119–123.

Richards, D.S. "Yaqut." Meisami and Starkey, *Encyclopedia of Arabic Literature*. 811.

Yusuf, Sa'di, 1934–

Web Sites

"Saadi Youssef." *Jehat.com.* http://www.jehat.com/en/
    default.asp?action=article&ID=41#1 (accessed 21 Apr. 2004) and http://
    www.jehat.com/en/default.asp?action=article&ID=92 (accessed 21 Apr. 2004).
    Includes translation of "Post Cards from Hajj Omrane," "A Vision," and another
untitled poem.

"Saadi Youssef." *Masthead* 7 (2003). http://au.geocities.com/masthead_2/issue7/
    youssef.html (accessed 26 Aug. 2003).
    Includes translations of "Elsinore, Hamlet's Castle," "Reception," and "Amer-
ica, America."

Saadi Youssef, Sa'di Yusuf, Saadi Yusuf, Sa'di Youssef. Ed. S. Davis, et al. http://
    www.humboldt.edu/~me2/engl240/student_projects/Youssef/Homepage.html
    (accessed 26 Aug. 2003).
    Compiled as a student project for an English class at Humboldt State Univer-
sity, includes translations of poems ("Departure of '82," "Nursery Song," "In Those
Days," "A Woman," "The Collapse of the Two-Rivers Hotel") with commentary,
biography, and bibliography.

"A Vision." *Free Verse: A Journal of Contemporary Poetry & Poetics* 3 (2002). http://
    english.chass.ncsu.edu/freeverse/Archives/Winter_2002/Iraqi_Poems/
    S_Yusuf.htm (accessed 26 Aug. 2003).

Yusuf, S. "Two Poems." *The Blue Moon Review.* http://www.thebluemoon.com/
    poetry/syoussef.shtml (accessed 26 Aug. 2003).
    Translations of "Shatt al-Arab" and " Thank You Imru Ul-Qais."

Autobiography

"On Reading the Earth." Trans. F.J. Ghazoul. Ghazoul and Harlow, *The View from
    Within.* 12–16.

Translations

Asfour, *When the Words Burn.* 122–124.
    Includes translations of "Evacuation '82," "The Fence," and "Six
Poems."

Jayyusi, *Modern Arabic Poetry.* 480–484.
    Includes translations of "Three Dispositions Regarding One Woman" and "The
Woods" by S. Boulus and N.S. Nye and translations of "Departure of '82," "A Hot
Evening," "Sentiment," "A State of Fever," and "A Woman" by L. Jayyusi and N.S.
Nye.

Modern Poetry in Translation 13 (1998): 114–115.
    Includes translations by K. Mattawa of "Algerian Glances," "Blue," "Electric-
ity," "Exhaustion," "A Fighting Position," "Flying," "Hoarding," "A Room," "Water,"
and "Where To?"

Without an Alphabet, Without a Face: Selected Poems of Saadi Youssef. Trans. K.
    Mattawa. St. Paul, MN: Graywolf, 2003.

Biography and Criticism

Moreh, S. "Yusuf, Sa'di." Meisami and Starkey, *Encyclopedia of Arabic Literature*. 815–816.

Simawe, S.A. "The Politics and the Poetics of Sa'di Yusuf: The Use of the Vernacular." *Arab Studies Quarterly* 19.4 (1997): 173–186.

Zafzaf, Muhammad, 1945–2001

Web Sites

"Death of the Godfather." *Al-Ahram Weekly On-Line* 19–25 July 2001. http://weekly.ahram.org.eg/2001/543/cu7.htm (accessed 26 Aug. 2003).

Translations

"Men and Mules." Trans. L. Jayyusi and T.G. Ezzy. *The HarperCollins World Reader: The Modern World*. Ed. M.A. Case and C. Prendergast. New York: HarperCollins, 1994. 1881–1886.

"Snake Hunting." Johnson-Davies, *Under the Naked Sky*. 142–148.

Biography and Criticism

Abu-Haidar, F. "Zafzaf, Muhmmad." Meisami and Starkey, *Encyclopedia of Arabic Literature*. 818.

———. "Zafzaf, Mohammed." Serafin, *Encyclopedia of World Literature in the 20th Century*. Vol. 4. 567–568.

Salhi, Z.S. "Zefzaf, Mohammad." Gikandi, *Encyclopedia of African Literature*. 584–585.

Zaqtan, Ghassan, 1954–

Web Sites

"Palestinian Poets, Ghassan Zaqtan." *Khalil Sakakini Cultural Centre*. http://www.sakakini.org/poets/ghassan-index.htm (accessed 26 Aug. 2003).
    Includes translations of "Guide," "Pillow," "Four Sisters from Zakaria," "Darkness," "Family Heirlooms," "A Mirror," and "An Incident."

Translations

Jayyusi, *Anthology of Modern Palestinian Literature*. 323–326.
    Includes translations of "Another Death," "How Did They Inform on You?," "An Incident," and "A Mirror" by L. Jayyusi and J.R. Jayyusi.

Modern Poetry in Translation 14 (1998–1999): 204–206.
    Includes translations of "Biography," "A Different Morning," "Defence," "Delighted with My Things," and "Winter 1981" by S. Simawe and E.D. Watson.

Zayyad, Tawfiq, 1932–1994

Web Sites

Magda's Night Gallery. Ed. Magda. Dec. 2002. http://www.geocities.com/SoHo/Cafe/1324/ziad.htm (accessed 26 Aug. 2003).
    Includes the following poems by Zayyad Tawfiq: "All I Have," "Here We Will Stay," "Pagan Fires," "Passing Remark," and "They Know."

"Taufik Ziad, Eight Years Gone." *The Israeli Communist Forum.* 9 June 2002. http://www.geocities.com/ic_forum/ziaden.htm (accessed 26 Aug. 2003).

Autobiography and Interviews

"Interviewed by Tawfiq Zayyad." Interviewed by A. Joyce. *American-Arab Affairs* 25 (1988): 48–54.

Translations

Elmessiri, *The Palestinian Wedding.* 55+.
    Includes translations of "The Bridge of Return," "The Crucified One," "The Fire of the Maji," "I Clasp Your Hands," "The Impossible," and "On the Trunk of an Olive Tree."

Jayyusi, *Anthology of Modern Palestinian Literature.* 327–331.
    Includes translations of "All I Have," "Here We Shall Stay," "A Million Suns in My Blood," "Pagan Fires," and "What Next?" by S. Elmusa and C. Doria.

———, *Modern Arabic Poetry.* 485–488.
    Includes translations of "Before Their Tanks," "Here We Will Stay," "Pagan Fires," "Passing Remark," "Salman," and "They Know" by S. Elmusa and C. Doria.

"Six Words." Asfour, *When the Words Burn.* 217.

Biography and Criticism

Suleiman, Y. "Zayyad, Tawfiq." Meisami and Starkey, *Encyclopedia of Arabic Literature.* 824.

al-Zayyat, Latifah, 1923–1996

Web Sites

Caesar, J. Rev. of *The Open Door. Middle East Studies Association Bulletin* 35.2 (2001). http://fp.arizona.edu/mesassoc/Bulletin/35-2/35-21Literature.htm (accessed 26 Aug. 2003).

Ghazaleh, P. "Eyes Wide Open." Rev. of *The Open Door. Al-Ahram Weekly On-Line* 8–14 Feb. 2001. http://weekly.ahram.org.eg/2001/520/bo1.htm (accessed 26 Aug. 2003).

al-Zayyat, L. "The Picture." *Gender Issues & Literature in the Middle East.* http://www.u.arizona.edu/~talattof/women-lit/introduction.htm (26 Aug. 2003).

Autobiography and Interviews

"On Political Commitment and Feminist Writing." Interviewed by S. Ramadan. Trans. L. al-Nakkash. Ghazoul and Harlow, *The View from Within.* 246–260.

The Search: Personal Papers. Trans. S. Bennett. London: Quartet, 1996.

Translations

The Open Door. Trans. M. Booth. Cairo: American U in Cairo P, 2000.

The Owner of the House. Trans. S. Bennett. London: Quartet, 1997.

"The Picture." *An Arabian Mosaic: Short Stories by Arab Women Writers.* Trans. D. Cohen-Mor. Potomac, Md.: Sheba, 1993. 65–75.

Biography and Criticism

Bennett, S. "A Life of One's Own?" Ostle, Moor, and Wild, *Writing the Self.* 283–291.

Booth, M. "al-Zayyat, Latifa." Meisami and Starkey, *Encyclopedia of Arabic Literature.* 825.

Ghazoul, F.J. "al-Zayyat, Latifa." Gikandi, *Encyclopedia of African Literature.* 584.

Taieb, H.D. "The Girl Who Found Refuge in the People: The Autobiography of Latifa Zayyat." *Journal of Arabic Literature* 29 (1998): 202–217.

Ziyadah, Mayy, 1886–1941

Web Sites

Khader, L. "In Memory of May Zeyadeh: A Torch in the Darkest of Ages." *Middle East and Islamic Studies Collection, Cornell University.* http://www.library.cornell.edu/colldev/mideast/mziydh.htm (accessed 26 Aug. 2003).

Melhem, E. "Saving May: How Antun Sa'adeh Tried to Save May Ziyadeh from the Ghoul." *Al-Zawba'ah.* Ed. E. Melhem. http://home.iprimus.com.au/fidamelhem/SSNP/May%20Ziadeh.htm (accessed 26 Aug. 2003).

Ziegler, A. "May Ziadeh Rediscovered." *May (1886–1941).* Ed. Mira. 22 Aug. 1999. http://leb.net/isis/z/ziegler.html (accessed 26 Aug. 2003).

Translations

"The Lady with the Story." *An Arabian Mosaic: Short Stories by Arab Women Writers.* Trans. D. Cohen-Mor. Potomac, Md.: Sheba, 1993. 85–94.

"Warda al-Yaziji." Badran and Cooke, *Opening the Gates.* 239–243.

Biography and Criticism

Booth, M. "Ziyada, Mayy (born Mari Ilyas Ziyada)" Meisami and Starkey, *Encyclopedia of Arabic Literature.* 826–827.

Gibran, K. *Blue Flame: The Love Letters of Kahlil Gibran to May Ziadah.* Ed. and trans. S. Bushrui and S. Kuzbari. New York: Longman, 1983.

Ziegler, A. "Al-Haraka Baraka! The Late Rediscovery of Mayy Ziyada's Works." *Welt des Islams* 39 (1999): 103–115.

Zuhayr ibn Abi Sulma, d. 609

Web Sites

"Pre-Islamic Arabia: The Hanged Poems." *Internet Medieval Sourcebook.* http://www.fordham.edu/halsall/source/640hangedpoems.html (accessed 26 Aug. 2003).
Scroll down to read the translation of Zuhayr's poem.

Biography and Criticism

Arberry, A.J. *The Seven Odes.* London: George Allen and Unwin; New York: The Macmillan Company, 1957. 90–118.

Montgomery, J.E. "Zuhayr ibn Abi Sulma." Meisami and Starkey, *Encyclopedia of Arabic Literature.* 827.

Zurayq, Qustantin, 1909–2000

Web Sites

"AUB Mourns Passing of Constantine Zurayk." *AUB Bulletin Today* 2.1 (2000). http://staff.aub.edu.lb/~webbultn/v2n1/html/07.htm (accessed 26 Aug. 2003).

Mattar, P. "Constantine Zurayk." *Middle East Studies Association Bulletin* 34.2 (2000). http://fp.arizona.edu/mesassoc/Bulletin/34-2/34-2%20Memoriam.htm (accessed 26 Aug. 2003).

Zurayq, C. "The University and Society." *IAU Newsletter* 6.1 (2000). http://www.unesco.org/iau/iaunew61.html#IAU%20Retrospective%20and (accessed 26 Aug. 2003).

Biography and Criticism

Faris, H.A. "Constantine K. Zurayk: Advocate of Rationalism in Modern Arab Thought." *Arab Civilization: Challenges and Responses: Studies in Honor of Constantine K. Zurayk.* Ed. G.N. Atiyeh and I.M. Oweiss. Albany: State U of New York P, 1988. 1–41.

Sluglett, P. "Zurayq, Qustantin." Meisami and Starkey, *Encyclopedia of Arabic Literature.* 829.

Index

About the Author

Dona S. Straley is Middle East studies librarian and associate professor of library administration at the Ohio State University libraries. She received her B.A. with distinction in history from Ohio State University in 1974, a Ph.D in Arabic and Islamic studies from the University of Edinburgh in 1977, and an M.L.S. from Indiana University in 1981.